# Edges of Truth
## The Mary Weaver Story

# Deb Brammer
### with Steve Brennecke

Library of Congress Control Number: 2013913698
CreateSpace Independent Publishing Platform
North Charleston, South Carolina

This riveting story about truth winning the victory in spite of nearly impossible odds will arrest readers from the first page and hold them captive until the stunning verdict. They'll want to stand up and cheer. This rare glimpse into the inner workings of a murder trial left me spellbound. I couldn't put the book down. Highly recommended!

**Adam Blumer,** author of *Fatal Illusions* and *The Tenth Plague*

The concept of shaken baby syndrome has acquired a cult like following, especially among pediatricians. As more evidence came forth that the entity does not exist, the experts espousing this concept became more ardent and venomous. They invented the concepts that the last person to contact the individual was the perpetrator, that there was no lucid interval after injury and retinal hemorrhage absolutely guaranteed that the child was shaken. The Mary Weaver case is a horrible example of science recruited for vengeance and not for the objective interpretation of injuries.

**Vincent J.M. Di Maio, M.D.,** witness for the defense in two of Mary's trials

Mary Weaver is a wife, mother, and God-loving person who is also known and respected in the community. Her trials of being arrested and ultimately put in jail, potentially for life without the possibility of parole, is frightening and a wake-up call for anyone who is ever involved in child care. The reason for the arrest and the method are both frightening and disconcerting.

Although I had the opportunity to participate in some of the proceedings of this case and was aware of the general outcome, few of the actual details were known to me until I read the book myself. The author's technique of looking forward and backward in time without revealing the outcome keeps the reader on the edge of their chair in anticipation of the outcome and the final verdict.

The story includes sad times, bright moments, sorrow and hope. This real-life story reads like a fictional adventure and is well worth the journey of reading from beginning to end.

**Ruth G. Ramsey, M.D.,** witness for the defense in all three of Mary's trials

The Mary Weaver Story is a good read. It explores a tragedy that begins with the death of a baby in an unlikely place like small town Iowa. This a story about never losing hope, of sorting through the complex reasons why the baby died, of family and friends developing deep and passionate support for a person they believed innocent. And a heroic fight by lawyers who overcame tremendous odds.

**Frank Santiago,** former reporter for the *Des Moines Register*

Deb and Steve have done an awesome job of telling Mary's story! What an encouragement for anyone who has been falsely accused. It is an intimate and courageously honest memoir about devastating loss, enduring trust, and finding the strength to carry on. What a journey Mary and I, and so many others experienced. It was definitely a faith walk!

**Marge Wolfe,** member of The Mary Weaver Support Group

# DEDICATION

*All glory for this book goes to God, the true Author, who wrote*
*Mary's story not in ink but in lives.*
*Mary wants to dedicate this book to Catherine and John whose lives,*
*like  hers, were changed forever because of this story.*

# CHAPTER 1

## FRIDAY MORNING, JANUARY 22, 1993

Mary settled Melissa into the car seat on the kitchen counter. The baby was just eleven months old, but forty-two minutes with this baby would change Mary's life forever.

Mary shushed the questions that taunted her inner peace. Was Melissa really over the flu that had sent her to the doctor earlier in the week? Would the illness spread to Mary's own children, Catherine and John? Why couldn't Tessia take one more day off work so Melissa would have the whole weekend with her mother to get stronger?

But Mary was just the baby-sitter, and the young mother wasn't asking for advice. Mary unscrewed the lid of the vanilla custard Tessia had sent. Tessia had already fed Melissa two bowls of cereal and eight ounces of milk for breakfast. Mary questioned Tessia's instructions to give the baby more midmorning when she'd been sick all week, but Melissa did seem to be feeling better. The fragile girl had not gained weight as quickly as the average baby.

Mary spooned some custard into the tiny mouth and gave her plenty of time to swallow. She captured the moosh that oozed out and added it to the next spoonful. The baby acted perfectly fine today, but if she did vomit, she was more accessible in the car seat than in the high chair. After all, a mother and a child care worker had to guard safety like a Doberman. Mary grabbed a towel and set it on the counter, just in case.

Mary caressed the bit of fuzz that covered the little head. "'Jesus loves me, this I know,'" Mary sang. She scooped another spoonful from the jar. "Jesus loves you," she said. "Mary loves you. Mommy and Daddy love you. They're a little young, and they've got some things to learn, but I'm sure they do."

After half a jar of custard was gone, Melissa turned her head away, avoiding the spoon. Mary glanced at the clock. 11:10. "Now it's time to pick Catherine and John up from preschool. They love you too. You're like a little sister to them. Now let's wiggle into your snowsuit so you'll be snuggly warm."

Mary spread the pink snowsuit on the thick carpet in the living room. Floors were safe. The wiggliest baby couldn't fall off a floor. She lifted Melissa from the car seat, positioned her on the snowsuit, and worked the tiny feet into the legs of the suit. Then Mary reached behind the baby and supported her head and shoulders. She lifted the baby forward at the waist to get her arms into the snowsuit.

Suddenly Melissa's eyes rolled back into her head. Her body became limp as a worn-out rag doll. Her chest failed to inflate.

Mary shook her gently and called to her with quiet urgency. "Melissa! Melissa!" she shouted. The baby didn't respond. Mary eased her back down, but the tiny chest never moved.

Stay calm. What did they say in CPR class? Check the mouth and throat for obstructions. Mary checked. Nothing. She carried the child into the kitchen and grabbed the phone. She dialed 9-1-1, waited for an answer. "I need an ambulance!" She needed someone with far more experience than she had—now! "I have a baby that's stopped breathing!" Melissa spit up, but Mary kept rattling off essential information as fast as she could.

# CHAPTER 1

"Ambulance service." Her call had been transferred, and she had to begin again.

"I need an ambulance." She gave the address. "I have a baby that's stopped breathing. She spit up, and she stopped breathing."

"Okay, and she's not breathing right now?"

"No."

Calm urgency colored the operator's voice. "Okay, you want to open up her airway and blow into her mouth."

Mary grabbed the towel, wiped away the vomit. Cradling the phone between her head and shoulder, Mary held the girl close, covered the baby's mouth with her own, and blew. No response. More vanilla custard erupted from the tiny lips like an overheated volcano. Mary's mother reflex tilted the child away from her, allowing the foul lava to flow to the floor.

"Oh, she just spit some more up."

Mary kept trying unsuccessfully to get Melissa to breathe on her own. Soon baby food was coming out of her nose and mouth. The dispatcher told her to brush that out of her mouth and try to get her breathing.

"Is she breathing yet?"

"No. It's still coming out of her nose."

"Okay, get her airway cleared out and put your mouth over her mouth and nose and try and force some air in."

Mary kept trying, and the dispatcher kept repeating the instructions.

"Put your hand on her chest and see if there's any movement there."

Mary felt a slight movement. "Well, yeah, she's still making noises and things."

More vomit. The dispatcher had to hang up and take another call. What could be more important than a baby who was barely breathing? Mary waved her hand in front of Melissa's glassy eyes and got no response. The dispatcher came back on the line. Mary told her what was happening.

"Maybe give her a couple more breaths."

Mary put the phone down and tried again. This wasn't working. She picked up the phone. "I can hear the breath going into her lungs, and her chest is rising, but she—there's something wrong with her."

Melissa had quit spitting up, but there was an ominous gurgling in her throat. Mary couldn't see any signs of breathing, and Melissa's heart was pounding.

After several long minutes of this, a siren screamed in the background.

Would the ambulance be able to find the house? The white numbers on the yellow house had never been easy to read, and delay could cost Melissa her life. Mary blew one more breath before she placed Melissa on the floor. She dashed out the kitchen door and ran through the garage to flag down an approaching police car. The ambulance must be close behind.

The brakes squealed, and the officer's door shot open.

Mary waved again. "Over here! Quick!"

She scurried into the house just ahead of the policeman.

Mary panted out information as the policeman knelt beside the pale body. "Her eyes rolled back and she—she just quit breathing! For no reason! I was putting on her snowsuit. I just lifted her up, you know, at the waist, sat her up. Then this!"

The policeman breathed into her mouth and counted five chest compressions, while Mary informed the 9-1-1 operator that help had arrived and hung up.

Soon another siren screamed, and three paramedics blew through the open doorway with a blast of bitter wind. The male paramedic cupped an oversized oxygen mask over Melissa's tiny mouth and tried to get air into her lungs, while one of the female paramedics knelt on the other side of Melissa. The airway was evidently obstructed.

Mary stepped behind the U-shaped island in her kitchen to give the paramedics room to work. The policeman, who was sturdily built like Mary, squeezed in beside her and one of the female paramedics. The officer asked for a glass of water and a clean towel. He evidently didn't have a mother's reflexes because vomit streaked down the front of his uniform. Mary grabbed a towel from the oven handle and handed it to him.

On the floor the male paramedic gave up on the oxygen mask. He flipped Melissa over his arm and struck her four times between the shoulder blades. That didn't help, so he turned her back over and thrust an instrument into her mouth.

Beside him the female paramedic hooked Melissa up to the heart monitor, then stood and asked Mary about what had happened. Mary reported lifting Melissa's upper body, the eyes rolling back, the way Melissa quit breathing, the vomiting. She gave pertinent information about Melissa's illness that week, allergies, medicines she had taken for the flu.

Mary shook her head in confusion. In her experience as a mother, the vomiting, loss of appetite, and tiredness had pointed to normal illness—not to the life-threatening horror story playing out before them.

Once Melissa was breathing the paramedic patted Mary's arm. "Don't worry, ma'am. We'll drive her to the Marshalltown Medical Center and take good care of her."

"Do you want me to call her mother?"

"Yes. Get the doctor's name and any further history, and call the ER."

They lifted the doll-sized body onto an adult-sized stretcher, grabbed poles on either side of it, and jogged out the door.

Mary followed them and watched the stretcher disappear into the ambulance with the paramedics. The vehicle sped away, red lights flashing and siren screaming. The policeman drove off close behind them.

*Please, Lord, give the doctors wisdom.* Mary planted some prayer seeds and watered them with her tears. *Keep Melissa safe. She's such a sweet baby, and she's Brad and Tessia's only child.*

She couldn't say "amen" because her prayer was only beginning. Melissa was in good hands now—the hands of health care professionals and God. Yet somehow Mary couldn't relax in the everlasting arms. Something was terribly wrong.

Mary stumbled back into the empty kitchen. What had just happened? Melissa had battled with flu all week. Lethargic on Monday. Home with her mom and dad on Tuesday, Wednesday, and Thursday. She'd vomited a bit, visited the doctor. Everyone thought she was recovering. What could have caused the horrifying incident that had just sent her away in the ambulance?

Mary had to call Tessia, but she had to calm down first. Tessia was going to have to drive to the hospital. Mary had to balance enough urgency to convince Tessia to drive there with enough restraint to get Tessia there safely.

Mary breathed deeply, stepped to the counter, filled a glass with water, and drained it. "Please, Lord, keep this little one safe and give me words to explain the situation to Tessia without upsetting her. Take her safely to the hospital. Please!"

She took another deep breath and willed her heart to quit beating so fast. She reached for the phone and dialed Hardee's. She was put on hold. Whirring machines, sizzling hot plates, and orders to the cooks filled the line until Tessia's voice came over the phone. "Yeah?"

"Tessia, something's happened to Melissa. She's going to be okay, but she's at the hospital, and I think you should go too."

# Chapter 1

Tessia hesitated. "But I'd have to leave work. Who would take my place?"

Mary allowed some urgency to enter her voice. "Surely someone can take your place in an emergency."

"Emergency?" Complacency changed to fear in her voice. "I thought you said she was okay. What happened?"

"She started vomiting again, and she's having trouble breathing. I didn't want to take chances, so I called the ambulance."

"Ambulance?" Panic built in Tessia's voice. "You called the ambulance? And she's not breathing? What's going to happen to her?" She was practically screeching now.

Time for restraint. "I'm not sure, but she's in good hands. Can you go down? I would, but I've got to pick Catherine and John up from preschool, and I think it would be better if you go since you're her mother. They'll need information about her that I can't give. Stay calm but get there as soon as you can."

Mary hung up the phone. Her mind started going in a million directions. She was already late getting the kids. Maybe she should call a friend to pick them up. Should she drive to the hospital? If so, someone would have to baby-sit her kids. Should she try to call Brad? Tessia could be too busy thinking about Melissa to call the child's father. Then Mary needed to call her own husband Jim, and Pastor Frost, and her friend April to get the prayer chain started. She ached for Melissa, whom she had watched five days a week for six months. Mary could picture the rag doll of a baby at the medical center, stretched beneath a tangle of wires and tubes and beeping machines.

Mary made a few quick phone calls, but soon new questions heckled her. Would Melissa be all right? What had caused the seizure? Had she responded with the correct lifesaving techniques? Would Brad and Tessia blame her for the incident? What could she have done differently?

Mary's phone buzzed with activity that day, while she checked up on Melissa and kept people informed. Tessia called, and Mary told her about her short time with Melissa and the incident that had led to this crisis. She offered to get someone to watch her kids so she could join Tessia at the hospital, but Brad's mom was already there.

Brad called midafternoon with a progress report. Doctors had performed a CT scan at the medical center, but they couldn't figure out why she wasn't breathing on her own. Then a helicopter had flown her to the University of Iowa Hospital in Iowa City. Brad's voice shook with worry. "Mary, I'm so glad you were with her when this happened. I know she wouldn't be alive today if she'd been at home. We wouldn't have known what to do. You saved our daughter's life." Brad's voice caught. "Thank you so much."

That evening Mary called the hospital to check up on Melissa. Tessia said two CT scans had failed to show why Melissa couldn't breathe on her own. Mary promised Tessia she'd keep praying and that she'd come to the hospital the next day.

Mary slept little that night. When she couldn't sleep, she asked the Great Physician to heal Melissa, but even after prayer, an uneasy feeling stole most of her sleep. Her eyes blinked open at 6:53 the next morning. She had just pulled on some clothes and started the coffee maker when a police car by the curb caught her eye. A young policeman had arrived.

When she opened the door he asked her to come down to the station. "We have a couple of questions to ask you. Whenever they send an ambulance out, they have to do a follow-up report."

Why were the police involved in this? Must be some sort of routine investigation about 9-1-1 calls. She'd give her statement quickly and drive on to Iowa City.

# Chapter 1

Mary ran her fingers through her unbrushed hair. "Of course. Let me grab my coat and keys. I need to wake my husband and explain things to him too."

At the station she was escorted to a room sparsely furnished with a table and a few chairs. A police detective introduced himself and seated the two of them around the microphone.

He blew into the mic and introduced the case number. "Conducting the interview will be Lieutenant Buffington. I will be speaking with Mary Weaver." He gave her address. "Mary, there was an ambulance call at your residence yesterday. You were baby-sitting a child. Can you go ahead and relate to me what happened and what led up to it?"

"Sure." Mary started with Monday and gave a fairly detailed account of Melissa's health day by day. Then she recounted the time she had spent with Melissa: picking her up from her home, buying a few groceries, feeding her, putting on her snowsuit, and the sudden eye rolling and cessation of breathing. Mary described the 9-1-1 call, the ambulance, everything. When she finished Lieutenant Buffington nodded, but he seemed to be waiting for more. She had no more to say and was eager to get to the hospital to be with Brad and Tessia.

The detective studied her eyes, measuring her. "Well, I don't know if you're aware of it or not, but the baby did die."

# CHAPTER 2

**M**elissa was dead? Impossible! She had suffered through several days of flu, but she'd seemed fine only yesterday morning. Flu might make a baby miserable, but babies didn't die of it—did they?

"Oh, no." Mary swiped at the tears washing down her face. "Melissa's become like one of my children. She's been in my house for six months, and then she's changed so much. When she first came to our house, she was really a fussy, sad little baby."

"What do you mean by 'fussy'?"

Mary explained that Tessia had used other baby-sitters, but Melissa hadn't settled in well with any of them. At Mary's house she'd become happy. She'd loved Catherine and John, and they'd loved her. She'd become like one of the family. "At my house she slept really good. She ate and slept and just—I can't believe she's dead."

Lieutenant Buffington explained that the police had to investigate and make sure everything was all right.

"One minute she was just fine," Mary said. "Then all of a sudden she just...When I put on her snowsuit, I just picked her up, and I set her down and just...I don't know what else to tell you. It just happened so quick."

"Now it's our job to investigate it."

This made no sense. Mary breathed deeply, calming herself. "Did the doctors find out what caused her death?"

"I can't answer that at this time because the medical reports aren't done. As soon as we find out, then we'll know which way to go. Right now there are no accusations."

"I understand that."

"We have to get the preliminaries, and you're the first place we've got to start. You've been very cooperative, and we do appreciate it."

Maybe the autopsy would reveal answers. Brad and Tessia must be devastated. Since she had been with Melissa when the incident first happened, maybe she could help them solve this puzzle. Mary searched the detective's eyes. "I'll do anything I can to help."

"That's good. And we'll be recontacting you."

"Just call if you need anything at all." She might not be able to do much to ease Brad and Tessia's pain, but if they could figure out why Melissa died, it would help bring them closure.

Today she would make some phone calls, report Melissa's death, and ask prayer for the family. Other than that she would just have to wait at home for the police to contact her.

That afternoon Lieutenant Buffington drove into the Weavers' driveway with an officer from Des Moines. The other detective strode to the door and banged on it. Mary opened it.

The detective flashed his badge. "I'm Agent Motsinger from the Department of Criminal Investigation. You know Lieutenant Buffington. May we come in?" His words asked permission, but his tone demanded entrance. This state official wore his rank like stars on a general.

Mary seated them around the dining room table and offered them a cup of coffee. Agent Motsinger declined. "We're not here for pleasantries, Mrs. Weaver. We just want the facts. Yesterday morning, January twenty-second, you placed a 9-1-1 call from this house. Tell us the circumstances leading up to the call."

This state guy was all business. Even though Lieutenant Buffington was older, he cowered in Agent Motsinger's presence. Her husband, Jim, crouched on the sofa, a five-foot-ten, blond watchdog.

"Where would you like me to start? When I picked Melissa up at her parents' house?"

Motsinger glared. "Everything you did with Melissa yesterday morning concerns us."

Mary blinked a few times at the harsh tone. "All right. If that's what you want."

His eyes shone like interrogation lights in an old movie. "I said it was."

Mary cleared her throat and recited the whole story again.

The state detective's dark eyes never wavered. If the local officer was the good cop, this guy was playing bad cop. "What else happened?"

Frustration pushed her voice a few notches higher. "Nothing else happened. I only had her for…" She glanced at Lieutenant Buffington. "We figured out it could only have been about forty-two minutes. That's all that happened."

Motsinger leaned his bulky body back in his chair, just enough for his suit coat to fall to one side. His badge shone from his belt. "I don't believe you. I think you're leaving something out."

"I'm not leaving anything out." Her voice shook; she could tell no more of the story without making something up. "That's all there is. I told them this morning at the station, and I'm telling you now. There's nothing left to tell."

Motsinger stood, stretching his medium height to maximum advantage, then leaned over the table, bracing his weight on his knuckles. "We found a two-inch skull fracture."

A skull fracture? Mary hadn't noticed any injury during those forty-two minutes. "What do you mean by 'a skull fracture'?"

"You tell me."

"I can't tell you because I don't understand what you mean." If Melissa had a skull fracture, wouldn't her head be broken open? Surely there would at least be a huge bruise. Mary touched a place on the back of her head. "Was it here?"

No answer. He just stared at her.

Mary moved her hand to a new spot. "Or here?" The injury had to have been covered by Melissa's hair, or she would have seen it. "Or here?"

His eyes accused her. "You ought to know."

What was that supposed to mean? Mary glanced at Jim, read the frustration in his eyes. He could feel it too. This detective had declared her guilty before he knocked on the door. Jim shook his head, rose, and walked away with his anger.

Mary breathed deeply, prayed for a calm spirit. "I'm just asking because yesterday morning I looked her in the eye, sang to her, fed her, and I didn't see any bruises or marks. It had to be in the back of the head."

"She's got a two-inch skull fracture, and someone had to do it."

"Well, it wasn't me." Mary stood beside her chair, hoping to hasten the end of this farce. "I spent forty-two minutes with her, and I didn't hurt her. Absolutely nothing happened during that time that could have injured her."

Motsinger folded his arms, unmovable. "I still don't believe you. In November I gave testimony for the murder of a seven-month-old boy in Boone County. In that case the baby-sitter did it. I believe that's what happened here."

Maybe that baby-sitter had killed that child, though Mary could hardly imagine it, but what made the detective so sure she had done the same thing? Mary knew she was innocent.

This was America. People were innocent until proven guilty—but Agent Motsinger must have missed that lesson at the police academy.

Mary stepped back, tripping over a tricycle with big plastic wheels. "Do I need a lawyer?"

Motsinger moved closer, accusation in his eyes. "You tell me. Do you need a lawyer, Mary? Do you?"

It was time to call her friend Steve.

✡ ✡ ✡

When the phone rang, Steve Brennecke was sitting on the couch, reading to his three-year-old son, Nic. "It rained, and it rained, and it rained. Piglet told himself that never in all his life–"

Kim, his pretty, young wife, interrupted the story and handed him the phone.

"Steve, this is Mary Weaver." The voice sounded worried but under control. "The police have just left my house. I think I need a lawyer."

What was wrong? He knew Melissa had died, that the police had questions about her death, and that Mary was helping them find answers. She could supply background information, but why would she need a lawyer? He rose from the floor and walked into the next room. "What's up, Mary?"

"The police questioned me about Melissa. I went down to the station this morning. I told them what happened, but they—they don't seem to believe me. They keep asking me the same things over and over. After I told them everything I knew, they told me Melissa died." Her voice broke on the last word.

"Yes. We heard about that over the prayer chain. We're sorry to hear that."

"I just can't believe she died! She had the flu all week, and she wasn't doing too well, but she died! And if that isn't bizarre enough, another detective just came to my house and he said…" Mary sniffed loudly. "Steve, she died of a two-inch skull fracture!"

Steve switched the phone to his other ear and tried to process this bombshell. They'd been praying for Melissa since yesterday when she was flown to Iowa City's university hospitals. The death of a baby saddened everyone, shocked the family. But for a lawyer, this new information pushed this tragedy to a higher level—allegations of child abuse, even murder.

Steve shifted into his lawyer mode, balancing cautious optimism with carefully controlled emotion. "I'm sorry to hear about Melissa, but don't worry, Mary. You've done the right thing. You've cooperated and given them the whole story. The truth will come out in time."

"But…they don't believe me."

"They're probably just fishing for information, just doing their job." Steve tried to sound hopeful, but the words rang hollow, even to him. He reached for a pen and scratch pad.

"But the detective…I told him what happened. He said he didn't believe me. He thought I was leaving something out, but I told him everything. Melissa was only with me forty-two minutes. How much can happen in forty-two minutes? He had just witnessed a murder trial for a baby-sitter in Boone County. She was found guilty of murder. He thinks I did the same to Melissa."

"Did he say that—in so many words?"

"He did."

Unbelievable! Steve jotted some notes. *Didn't believe her. False accusations. Innocent until proven guilty. Idiot!* But he was supposed to be reassuring Mary, calming her down, even though anger pumped his own heart faster. "Sounds like they are getting adversarial, and they have no call to do that when you have been so cooperative. Don't answer any more questions. It's time to tell them to talk to your lawyer."

"You think I need a lawyer?"

Steve was certain of two things: This gentle friend from church would never harm any child, much less inflict a two-inch skull fracture on an eleven-month-old baby. And she did need a lawyer.

# CHAPTER 3

## MONDAY, JANUARY 25, 1993

Mary's morning echoed with a strange emptiness. She should be watching Melissa now, but Melissa was gone, forever. Mary would miss the baby's antics, but she also wondered what would come of the detective's questions. She replayed Steve's words. *You've done the right thing. You've cooperated and given them the whole story. The truth will come out in time.*

She trusted Steve. The blond lawyer was on the small side of average, but she could picture him digging his toes into an issue to fight for what was right.

The phone rang, interrupting her quiet reflection. "Mrs. Weaver, this is Lieutenant Buffington again with the Marshalltown Police Department. We are trying to clear up details about the death of Melissa Mathes. Would you be willing to take a polygraph test in Nevada this afternoon at one?"

Mary answered immediately. "I'll have to contact my husband first and see if he can baby-sit. Can I call you back in ten minutes?"

She called Jim quickly. Also Steve. He'd told her not to answer any more questions without him, and this gave her a chance to consult him.

Steve seemed to think the test was a good idea. "Polygraph tests are subjective," he said. "That's why they aren't admissible in court, but we don't know how the Lord will use this. Maybe it will show your innocence. Then the police can move on to find the person who hurt Melissa."

Mary tried to think positively. After all, God was in control. He would use this test for his good purpose.

She called the lieutenant within ten minutes of his original call. He said he would pick her up at noon.

She had nothing to hide. A lie detector test could help her clear her name so the police could find out what had really happened to Melissa.

Only liars need to fear lie detector tests. Mary told herself this, but the suspicion and finger-pointing robbed her of her normal peace. Would that anxiety affect the test? She recalled stories about lie detector tests. Results weren't always straightforward. Would the test reveal the truth or obscure it?

They think I'm guilty. The thought nagged at Mary's mind as she changed clothes and grabbed a sandwich. Each time she countered with truth from God's Word. The truth will set you free.

The lieutenant arrived at noon.

"We'll have to wait a few minutes," Mary said. "I have a friend who would like to ride along if that's okay."

"Who's your friend?"

"Steve Brennecke. He's a local attorney."

At the sheriff's department in Nevada, Iowa, things didn't go as planned. Steve had followed correct procedure. Mary had exercised her right to have her attorney present. But in spite of the fact that they were voluntarily undergoing the polygraph test, Sergeant Fosse said proper protocol dictated that Steve wait in a conference room with Lieutenant Buffington. Mary hoped

Steve had something in his briefcase that would allow him to use the time for some profit.

Inside the examination room Sergeant Fosse attached two rubber tubes around Mary's chest to monitor her breathing, then strapped a blood pressure cuff around her arm. Next he strapped sensors around her second and fourth fingers. "Monitors perspiration," he explained without a smile. He clamped the pulse oximeter on Mary's middle finger to complete the picture.

What was this—a polygraph test or minor surgery? Mary hated blood pressure cuffs and already felt sweat trickling down her neck. Would her nervousness affect the reading?

Once the instruments were settled, Sergeant Fosse proceeded without emotion. "State your name and address."

She did.

"Are you married?"

"Yes."

"To whom?"

"Jim Weaver."

"What is his occupation?"

She described his management of an auto parts store, which he owned with his family.

"How many children do you have, and what are their ages?"

"Two children. Catherine is four. John is two."

He asked more general questions, then moved on.

"What is your relationship to Brad and Tessia Mathes?"

Mary explained that her mother-in-law was a cousin to Brad's mother and that she had been providing child care for Brad and Tessia.

More intrusive questions followed: Did you have a good relationship with them? Were there problems? How did Melissa act during the week prior to her death? Were you worried about Melissa? Did you mention your concerns to Brad or Tessia?

Mary answered each question in a straightforward manner, reminding herself to keep her replies simple. She had already responded to these same questions for the police anyway.

"Are you aware that Melissa had a two-inch skull fracture at the time of her death?"

She should have expected this question, but it still jolted her like a slap across the face. Her hand twitched, and the pulse oximeter fell off. Sergeant Fosse readjusted it and repeated the question.

"Yes," Mary said, "I knew about the skull fracture."

"Do you know of any accident that could explain an injury of this sort?"

"N-no."

Mary thought about the long, narrow bruise she had seen on Melissa's leg months earlier. Tessia had said that Melissa fell on the rocker of a rocking chair. Her explanation seemed strange at the time because Melissa was barely crawling, not really pulling herself up. Melissa had come back from Christmas break with a few bruises too, but as Tessia explained them, they sounded like normal falls of a baby learning to walk. Then Becky, Brad's mom, had told Mary that Tessia had held Melissa upside down by the ankles. Melissa wriggled out of her hold and fell a couple of inches to the carpet, but that wouldn't have caused an injury like this, would it?

Mary had already told Lieutenant Buffington about these incidents. Was she supposed to bring up these past incidents now? Did the machine sense her hesitation?

"Melissa was trying to learn how to walk," Mary finally added. "She got bumps and bruises, but I don't know of anything that could cause an injury like this."

Sergeant Fosse eyed Mary carefully. "Someone hurt Melissa. Do you know who hurt her?"

# CHAPTER 3

"No."

Sergeant Fosse waited for more, but Mary chose to keep it simple.

"Did you hurt Melissa?"

"No! I didn't hurt her. I would never hurt her." Sweat beaded her skin. Her blood pressure must be going crazy, and she could only imagine what kind of line the needle was sketching. They would think she was lying. She took a deep breath and forced herself to speak in a more natural tone. "I have never hurt Melissa in any way."

"State your name and address."

That again? The examiner asked the same questions over again several times. He mixed simple, informational questions with insinuations about Melissa. Each time he asked about Melissa, he paused longer than he did with other questions. Was he hoping to get her to say more, or was he merely trying to unnerve her?

Each question probed deeper until she felt the questions would never end. When the end did come nearly two hours later, Mary was never so glad to have finished anything in her life.

Around noon the next day, the phone rang again. Mary answered it and found the caller to be Lieutenant Buffington again. "Mrs. Weaver, I wonder if you could come down to the station. We need to ask a few more questions so we can wrap up this matter with Melissa Mathes."

"Wrapping the matter up" sounded promising. A few more questions, and the dark clouds of suspicion could hang over someone else's house for a change. Of course, she would coop-erate. She glanced at the little girls playing at her feet. She was baby-sitting for the day but said she could come after Jim got home. A tiny warning whispered that she should call Steve first, but this didn't sound very serious, and she didn't want to take him from his family on this Tuesday evening.

Mary finished her baby-sitting, greeted Jim, and dropped Catherine off at her dance class at 5:30 on the way to the station. A man in blue led her to an interrogation room.

Moments later Agent Motsinger strutted into the room, chasing away any illusions she'd had that the end was in sight. He towered over the chair where she sat while Lieutenant Buffington stood guard on the sidelines. The questions started pleasantly enough, but Agent Motsinger soon changed his tone.

"You flunked the lie detector test big-time, Mrs. Weaver. Why don't you tell us what really happened when you were with Melissa?"

Not again. Mary searched for an answer that would satisfy the relentless detective. "I told you what happened."

"You must have left something out. Why don't you try again?"

Impatience crept into her voice. "I told you on Saturday. I picked Melissa up, fed her some baby food, laid her on the floor to put her snowsuit on, lifted her up carefully from the waist, supporting her head and neck. Then her eyes rolled back, and she quit breathing. I called her name. 'Melissa. Melissa.' I called 9-1-1. I tried to administer CPR. I flagged down the ambulance. That's it!"

"When you called her name, did you shake her to get her attention?"

"I may have, a little bit. Like this." Mary shook her hands gently, the way you would wake someone who was sleeping.

"You're sure you didn't shake her any harder than that?"

"Absolutely. It wasn't a rough shake. No more than that."

"You must have done something else. Something had to cause Melissa's seizure."

## CHAPTER 3

"I didn't. I have spent hours thinking about this, asking myself if I could have possibly done anything to hurt Melissa, but I didn't."

"So what caused the seizure?"

Her volume rose slightly. "I don't know. That's all that happened. I didn't do anything to harm that baby."

Agent Motsinger slammed a manila folder onto the table. "See this folder? In it I have medical reports from doctors in Iowa City that prove you are lying. Why don't you tell us what really happened?"

Over and over Agent Motsinger slammed the folder around and asked the same probing questions he had asked on Saturday. Mary stretched her patience thin to cover the answers. She wanted to help them solve this puzzle, but it was impossible. It was like a fill-in-the-blank test. They wanted her to fill in blanks, but she had no idea what answers they were looking for. Worse than that, they seemed incapable of believing she was innocent.

Agent Motsinger talked on and on. His voice grew louder as he repeated the same accusations. Maybe it was the desire to end this argument, or maybe it was her mother's instinct, but Mary suddenly checked her watch and realized Catherine's dance class was over.

Finally Mary leaned forward and challenged the detective's accusing eyes. "I don't know what you want me to say. Nothing. Else. Happened. You keep accusing me. Are you going to arrest me? Because if you are, I want to call my lawyer."

At the mention of a lawyer, Agent Motsinger straightened and lightened his tone. "We aren't arresting you. You are free to go anytime."

She stood up and grabbed her purse. "Then I'm out of here." Mary sped out the door so fast, she kicked over a small trash can.

✿ ✿ ✿

Steve was furious. Mary had made a mistake by not taking him with her for the interview. She didn't like to bother him; he understood that. But according to her teary phone call, Agent Motsinger had yelled at her and accused her of lying—again.

As an attorney Steve had always had a good relationship with the police, but this time they were crossing the line. He had to stop them. Mary's truthfulness and cooperation had been repaid with accusations and bullying. Melissa had died less than four days ago, and these detectives had already decided Mary was guilty. So much for gathering all the facts first.

Steve looked up Lieutenant Buffington's home phone number and dialed.

"Lieutenant Buffington? Steve Brennecke here. I am very unhappy that you allowed Agent Motsinger to question my client, Mary Weaver, without me being present."

Buffington shifted into defense mode. "Mrs. Weaver didn't have to answer our questions. We advised her of her rights. She was willing to talk. She signed an affidavit to that effect."

"You're not playing fair here, Lieutenant, and you know it. Mary has given you three interviews willingly without her attorney present. She has answered all your questions, in spite of the fact that she has been treated rudely and accused of lying. She took your polygraph test. Most attorneys wouldn't let their client take a polygraph, let alone accompany them to the polygraph. We have cooperated in every way, yet when Mary refused to agree with Agent Motsinger's false accusations, he yelled at her."

"Agent Motsinger didn't yell at her. Voices were raised, yes, but no one yelled at her."

"Mary says Motsinger lost it, and I believe her. I've never known her to exaggerate. You and Motsinger, on the other hand, are police officers. You have betrayed the good faith Mary showed in repeatedly answering all your questions. I'm not happy about the way she was treated. In the future you are not to talk to Mary without my permission or without my presence!"

✿ ✿ ✿

Weeks later Steve received a disturbing phone call. A week and a half after Mary had taken her polygraph test, Brad and Tessia had been asked to take one too. Steve studied the notes he had scribbled on a napkin. How could he put a good slant on the call he had received? This kind of thing happened all the time, but it could shake a client's confidence, and his job as lawyer was to inspire confidence. The fact that Mary was a friend as well made his job imperative.

Steve rang Mary's number and waited for her to pick up. He softened the blow with a bit of small talk first. Then: "I got the results of the polygraph tests. They tested Brad and Tessia too. They decided your test was deceptive, and Brad and Tessia's were inconclusive."

"What's that supposed to mean?" Mary asked.

"They told you when they first questioned you that they thought you were guilty. Now they think you're deceptive. You didn't give them the answers they wanted." Steve sighed. "Sounds like the tests were a waste of time."

"So do they think I'm lying or what?"

"They know polygraph tests aren't conclusive."

"Did they give you any details?"

"They would only give me the labels. I may get an official letter later, but we probably won't get any details. We don't know what questions the examiner asked Brad and Tessia. We don't know how he approached them. He may have been gentler with them since they are grieving parents. He may have made it sound like the police just wanted to rule them out, whereas with you they were very adversarial."

"They sure were. They kept probing until I almost felt guilty. You can't imagine how it felt. I can see how people flunk those tests."

"And you know that manila folder that you said Motsinger was slamming around at the interview?"

"Yeah."

"Whatever was in that folder, it wasn't medical reports that showed you were lying. They hadn't even been released at the time."

"Do they really think I'm guilty?"

"I'm convinced of it. They don't seem to be looking at anyone else."

"So how am I going to prove my innocence?"

"Shouldn't have to. 'Innocent until proven guilty.' It's the foundation of our legal system." Steve took a deep breath, forcing the anger from his voice. "But remember, we're not at the mercy of the legal system. We're at the mercy of God."

"I'm counting on that."

✿ ✿ ✿

Months passed, but Mary couldn't forget the scowling Agent Motsinger. He had bulldozed over her simple truth while she'd shivered like a fawn in the headlights. No bully could have scared her more.

Mary went about her daily activities, but Melissa's death glowered in the background like a dark funnel cloud that couldn't decide where to touch down. She tried to ignore the storm warnings, but someone had injured Melissa. The police would continue to search for answers.

# CHAPTER 3

Did the police still think she was guilty, or were they questioning other possible suspects? If they suspected someone else, why hadn't they arrested anyone? Since Steve had warned them not to talk to Mary without his presence, the police weren't talking to her at all. Mary didn't know what was worse: knowing they thought she was guilty or having no idea what they were thinking.

Mary pushed the incident from her mind and reached out to Tessia and Becky. At least they didn't think she was guilty. Both Brad and Tessia had thanked her for trying to save Melissa's life.

But Tessia and Becky didn't respond warmly to these gestures. Several times Mary called Tessia and invited her to lunch, but the grieving mother always made excuses. Mary saw Becky now and then, but Mary could feel their friendship cooling.

"I feel bad for Becky," Mary told a friend one day. "She's lost her only grandchild. I want to comfort her as a friend. I don't want it to be like this."

The friend squeezed Mary's arm. "It's a hard time for Becky too. Maybe seeing you reminds her of Melissa's death. Maybe you should just pull back and give her some space."

Perhaps the friend was right. Maybe the mom and grandma needed to grieve on their own. Mary understood the need to grieve. She had cared for Melissa every weekday for about six months. The fact that this sweet baby girl had evidently been intentionally injured by someone made her death more disturbing than usual. Yet the uncertainty of the police investigation made grieving difficult. Mainly Mary just tried not to think about it.

Mary moved on with her life, keeping house, making meals, playing with her kids. But when months went by with no arrests, she could sense that funnel cloud of suspicion rotating above her.

✿ ✿ ✿

## WEDNESDAY, MAY 26, 1993

The legal tornado hit without warning.

The day started hot and humid, but Mary refused to let it affect her. She hefted the box fan from the basement and pre-heated the oven. Catherine colored Care Bear pictures on the kitchen table while John raced sports cars around the table legs. Mary was humming to herself and pulling bread from the oven when a knock sounded at the door.

Probably just a neighbor wanting the kids to come out and play. Mary set the pan on the stove and headed for the front door. She finger-combed her shoulder-length hair and dusted flour from her apron.

When she pulled the door open, she found two uniformed policemen standing on the top step. Catherine and John hovered around her ankles.

"Are you Mary Weaver?" one of the policemen asked.

Melissa had been dead four months, but Mary feared the tempest had only begun to rage. "Y-yes."

"We have a warrant for your arrest."

No. She hardly dared to ask the obvious question. "On what charges?"

"First-degree murder and child endangerment."

# CHAPTER 4

Arrested! Mary had never received anything more serious than a speeding ticket, and now this. Two innocent little faces stared up at her. Confusion was written across their faces. *Policemen are our friends,* she could imagine them thinking. *What are they doing to our mommy?*

Mary pulled John close. "I…I just can't leave these kids here like this. Can I make a couple of phone calls?"

The officers said she could. She called Jim and Steve and her friend April to ask her to watch the kids. Then she and the kids piled into the squad car. April met them in front of her house. The kids clung to Mary and didn't want to get out of the car.

Mary hugged each of them. "I need you to go with Aunt April now. Everything will be all right."

Mary watched out the car window as April led the kids away. As they drove away, Catherine and John stared at them from the front porch.

The squad car pulled up to the Marshall County Jail. One of the policemen opened her door. "Mrs. Weaver, I'm going to have to handcuff you. I should have done it at the house, but I didn't want to do it in front of the kids."

Mary nodded and held out her hands. The policeman cuffed her and led her inside to a solitary confinement cell. She couldn't share a cell with men, and all the other prisoners were men, so this steel cage was the logical place for her. She exchanged her jeans and T-shirt for a navy jumpsuit and settled down to study her surroundings.

One high window with bars let in light. A single metal bunk bed and pillow completed the furnishings. This was temporary. God knew she had never hurt Melissa. All the suspicion in the world would lead nowhere because she was innocent. But what was her family thinking? Were her children scared? Right now she needed only one thing. When Steve came by for a visit, she asked him to bring her a Bible. He made sure she got one.

Worries about her family buzzed around her head like ruthless mosquitoes. Catherine and John must be so afraid. What would Jim tell them? She leafed through her Bible until she found Matthew 7. "What man is there among you who, if his son asks for bread, will give him a stone? Of if he asks for a fish, will he give him a serpent? If you then, being evil, know how to give good gifts to your children, how much more will your Father who is in heaven give good things to those who ask Him!"

Mary caressed the verse with her fingers. "Lord, I believe. You are a good God. You are in control. You will take care of my family."

She remembered God's promise, "Ask and it will be given to you." Mary prayed for her family, for wisdom for Steve, for her own release. But when she opened her eyes, steel bars still surrounded her.

That night she focused on her verses. Peace came, and sleep came easily. Only later did she find out that her friends hadn't fared so well. Pastor Shomo had called the prayer chain, and her friends had prayed and worried more than slept.

Time passed slowly in jail. Bail was initially set at one million dollars, but Steve convinced Marshall County Attorney Diann Wilder-Tomlinson to agree to posting the deed to the Weavers' house instead of the bail money. Within days Mary was released to return home to a new and unsettled state of "normal."

✿ ✿ ✿

Steve left the prison with a heavy heart. He had informed Mary of her right not to speak to the police anymore, especially without his presence. He assured her that she'd cooperated with the police in those early interviews, giving them good answers to help them find out what happened to Melissa. But his job as a lawyer had just kicked into a much higher gear. Now Mary was a murder suspect awaiting trial. The state wasn't going to back down from this. They were going to try to put her in prison.

He'd been a courtroom lawyer with his own practice for all of three years. In most of his cases he represented guilty clients. He'd become a lawyer to help people with their problems. Guilty people had problems and needed his help. He gave them good representation and tried to negotiate an acceptable plea.

But Mary was innocent. Though he'd known her for only a short time, he knew she was a patient, caring mother who would never murder a child. Mary needed representation, and she had chosen him to do it.

It was natural that she would choose a lawyer she knew, a friend from church, but this was the biggest case Steve had ever taken. Was he up to it?

Steve didn't mind a challenge. When they'd moved to Grinnell a few months ago, he and Kim bought an old mansion that needed lots of work. Sure, it needed totally new wall linings and major work on the roof, but they could hardly wait to restore it to its former glory. They would just work on one project at a time until they were finished.

Mary's case would be a challenge too. He was relatively inexperienced, but he knew the rules and procedure and case law. He'd studied law and seen some good trials played out before him. He would work especially hard on this case because he was convinced of her innocence.

Actually her innocence made this case far more intimidating than usual. With a guilty client Steve could be content to provide adequate representation and negotiate the terms of the sentence. If he failed in Mary's case, however, an innocent mother of two small children would spend the rest of her life in prison.

Never had he taken a case with greater need—or greater risk.

But they didn't have to prove Mary's innocence. The state had to prove her guilt beyond reasonable doubt. And Steve saw reasonable doubt in every direction.

As a bonus, if he won this case, his career would sprint forward. On the other hand, losing his first big case would damage his career.

Steve added it up. Great cause + great prospects + good training + God = the greatest case of his life. If Mary was willing to hand over her fate to a relatively inexperienced lawyer friend plus God, how could he say no?

Following the bail hearing and Mary's release, Steve cleared his schedule and began to read through the official autopsy report. His training was in law, but he would need to educate himself in the medical issues Melissa faced. Otherwise doctors could shade the meaning of their findings, slanting the case their way without his realizing it. He would have to be able to understand the medical issues to challenge their conclusions.

First he read the report from cover to cover without stopping. Then he started over, this time with a highlighter, reading carefully, marking things he had questions about. He made a list of the injuries and sorted the older injuries from the acute ones.

skull fracture—7–10 days old
subdural hematoma (under fracture)—1–2 weeks old
clot, sagittal sinus (top of head)—7–10 days old
contusion, frontal cortex (bruise on brain in forehead)—acute
hypoxic injury (lack of oxygen)—acute
cerebral edema (brain swelling)—acute
retinal hemorrhaging—no age listed
DIC's (look this up)—acute

He found medical definitions in his dictionary. The picture of Melissa's injuries began to form in his mind.

Mary had had Melissa for only about forty-two minutes that Friday morning. Something catastrophic must have happened to Melissa long before Mary picked her up that day. Old injuries pointed the finger of suspicion at other caregivers and away from Mary. Steve found himself growing confident of their defense just by studying the state's evidence.

But the autopsy implied that there had been a new incident of abuse, a second scenario by which Melissa had been reinjured. Since Mary insisted that Melissa had seemed fine that morning when she picked her up, in the mind of the state Mary looked guilty. The report concluded that the new injuries had caused Melissa's death.

To a nonmedical person, however, the report left more questions than it answered. What had happened to Melissa seven to ten days before her death that had fractured her skull and caused bleeding in her brain? Why wasn't she taken to a doctor then? How could she have acted so "normal" only to succumb to these lethal injuries days later? How could the state believe Mary had inflicted lethal injuries on Melissa when not even the ER doctor could see any outward sign of those injuries?

These questions sent Steve searching for his own answers. The state seemed content with its medical experts, who had decided Mary was the murderer. Steve knew she wasn't. He needed an expert who would look at the facts objectively and give a second opinion.

Steve talked with his lawyer friends. One recommended Dr. Earl Rose. He'd been deputy chief medical examiner for the state of Virginia and city and county medical examiner in Dallas, Texas. Then he'd practiced pathology, taught, and done research for the University of Iowa for more than twenty years. Though he'd retired a few years earlier, he enjoyed a stellar reputation from a lifetime of medical practice.

Steve was told Rose wasn't flamboyant, but he told the truth and stayed within the boundaries of what science could prove. He stuck to the facts and wouldn't be impeached on cross-examination. Just the kind of guy they needed.

Steve could feel God's blessing when Dr. Rose agreed to look at the autopsy and discuss it with him. Steve made an appointment to meet with Rose in the doctor's home.

On the day of the appointment, Steve drove into Iowa City, the town that held the answers. He drove along through the familiar neighborhoods, past the law school he'd first attended only ten years earlier. Though Iowa City was known as a wild college town, for Steve it brought back memories of his spiritual awakening. The Iowa City Bible Fellowship was the first church Steve had attended after becoming a Christian. Here in the midst of law school, when he was looking for answers to the bigger questions of life, he sought out God in the pages of the Bible and found him. With the encouragement of Christian friends, he began to grow in his faith, a faith that was about to be tested.

Here also Melissa had clung to life, fighting through the final hours before she passed away. Doctors conducted the autopsy here and concluded Melissa had been murdered. Now they were focusing all their accusations on Mary.

Steve pulled up to the curb in front of a century-old home and walked to the door. Dr. Rose met him at the door, introduced himself, and seated him in a tastefully furnished room trimmed in oak and accented with fine oil paintings.

As they chatted over steaming coffee in china cups, the two discovered they had graduated from the same alma mater in Dallas. Dr. Rose had studied law while serving as medical examiner in Dallas.

"I didn't know you were a lawyer," Steve said. "I understand you were supposed to have done the autopsy on JFK when he died."

"By Texas law I should have, but Mrs. Kennedy wanted the autopsy moved to Maryland, and the fact that I wasn't allowed to do the autopsy has only fueled the conspiracy theories. That's what happens when you don't follow protocol."

Steve nodded toward an envelope on the table. He recognized it as the autopsy report he had sent. "Do you think they followed protocol in Melissa's autopsy?"

"Well, this is a complex case, Melissa's."

Dr. Rose set his cup down on the saucer and began to teach Steve as he would have a class. "You see, you've got old injuries. Severe old injuries. And they complicate anything you're trying to do now. While they are old, they are still operative. They continue to impact her condition; they're not resolved."

The doctor gestured with his hands as he explained the various layers of the head, starting with the skin, then the bone, the shoe leather layer called the dura, the arachnoid membrane that was as thin as cellophane, and the brain tissue inside. Melissa had suffered a subdural hematoma, bleeding between the dura and the brain. When the bleed began, it inflated like a small balloon, pressing on the brain.

"What happens to the patient with a subdural bleed?" Steve asked.

"You mean, what does the patient feel?"

Steve nodded.

"As a pathologist I don't treat live patients, but I understand they have one big headache. When the subdurals heal, they leave only an iron stain on the inside of the skull. Melissa's subdural hematoma had only started to heal when she died."

"So we have the subdural hematoma; what else here is significant?"

"Let me be clear. She didn't die from just the subdural bleed. There are other injuries and processes that led to her death. Some were old injuries."

"How old?" Steve began to realize that the age of the injuries was one of the keys to Mary's defense.

"Same age roughly. It is hard to tell exactly, and that's why they give these old injuries a range. 'Seven to ten days,' for example. Take the skull fracture. It ran from the thick, bony prominence at the base of her skull"—he paused, reaching his left hand to the back of his head—"all the way up to the crown, where her hair swirled around."

Steve felt the back of his own head, listening.

"And the skull of an eleven-month-old child isn't brittle like us old folks' bones." He clinked his index fingernail against the lip of his china cup. "They're supple, somewhat flexible. So this fracture is really more of a tear in a thick, difficult skull bone."

Dr. Rose launched into a discussion about the healing of bone tissue. He estimated the skull fracture to be seven to ten days old. The subdural hematoma was about seven days old. It had also been healing.

"What else is there?"

"In terms of old injuries, there is a blood clot in her sagittal sinus, adherent to the left side of her brain. The clot has partly plugged up the blood as it flows out of the brain. This was increasing pressure in her skull along with the subdural bleed."

"She was a mess."

"Yes, she was a very critically injured child."

"Mary Weaver, my client, only had this child for about forty-two minutes that day."

"These injuries predate that by far. And the report refers to necrotic tissue." He spoke slowly, emphatically, tapping the side of his head with his fingers. "Her brain was dying. There was dead and dying tissue behind the clot."

"Is that what killed her?"

"Can't know for sure. Can't say emphatically. We'd have to do a study of eleven-month-old children—line them up and give them these particular injuries—and then sit back and study what happens to them. Can't do that."

"Well, what do you think happened?"

"It is likely that she had a rebleed of the subdural hematoma. The report noted new blood there as well as the old, organized clot. The rebleed would have added sudden pressure to her brain, and she would have just shut down."

Dr. Rose had already said he didn't know for sure what happened, but for Mary's sake Steve felt he needed to press on to the point of being pushy. "So did she receive a new injury at that moment on Friday morning that caused her to collapse? That's where they are going with this, you know."

"Not necessarily. Under these conditions, with the injuries Melissa had, just sitting up could change your intercranial pressure, the pressure inside your skull, and you could rebleed and die. Sitting up in bed could kill you."

Steve sat in stunned silence for a moment, not knowing what to say. "Do you know what Mary said Melissa was doing when she passed out?"

"No. I have only examined what you sent me, the autopsy report."

"Mary was slipping Melissa into a one-piece snowsuit. Melissa was lying down on a carpeted floor on her back. Mary put her feet in, then pulled up the snowsuit behind her, then reached behind her head and upper back, and lifted her up into a sitting position so she could put her arms into the snowsuit. Melissa's eyes rolled back in her head at that moment, and she quit breathing."

Dr. Rose nodded.

Steve smiled. Already they had a medical expert to challenge the assumptions of the autopsy.

# CHAPTER 5

## AUGUST 1993

Six months had passed since Melissa's death, and the police still didn't seem to be considering any suspects other than Mary. Why wasn't anyone investigating the older injuries? With the injuries Melissa had when Mary picked her up, sitting up could have killed her. But police seemed to be ignoring the old injuries and focusing on the new ones.

Police were taking their cues from doctors. Steve had to understand the doctors because the word of medical experts could convict Mary of murder. The fact that police weren't searching for other suspects made him suspect that at least some of the doctors believed Mary was guilty.

In the next few days he would depose six doctors who had taken part in the autopsy or reviewed it. He would learn a lot about Melissa's injuries and the cause of death at that time. While he was learning about medicine, he could also spy out the state's arsenal of ammunition against them. These depositions would allow him to pin down the doctors' testimony and solidify Mary's defense.

Three of the doctors seemed to work closely together. Bennett, Smith, and Alexander had coauthored articles on serial abuse and shaken baby syndrome (SBS). As state medical examiner,

Bennett shared dozens of cases with Smith and Alexander, who served together on a subcommittee on abuse and neglect at the University of Iowa Hospital. Alexander specialized in recognition of child abuse injuries and patterns. Smith was usually notified in a child abuse case that involved imaging.

Bennett had reviewed Melissa's autopsy and overseen the whole process; he would testify as the foremost authority, the state medical examiner. Smith had administered Melissa's second CT scan and reviewed all the radiology. Alexander had met with the autopsy team.

These three would testify for the state. They would be determined to sniff out child abuse and prosecute it. Stamping out child abuse was a worthy cause. Steve hoped they would use their expertise to find Melissa's true killer. On the other hand, if they decided Mary was that killer, they would be tough opponents to shake.

The day before the depositions, Steve flipped open a copy of Dr. Wilbur Smith's police statement. Lieutenant Buffington had interviewed him over the phone from El Paso, Texas. Smith may have been unaware that the call was recorded, but this statement, on its own, could help them.

Smith had reviewed the radiology work—the CT scans and X rays. According to the autopsy, the skull fracture had been healing for seven to ten days. Buffington told Smith that "Melissa was 'happy-go-lucky' when Mary picked her up; then at 11:13 she called 9-1-1 with an unconscious baby."

Smith explained that the pattern on the CT scan was called a cerebral edema pattern, which began more slowly. They would have to look at a wider window of time for it. To Steve the meaning was obvious. The injury that killed Melissa had started before Mary picked her up.

Steve chose a yellow marker and highlighted Smith's next paragraph: It's not that massive of an injury, so it depends on how reliable the babysitter is…You can get fooled by a little baby with cerebral edema. Smith said that, based on the scans, the injury, if there was a new injury, couldn't be pinned down any closer than twenty-four hours from her seizure.

Mary had insisted that Melissa was behaving normally Friday morning, and Smith seemed to agree. He said that with her injuries Melissa could act normally and then rapidly deteriorate and have a seizure.

From what Smith said in his statement, Melissa's X rays and CT scans showed solid medical reasons to doubt Mary's guilt. And with presumption of innocence, doubt was all they needed.

The next day Steve prepared for the depositions in a conference room in the University of Iowa Hospital. Mary joined him as well as Ms. Wilder-Tomlinson, who would serve as Mary's prosecutor, and the court reporter.

Alexander's deposition went as expected, but Smith's deposition exploded Steve's hope that the case would be simple.

Smith's dark hair and rapidly receding hairline framed a face that would fit the president of the chess club. His tie was knotted with precision, his pants perfectly creased.

Smith agreed that Melissa had received severe older injuries, but the notion of re-injury held great risk for Mary. Steve led the questions in the direction of the timing of the acute injury, hoping to pin down the twenty-four-hour time frame Smith had given in the police report.

"The injury occurred," Smith said, "within four or five hours of the first CT scan."

Four or five hours? Steve's mind recalculated the new numbers, weighing the consequences of this new time frame. Mary had picked Melissa up at 10:20 a.m. Doctors performed the Marshalltown CT scan just past noon—about 12:30. He avoided

Mary's eyes, refused to flinch, and masked his emotions with a calmness that belied his pounding heart.

"Four or five hours of the Marshalltown CT scan?" Steve asked.

The doctor peered at Steve over a pair of half-lens reading glasses slung low across his nose. "Yes."

The time of the reinjury had moved. They were trying to blame Mary for this. The circle of blame was now much, much smaller. "Can you pinpoint it any better than that?"

Dr. Smith studied Steve over the top of his glasses. "I don't think I can, no."

Steve moved on, asking if this injury could have come from a fall against a padded recliner. Tessia had reported this injury earlier Friday morning.

Dr. Smith didn't think it was likely but didn't completely rule it out. Any relief Steve felt from this statement, however, was short-lived.

When the prosecutor, Ms. Wilder-Tomlinson, was given her turn to examine Smith, she quickly aimed her questions at the same target. "Can you quantify closer to time as to when that event would have occurred? You said, I believe, four to five hours before she ended up at the hospital for the CT scan."

"That's the outside, before the CT scan."

"What would be the inside?"

"Oh...an hour or two."

"Could it be within the hour?"

"Yes, could be."

Wilder-Tomlinson asked only few more questions, and Steve had one more chance.

Steve consulted his notes, glancing down to Dr. Smith's quote to Lieutenant Buffington. "Is it possible to get fooled by an infant with cerebral edema?"

Confusion clouded the eyes that peered over the half lenses. "Fooled?" He had no way of knowing Steve was staring down at his police statement.

Steve decided to keep the police statement to himself. He asked if Melissa could have received the fatal injury and come into Mary's care without Mary recognizing the symptoms, then gone into seizure without further injury.

Dr. Smith maintained it was impossible for Melissa to have received the fatal injury before her time with Mary and still look normal enough that Mary wouldn't have noticed.

His testimony had already changed in two different aspects from his police interview, and both aspects moved closer to blaming Mary for the newer injuries.

Bennett came last in the two days of deposition. He bounded into the room in blue jeans and sport shoes, and chatted with them like college buddies. During the deposition he actually unwrapped a sandwich and started eating it. Clearly the doctor was a busy man, but this seemed a bit informal for the deposition of a trial for first-degree murder.

Steve struggled to size the doctor up. Maybe he was trying to be friendly, but he came across to Steve as unprofessional and arrogant. A witness like this could strangle his own credibility with overconfidence, but he could also persuade a jury to convict. Steve had to be careful.

Steve began the deposition, asking Dr. Bennett about his background, education, training, and boards he'd been on. The doctor was clearly comfortable airing his accomplishments and credentials. Steve asked him to give his interpretation of the observations from the autopsy and to explain where he differed from the various doctors who had done the actual cutting and documentation.

Dr. Bennett warmed to his subject and answered in great detail. He chomped away on his sandwich and brushed crumbs from his mustache while reciting autopsy details—brain cutting, retinal hemorrhages, skull fracture, and bruises. Often he started answering a specific question, only to veer off on his own verbal side road. Bennett had the looks of a Hollywood actor, and he played his part well, using word choice, volume, tone, and pauses for dramatic affect.

Steve asked him to describe the injuries that he thought were seven to ten days old. Dr. Bennett believed they had to be the result of a shaking-and-slamming injury.

Steve worked for clarification. An injury could be consistent with shaken baby syndrome, but that didn't rule out other causes. If the injury was diagnostic of SBS, on the other hand, that ruled out other causes. Steve probed the doctor's eyes. "Are you saying that findings are consistent with that, but not diagnostic of, shaken baby syndrome?"

Dr. Bennett entered the stare down. "No. They're indicative of an episode of the shaking and slamming, shaking and impact."

Steve held his ground. "So you're very confident saying there was a shake-and-slam incident that day and that there was no other means of inflicting that type of combination of injuries?"

"That's correct."

Steve stared at his notes, giving himself time to process the reply. How could Dr. Bennett say there was no other means of inflicting a skull fracture? No other means than shaking and slamming? Surely one could inflict this injury some other way, perhaps in a car accident, but to Dr. Bennett, there was only one way–his way.

Steve moved on to the more recent injury Dr. Bennett thought happened closer to the time of Melissa's death. What was his opinion about the timing of that injury?

Dr. Bennett stated there had to be another shaking-and-slamming injury, which happened within one hour of Melissa's admission to the hospital. He said Melissa could not have been acting relatively fine one minute and then gone into respiratory arrest without a new injury.

With each new confident opinion Dr. Bennett narrowed the target. Shaking-and-slamming injuries were intentional abuse. Only Mary had been with Melissa just prior to the respiratory arrest.

Steve had to get Dr. Bennett to consider other options. His mind flicked back to Dr. Smith's quote about cerebral edema to Lieutenant Buffington.

"Dr. Bennett, is there no possibility of a more slowly developing cerebral edema pattern, which builds to the point that there's a loss of function, loss of breathing?"

"Can that occur? I suppose that can occur." Bennett paused, allowing the drama to build. Then he glared at Mary, eyeing her like a bull's-eye. "Did that occur in this case? No."

Steve stared, working consciously to keep his mouth from dropping open. How could anyone state with absolute certainty what did or didn't occur in this case? But Dr. Bennett asserted this strongly, as if the sheer force of his statements would make them true.

Near the end Steve read a quote from Bennett in Melissa's medical record. "Dr. Bennett stated there was still shake and slam within an hour before the baby was admitted to the Marshalltown hospital." He gave the doctor one more chance to admit any uncertainty about his conclusion by asking him if that was his statement and what he based it on.

Dr. Bennett mentioned the history that had been reported in Melissa's case—that she had been acting fine and eating at one point and then suddenly became unresponsive. "Then the findings of shake-and-slam incident had to occur within an hour prior to the presentation at the hospital or that 9-1-1 call—within the hour."

In other words, Mary was guilty.

Alexander, Smith, and Bennett had witnessed the aftermath of child abuse many times and were determined to stamp it out. Of course. But they were also doctors, scientists who were trained to consider the facts objectively. Surely they would be open to new evidence.

Steve hoped the doctors would follow Mary's case and the arguments of other doctors, and question the certainty of their current opinions. They had to understand that the fine line between doubt and certainty meant the difference between conviction and acquittal for Mary. They had to know that their word as doctors weighed heavily on the jury's decision.

Steve refused to be cynical. Even strongly opinionated doctors could change their minds. Yet Steve caught glimpses that these were more than three men who hoped to convict child abusers. They were more like a child abuse SWAT team who had identified their target and were merely waiting to fire.

# CHAPTER 6

"There is a way to resolve this case without the risk of life in prison."

Steve swiveled his chair away from Mary and listened without revealing his emotions. Wilder-Tomlinson had managed to call just when Mary was in the office. With the depositions done, they were preparing for the trial ahead.

"What do you have in mind?" he asked the prosecutor.

As the call ended, he swiveled back to face Mary. "Ms. Wilder-Tomlinson called. They want to offer you a deal."

Mary fingered her car keys, processing the words. "What do you mean, 'a deal'?"

"They want to offer to let you plead guilty to something that won't carry the risk of life in prison." Steve glanced at his shelves of law books, but none of his training made this any easier. He met Mary's eyes again. "You know, Mary, in Iowa a lifer is a lifer. You never. Get. Out."

Mary's eyes watered. "But I didn't do anything, Steve. You've got to believe me."

"I know that, Mary. I do believe you." He was certain of Mary's innocence but less sure of his own ability to successfully defend her. "I have an obligation to convey the prosecutor's offer to you, since you're my client. That's all."

"But...I'd have to lie to plead guilty to anything."

"I know."

"So I'm not interested in anything she offers."

"I'll let her know."

Steve turned back to the papers before him, but his energy for the task had deflated. Something in the prosecutor's voice had sent a warning that, though Mary was innocent, the outcome was far from guaranteed.

✿ ✿ ✿

Mary couldn't decide whether the prosecutor's plea bargain offer was a good sign or a bad one. Maybe Wilder-Tomlinson knew she couldn't prove first-degree murder, murder with intent, so she was offering a plea for second degree. Or did she think Steve and Mary had their backs to the wall and now would accept a lesser plea? Mary only knew that she wasn't guilty, so it made no sense to enter a guilty plea.

Mary pulled a cake from the oven, tossed a few remaining toys into a basket, and cuddled up in the recliner, alone in the silent house. Jim was at work. Catherine and John were at preschool. These quiet times with God helped her get through each day when fear clouded her future.

Six months had passed since Melissa's death. The investigative wheels rolled so slowly and in this case seemed to be stuck in neutral. The police had quit looking for other suspects. What if she were convicted?

Many in Marshalltown knew her and and seemed convinced of her innocence. Instead of treating her like the out-on-bond criminal suspect she was, friend after friend had assured her that they just couldn't believe this was happening to her. Still the police seemed so sure she was guilty that they weren't looking for anyone else.

Could the unthinkable happen? Even Steve couldn't guarantee acquittal. Alexander, Smith, and Bennett had studied the medical evidence and believed Mary to be the killer. What if she was convicted? Would God let that happen?

She reminded herself that the trial was still months away. The police could be gathering evidence they had yet to reveal.

Mary tried to silence the what-ifs by opening her Bible to the place she'd been reading the day before. Jeremiah was an intriguing Bible character. He'd lived during Israel's darkest days and earned the title of the weeping prophet. Some found the book of Jeremiah depressing, but Mary was finding new hope here.

Jeremiah lived in dark days, when his nation's stubborn rebellion and persistent sin had finally exhausted God's patience. God allowed them to be taken away from their homes and forced to live in captivity in Babylon. God spoke words of comfort to Jeremiah to pass on to his people.

"I know the thoughts that I think toward you…thoughts of peace and not of evil, to give you a future and a hope," God said.

Hope in dark days, like ice water in a desert.

"Then you will call upon Me and . . . I will listen to you. And you will seek Me and find Me, when you search for Me with all your heart."

Mary had already found God to be real and near. Now she was seeking comfort from a God who specialized in it.

"I will bring you back from your captivity."

Mary underlined the words of Jeremiah 29:11–14 and marked the place with the ribbon bookmark. God allowed the tragic, dark days of captivity, but he also promised they would end. He promised the Jewish people a bright future.

Somehow these words flashed at Mary like a neon sign. God seemed to impress them on her heart in an unusual way. All children of God could be assured that God had a future and a hope for them, but Mary felt God was promising her something extra. She would go into "captivity," but she would return. She didn't know exactly what "captivity" meant for her. Maybe it was these long days of waiting and preparing, and the trial which would end this chapter of her life.

Melissa's death would have been hard enough if it had been a simple accident. The fact that Mary was accused of murder made it much harder. She couldn't imagine what it would be like to sit through an entire trial and listen to people accuse her and testify against her. But it wouldn't last forever. She could claim this promise. God had a future and a hope for her.

Perhaps she would actually go to prison, but if she did, she knew she wouldn't stay there forever.

☆ ☆ ☆

Steve thumbed through the files that littered his desk. The experts were going to try to pin the uncertain, newer injuries on Mary. He needed to emphasize the older injuries. If he could get the prosecution to focus on the person who had inflicted the older injuries, the jurors might be able to consider Mary's innocence. He would raise doubt by showing that other people could have killed Melissa.

The ringing telephone interrupted his strategizing. Steve prayed it would be good news this time. His secretary transferred the call.

"Hello. This is Steve."

A nervous young woman's voice answered. "You represent Mary Weaver, right?"

"Yes, I do."

"My name is Kim Smuck, and I...I know some information about her case that I need to tell you. I wasn't going to tell anybody about it until after I saw they charged Mary with murder. But I can't be quiet about it any longer."

Steve leaned forward in his chair and began taking notes as she spoke. When the call ended, he filled in some gaps in his notes, then stared in amazement at the strange new information. The Lord worked in mysterious ways, but this was downright weird.

# CHAPTER 7

## DECEMBER 1993

"9-1-1 Emergency."

"I need an ambulance. I've got a baby that's stopped breathing!" Mary's urgent voice filled the courtroom. The jury barely moved as the audiotape played the dispatcher's instructions and Mary's vain attempt to get Melissa breathing again. Steve could picture the scene: Mary with a phone receiver wedged between her ear and shoulder, holding a limp Melissa close, trying to talk, listen, and save a life at one time. Ominous gurgling sounds and occasional gasps for air punctuated the conversation.

For nearly ten minutes the tape ran, replaying the horror of a baby fighting for life and a baby-sitter fighting to save her. No wonder it left the jury visibly disturbed. This was no TV drama. This was real life–leading up to real death. The state wanted to prove this was first-degree murder and child endangerment, and would try to prove the charges they had read just prior to the disturbing tape.

Steve was relieved to have the trial begin. The state had opened it by presenting their evidence with this 9-1-1 dispatcher.

In the chair beside him, Steve noticed Mary blotting a tear from the corner of one eye. Reliving the scene that had led to

Melissa's death had to be difficult. Steve jotted a note to her. "This helps us." He believed this was some of their best evidence. It was raw, unblemished sound, an unbiased witness—one of the few on the state's list of witnesses, in Steve's opinion.

Steve thought the jury could clearly see Mary's concern for Melissa in the taped call and her desperate effort to save Melissa's life. But the prosecutor, Wilder-Tomlinson, began to paint a different picture.

The prosecutor sat at her table, consulting her notes. No courtroom antics for this prosecutor. She rarely rose from her seat unless she needed to hand something to a witness. "Did you find anything unusual about that call?" she asked the dispatcher.

"Yes. After the first few seconds, maybe a minute, the caller wasn't as agitated as a lot of the callers are. I get a lot of callers, and this one was unusually calm."

Steve thought Mary sounded frantic on the tape, but the dispatcher complained that Mary had been too calm, as if calmness during a crisis was a fault. They were trying to portray her as a cold-blooded killer.

During Steve's cross-examination he led the dispatcher to admit that she didn't know how Mary acted under pressure and that some callers were, like Mary, not as agitated as others.

Officer Devenney testified next. He had been the first person to arrive at Mary's house in response to the 9-1-1 call.

The officer answered questions clinically, as if he were reading his report. He spoke of driving up Mary's street and seeing her run out of the garage to flag him down. "We entered right into the kitchen, and on the floor there I saw a child on its back. It was unconscious. There was vomit on the face and the clothing of the child and on the floor and on the kitchen table."

The prosecution could use this to say that Mary should never have left Melissa lying on her back—that she could have choked on her own vomit. But this was no evidence of guilt. Melissa was not responding and Mary was desperate to have the police officer find them quickly. Was it any wonder she made one mistake in the whole process?

The officer detailed how he' administered mouth-to-mouth resuscitation, trying to help the tiny child breathe. He had cleared her airway, checked her mouth for any obstruction, placed his mouth over Melissa's mouth and nose, and breathed into her lungs. Her little chest would rise and fall as he repeated breaths of air. Steve could sense the officer's relief when he told the jury that within a minute of his arrival, he heard the sirens of the ambulance approaching.

"And where did you go when the paramedics took over?"

"I asked Mrs. Weaver for a drink of water to wash out my mouth and wash up my hands and stuff."

"Did you notice any vomit or anything on the defendant?"

"Not that I recall, no."

"Did you ever see her have to rinse her mouth?"

"No, I did not."

Was the prosecution trying to imply that Mary hadn't done CPR? Couldn't the whole courtroom hear her doing it over the 9-1-1 tape? Frustration burned inside Steve, but he kept the glow hidden inside.

"Did you find anything unusual about this call?"

"It struck me unusual while I was there that Mrs. Weaver seemed awful calm about the whole situation. Compared to other ambulance calls I have been on, there is usually a level of excitement, confusion. She just seemed awful calm for the situation."

"You felt the defendant was atypical—correct?—in her emotions?"

"That's correct."

When Devenney stepped down, Steve stole a glance at Mary. Worry was beginning to cloud her face. He shot her what he hoped was a reassuring look. As he had told Mary before the trial, "You're the innocent one here. You need to let the jury see that in your demeanor."

Several paramedics who had responded to the call testified next. Each felt that Mary was unusually calm, that she wasn't screaming or crying. Wilder-Tomlinson asked one if she noticed anything unusual about the home.

"It was immaculate."

Steve scrawled on the legal pad, smiled, and slid the note over for Mary to read. "You're accused of housecleaning."

She scribbled a note and passed it back. "I'll plead guilty to that."

The prosecutor continued. "Did you see any vomit on the defendant?"

He hadn't, though there was some on the floor by the baby and on the table.

What was this picture the prosecution was trying to paint? That Mary beat the baby to death without emotion, cleaned the crime scene, then immediately called law enforcement officials? Did they want the jury to believe she called 9-1-1 but only pretended to do CPR? The prosecution might be trying to paint premeditation, but surely the jury would see this strategy as nothing but absurdity. Still, if experienced EMT workers seemed to buy this absurd picture, how could they be sure the jury wouldn't buy it as well?

Dr. Thomas testified next. He was the on-call doctor for the ER on the day Melissa was brought in at 11:37 a.m. He arrived at the ER just minutes before the ambulance. He found Melissa unconscious and making no effort to breathe on her own. Within minutes he recognized that she was critically ill and called the on-call pediatrician. Around noon the two doctors decided that Melissa needed the help of a specialist who wasn't available in Marshalltown. They made arrangements for the Iowa City helicopter to take Melissa to the University of Iowa Hospital. While waiting for the helicopter, they did a CT scan to provide valuable information for the university hospital.

While Melissa was at this first hospital, doctors and the nurses examined her. "We examined her head and underneath her head to see if there was anything abnormal there," Thomas said, "any signs of a bump or bruise or deformity of her skull and could not find any. Now admittedly, we did not roll her over to look very carefully and shine a light on the area on her skull because she had this tube in place and we couldn't roll her over, but we felt underneath, lifted up her head a little bit to see if there was anything obvious there, and there was nothing obvious to either of us at that time." They went on to examine her arms, legs, heart, and lungs. But in the end, Dr. Thomas said, "there were no outward signs of trauma to this little girl."

At the time Thomas felt that something catastrophic had happened to Melissa that morning to injure her brain and nervous system. Based on the history that Melissa had been acting normally that morning and the fact that she was in a life-compromising situation by noon, he believed something terrible had happened to her that day. After Melissa left in the helicopter, he discussed the case with the other doctor, the nurses, and the social worker. They didn't know what was going on with Melissa. They had seen no signs of injury or trauma on Melissa and to their knowledge, the injury was not child abuse. They made the conscious decision not to report it.

When Steve got his turn to cross-examine the witness, he asked Thomas whether there could be another explanation for the retinal hemorrhaging. Could the CPR have caused it? Were there other possibilities?

"My job is to report a condition that is consistent with child abuse to the authorities and let them decide if any child abuse has occurred," Thomas said.

"And retinal hemorrhages were the only signs of child abuse that you saw that morning?"

"I didn't even recognize it as a sign of child abuse that morning. I saw no other marks on her body and nothing else that would fit with abuse that day."

Steve hid a smile of satisfaction. Dr. Thomas' testimony was an anchor for his defense. Thomas knew that something catastrophic had happened to Melissa that morning. The doctors didn't understand it but it didn't look like abuse.

To Steve this emphasized that the catastrophic happening was due to older injuries, which had only later been revealed. If the jury made the same interpretation, they would understand that Mary wasn't guilty.

Dr. Kathleen Grauerholz stepped to the witness stand next. She was a young doctor who was fairly new to her profession in the same way Steve was. She had been Melissa's pediatrician, the main doctor Melissa had seen during her eleven months of life. She must hate this courtroom, where her work as a doctor would be examined, where her interpretation of the evidence was crucial to a murder case. Steve knew it was a world doctors generally hate.

Dr. Grauerholz's hands shook a little, but she testified clearly and carefully. During Melissa's short life the baby had experienced no major illnesses, just regular childhood things like ear infections.

Early in her testimony the prosecutor offered Melissa's medical records into evidence, approached the witness stand, and handed the doctor the records she knew so well.

Wilder-Tomlinson asked if the doctor had any concerns about Melissa's development. Grauerholz explained that she had watched Melissa's weight gain more closely than usual. Otherwise she was developing normally, following the usual markers.

"Did you ever have any concern about abuse of Melissa?" the prosecutor asked.

"I never observed anything that made me concerned."

"Never noticed any bruises on Melissa that you thought were suspicious?"

"I didn't. Brad and Tessia did bring Melissa to me one day with that question in mind, but I never observed anything that was unexplainable."

"And their concern was what?"

Dr. Grauerholz consulted her records again. "My records remind me that Mother was concerned about the possible problems with the baby-sitter. They showed me some scratches on Melissa's neck and a perianal tear, a skin tear that they wanted me to check and make sure they were not signs of abuse. I examined her, and I recorded that she had some scratches on the left side of her face and the back of her neck. The mother had reported to me that she would often scratch at her neck when she was tired. Regarding the perianal tear, in babies, if there is a little constipation or inflammation of the skin, it's possible to have these superficial skin tears just because of the hard stool. I explained that to the parents. I said that all of the things that I could see I felt we had explanation for based on her history, but that if they had any concerns at all about the baby-sitter, that they should document these things and perhaps seek another child care provider. If they had any other questions, they should return for examination."

Steve remained calm. He and Mary had known these statements were coming. He soon got his turn to cross-examine her.

He asked the doctor more details about Melissa's growth curve. The baby had remained within the normal range throughout her life, but the overall trend in Melissa's weight did drift downwards. She started out her life at the fiftieth percentile in weight, an average weight of all babies, and wound up in the fifth percentile, with 95 percent of babies weighing more.

Steve appreciated the doctor's careful answers. She stuck with the information she knew and didn't speculate wildly about matters for which she had no proof. If only every witness would do the same.

When Steve cross-examined her, he asked Grauerholz about her appointments with Melissa during the last week of her life. Melissa had sat on her mother's lap and leaned her head back on her mom's chest. The doctor never saw any signs of a skull fracture during her examinations, but it was well documented that skull fractures didn't always have clinical signs and symptoms. Doctors sometimes found them only through X rays or something like that. She had examined Melissa in different positions, held her head to look in her ears, and Melissa never cried suddenly at the doctor's touch. Grauerholz had seen no sign of the older fracture. Melissa was a little fussy but never seemed to be in any obvious distress.

Steve hoped the jury could see that her life-threatening injuries weren't obvious. Grauerholz was a good and careful pediatrician, but she hadn't noticed the skull fracture during three visits with Melissa in that last week.

Several other witnesses testified, and then on Wednesday morning Agent Motsinger of the State Department of Criminal Investigation claimed the chair with the authoritative bearing of a long-time law enforcement officer. As the prosecutor questioned Motsinger, a clear picture emerged of his investigation on the day Melissa died. Lieutenant Buffington had already conducted his interview with Mary when Motsinger arrived. Buffington briefed him, and he listened to a tape of Mary's morning interview.

That afternoon Motsinger interviewed Brad and Tessia. During the interview Dr. Bennett called. Bennett had contacted Dr. Alexander, and both doctors felt the injuries were consistent with shaken baby syndrome and that the trauma happened shortly before Melissa was admitted to the Marshalltown hospital. They believed that once this trauma happened, Melissa would have shown signs immediately, moving quickly to unconsciousness and death. Bennett said that without medical intervention, Melissa would have been dead within an hour of injury.

That conclusion seemed to mark the end of the detective's search for other suspects. He didn't split Brad and Tessia up for the interview so that he could compare their stories. He hadn't considered them suspects.

"Why were Brad and Tessia interviewed?" Steve asked.

Since he believed that this was shaken baby syndrome and that the symptoms would have begun immediately after the trauma, he wanted to talk to everyone who had taken care of Melissa that last day.

Motsinger clearly went to Mary's interview assuming Melissa had died of shaken baby syndrome, believing Mary had inflicted the injuries. Mary told him the same story she had told Buffington that morning.

"I told her that, 'Well, Melissa did suffer a skull fracture,'" Motsinger said. "And at that point, she placed her hands on the back of her head. 'Well, was the skull fracture located here?'"

The detective imitated Mary's touch with his own large hands.

"Well, I looked at her, and she is looking at me looking at her. And I mean, it couldn't have been more than a second or a second and a half, but it seemed like, you know, we both noticed each other looking at each other. And then from there she touched a different place on her head and went, 'Oh, was it here or here or here or here?'"

"You felt that was unusual?" Wilder-Tomlinson said.

"I did."

Motsinger moved to the next interview with Mary a few days later on Tuesday evening. "I went over again with Mary Weaver her statements that she had made earlier to Lieutenant Buffington, what she had stated to me, and told her that the statements that she was giving me did not stack up against what medical evidence I was receiving from all these doctors. And I told her I didn't believe her statement. Finally, then she stated, well, she may have shaken Melissa a little bit." He shook his hands lightly. "She didn't move any more than what I am showing now, just a very small movement."

After that he started to have daily contact with doctors. Sometime later, probably about a week later, the doctors told him there were two distinct and separate shaken baby events, both with trauma. The skull fracture had started to heal, so it had to be an older injury.

Waiting to cross-examine him, Steve felt anger flame inside him. During those crucial first few days Motsinger didn't investigate any suspect except Mary. His focus didn't change even after the doctors informed him of the older injuries. After talking to Bennett, Motsinger decided first that Mary killed Melissa, then set out to prove it.

When Steve's turn to cross-examine came, he didn't mess around with formalities. With the first question he went straight for the throat. "Did you have any other suspects?"

Motsinger said he had tried to contact everyone who had care and custody of Melissa–the baby's parents, Sally Jones, Brad's sister who baby-sat Melissa the Saturday night before her death, baby-sitters at the bowling alley who often watched Melissa on Thursdays.

Steve glared at him. "But did you have other suspects?"

Motsinger squirmed, then talked at great length about the effort they had made to contact a list of people. He gave the names of those people but finally admitted that, after talking to Brad and Tessia and Mary on the day Melissa died, they didn't suspect anyone else.

He talked to Sally Jones on the phone in February but didn't interview her until October 19. Steve hoped the jury would notice that Sally baby-sat at a key time when Melissa had started crying a lot and not acting like herself. Yet even then, the detective didn't do a face-to-face interview with her for more than nine months.

Motsinger got a typed statement from Officer Devenney, the first person Mary talked to after the incident, but didn't interview him. He hadn't talked to Jim Weaver or Janet Smith and Lisa Murphy, two friends Mary had talked to shortly after the ambulance left.

"Did it ever occur to you," Steve asked, "that Mary might have told Janet Smith, Lisa Murphy, and her husband what had happened that morning to Melissa?"

"Mary Weaver told us what had happened that morning," he shot back.

"Okay. I'm going to ask you to answer my question. Did it occur to you that Mary Weaver might have told Jim Weaver, Janet Smith, and Lisa Murphy what had happened to Melissa Mathes at her home on Friday morning?"

Motsinger hadn't known about the ladies. He had asked Jim during Mary's second interview what he knew about the incident, and Jim said he didn't know anything about it. Jim wasn't there when it happened. It didn't make any difference what Mary told Jim. She had already told Motsinger what happened.

"Well," Steve said, "wouldn't it make a difference if she made a contrary or contradictory statement to somebody else?

# CHAPTER 7

Wouldn't you then confront her with that and say, 'Mary, that's not what you told your husband?'"

No. He wanted to hear it from her. She gave him the same story all the time. He didn't confirm it with anyone else. "After Tuesday evening, she stated that we would have to go through her lawyer if we wanted to talk to her anymore. So I didn't have any more communication with Mary Weaver."

"But up until the point on Tuesday evening when it got pretty heated, she had cooperated and talked with you at every beck and call?"

He admitted she did.

"Did you ever raise your voice with Brad or Tessia Mathes?"

"No."

"Did you ever tell Tessia or Brad that you didn't believe they were telling you the truth?"

"No."

"Was there any evidence of somebody else who might have been the perpetrator?"

"From the medical evidence, no."

Steve asked him if he had checked into Tessia's background, if he had heard she'd been abused as a child. This question prompted an objection, an off-the-record discussion, and a decision to order the jury to leave the room. In the end Judge Baker allowed Steve to ask the question. Motsinger revealed that Tessia had been physically and sexually abused as a child, and had received counseling for the abuse.

Near the end of his cross-examination, Steve asked, "Do you recall making the statement that Saturday morning that 'it's not looking good for the baby-sitter at this point'?"

"Oh, I imagine I had made that statement."

"And that was the day Melissa died."

"It would have been after I had received the medical evidence later that day."

"But the same day she died?"

"Right."

Bennett had briefed the detective and shared his opinion that Mary had to be the killer. Agent Motsinger accepted his conclusion and quit looking for anyone else.

Steve paused. He was about to take a gamble. He'd been trained never to ask a witness on the stand a question unless he already knew the answer. But Motsinger didn't have any evidence apart from the doctors' opinion. Steve had already scored some points with the jury, and this question could nail down the fact that this was a one-sided investigation from the start.

"Tell me exactly what evidence you have that indicates that Mary Weaver inflicted these injuries on Melissa Mathes."

"It would be the statements made by the doctors to me that when Melissa received the trauma, that the symptoms would be instantaneous from that time on, and that she would not be a happy, playful, talking child. Mary stated that Melissa was fine when she picked her up, and the doctors have told me that the trauma happened after that point, and that would have been while the baby was in her care and custody."

"Other than the doctors' statements, what evidence do you have that Mary Weaver did this?"

Motsinger lifted his chin. "None."

Steve glanced up at Judge Baker. "We have no further questions of this witness, your honor."

During lunch break Steve pulled overshoes over his dress shoes, zipped up his parka, and headed toward his office. Waiting at a DON'T WALK sign, Steve noticed a poster in a shop window. These words were stamped across a baby's forehead: "Fragile: Do not shake!" The picture was edged by these words: "Never, ever shake a baby!"

Good advice for caregivers, but police needed to realize other injuries could look like injuries inflicted by shaking, yet come from other causes. Steve had read in his law journals of several apparently innocent parents who had been convicted of murder by SBS simply because they were with a baby at the time of death. In Mary's case, the baby had been slammed as well as shaken, but the doctors ignored those older, severe injuries.

When police suspected SBS, they often focused their entire investigation on the last person who was alone with the baby, believing that person must be a killer. They ignored other possible causes of death and other possible suspects who could have inflicted injury. Mary's situation wasn't the first case in which the baby wasn't the only innocent victim.

Steve stared at the poster long after the WALK sign started blinking and other pedestrians crossed the street. He'd like to add another poster beside the one with the baby. Stamped across an adult's picture would be these words: "Fragile: Caretakers will be suspects! Never ever be alone with a dying baby!"

When a baby died of mysterious causes, "innocent until proven guilty" didn't always work. Any adult who was alone with a baby when the baby died was in grave legal danger.

# CHAPTER 8

That afternoon Ms. Wilder-Tomlinson eyed the grieving father in the witness stand with compassion. "Did you have any concerns that the defendant was physically abusing Melissa?"

Steve had been expecting this question and had prepared Mary for it.

Brad stared at his hands, glancing up only long enough to answer each question. The dark-haired young father seemed lethargic, exhausted.

Brad talked about the anal tear. Tessia had been upset about it, but Brad thought she was being overprotective. Tessia pointed out other bruises to him. She had talked to Mary about them and gotten explanations. They seemed to be normal bruises for a baby who was crawling and doing baby things.

The prosecutor ignored the seven-to ten-day period before the death, when other caregivers had taken care of Melissa. Mary had baby-sat Melissa eight to ten days before her death, but everyone agreed that the baby was fine then. So Wilder-Tomlinson moved directly to the Monday before Melissa's death. If she could make Monday look like a possible date of injury and get the medical experts to agree to a five-day time frame for the older injuries, she could blame Mary for the older injuries *and* the acute ones as well.

Brad's answers gave the prosecutor just what she needed. He said Melissa had acted normally before he went to work that Monday. When he picked her up, she didn't move or wiggle. She just lay there. She wasn't responsive in the car, and she didn't babble like she normally did. When he got home and gave her a bottle, she drank just a little bit and threw it back up on him.

Steve's cross-examination brought the focus back to the beginning of the seven- to ten-day time frame. He asked who else had baby-sat Melissa on each of those days. It was time to turn the spotlight on others who should have been suspects.

On Saturday, day seven, Tessia's sister, Sally Jones, had watched Melissa while Brad, Tessia, and his parents went to the casino. Brad thought another sister, Cindy Nehring, had been at Sally's apartment too. When Steve asked for details about picking Melissa up, he sensed Brad's resistance.

"Now, Melissa was crying when you picked her up, wasn't she?" Steve said.

"Not that I remember."

"And she was crying when you put her in the car?"

"Not that I remember."

"She was crying on the way home?"

"I think she fell asleep on the way home."

Steve stood up, breaking the tempo. He glanced at a police report, refreshing his memory. Then he probed the eyes of the nervous, young father. "Are you aware that your mother has indicated that Melissa was crying on the way home?"

Brad stared at his lap a moment, considering. "Yeah, she said she said that."

"She told you that she went to the police and talked about Saturday night?"

"Yeah."

"Did she relate to you what she told the detectives?"

"Objection, Your Honor!" The prosecutor's voice rang across the courtroom. "I believe the witness is about to testify to hearsay."

Brad eyed the prosecutor like a man in a burning building eyes a fire extinguisher that's just out of reach.

After several objections and clarifications, Steve was allowed to proceed. He restated the question. Brad said his parents did have a chance to observe Melissa that evening.

"Did you talk to your mother after she went to the detectives and told them about Saturday night?"

"Yeah."

"Did you indicate anything to her about whether she should do that again?"

"If I remember right, I told her I didn't think there was anything unusual about Melissa that night."

Brad shifted in his seat, and his evasive answers hinted that he didn't want to talk about this subject—a lawyer's cue that it must be worth exploring. Steve always tried to ask the same questions the jury would want to ask, and he knew they'd want to know more about this.

Steve held his copy of Brad's mother's police report high so the jury could see the importance of the information that was generously highlighted in yellow and underlined in red. He scanned the words silently. He knew he walked a tightrope of risk here. The prosecutor might call this report hearsay, and he didn't want to lose too many evidentiary arguments with her. That could make Mary look bad. But the jury needed to see he was the good lawyer who was trying to give them the evidence they wanted. Meanwhile, every time she objected, Wilder-Tomlinson gave the impression she was trying to hide the truth.

Steve accepted the risk. "And regarding the report that your mother made, are you aware that she was reporting to the officer that this was her conclusion and the conclusion of your dad and your brother as well?"

Brad cleared his throat. "I remember them speculating on that. I don't remember a conclusion that they had come to."

Now he was playing word games.

"When you say they were speculating on that, basically they were thinking that something had happened Saturday night to Melissa?"

"They had thought her cry seemed funny and were wondering. I mean, this was at a time after Melissa had died and, you know, we were all just thinking back as far as we could, what might have happened, or could have happened."

"And that was their opinion?"

"Yeah. They had speculated at that."

Brad could have won more of the jury's sympathy by sticking to the role of the grieving dad and not quibbling about words. His mother's clear statement would be revealed in time. The jury could understand that when Brad's mother voluntarily drove to the police department to record a statement, she had serious questions about what had happened to Melissa on that Saturday evening seven days before her death.

Steve moved on to the next day and questioned him about Sunday afternoon, six days before the death, when Brad's folks had stopped at his and Tessia's house. They wanted to see Melissa but weren't allowed to because she was sleeping. That had never happened before.

Would the jury see the possibilities this suggested? Saturday night Melissa was whining and crying. On Sunday the grandparents stopped by, perhaps out of concern for the baby. They weren't allowed to see Melissa. Was Melissa in need of medical care at that moment?

Steve asked Brad if he had talked to Mary at the funeral. He said he had. That they were grieving and that Mary was grieving too.

"Did it occur to you that for half or a majority of Melissa's life, she had spent her days with Mary?" Here was a chance to show that Mary's grief was real through the observations of others.

"At some time me and Tessia had talked about that."

Now that the questions had moved away from the time frame of Melissa's injuries, Brad seemed more at ease. His voice was no longer colored with resentment. But the jury wouldn't forget that his mother had filed a police report. Her observations had clearly compelled her to do so.

Next Dr. Robert Schelper took the stand. He was a forensic pathologist at the University of Iowa with expertise in brain injury due to trauma. He had autopsied the brain. He taught the jury like medical students, drawing them into his world where dissected brains held clues to solving mysteries.

In Mary's defense, the dating of the injuries was the most important part, and timing was one of Dr. Schelper's areas of expertise. When Steve cross-examined him, he asked the doctor whether the injury dating was exact or estimated.

"Everything has a range." Schelper explained why in medical terms.

"Is five days outside your range," Steve asked, "even though you have written seven to ten days in the autopsy?"

"Well, yeah. We spent a lot of time thinking about these time intervals, and the time intervals that we have listed here are our very best estimates. If you get outside of these time intervals, it becomes more and more statistically unlikely that that happened at such a time. As soon as you begin to deviate away from that, then you start getting out to rare, rare events."

"Would a history that could possibly explain the older injuries have helped you? You didn't have that history, I know."

"Of course, the more history you have, the better your information is, and the better you can refine your estimates. We have what we consider to be two different ages of brain injury. There is an acute one, which is probably related to the history of having a respiratory arrest, this hypoxic injury. This contusion in the frontal area was brand-new, fresh."

Dr. Schelper explained that the old injury came when the child's skull came into forcible contact with some big, heavy object. For example, if she were thrown on the floor or her head was pounded on the table, door, or floor.

"The newer injuries, the hypoxic event, you can explain because of the respiratory arrest. Why did the kid have a respiratory arrest? Well, the brain had obviously already been injured from the incident that caused that old fracture. So the brain would be more susceptible to deciding to quit, if another insult is heaped upon it. So you could develop a respiratory arrest. So, if you were shaken, then a little baby that doesn't have much muscle–their head would whip back and forth, shaking that part of the brain stem with those whipping actions where your respiratory centers are. And you can turn them off. On the other hand, I think that there was another impact to this child's head. Something else hit this child's head within the last day of life."

Steve consulted his notes. "Can shaking also cause the results that you are talking about that are acute?"

Schelper said Melissa may have been shaken acutely, but the skull fracture meant her head must also have been slammed against something previously, seven to ten days earlier.

Steve asked whether the newer injury could be the result of the older injury re-bleeding. Dr. Schelper said that was possible.

"And that can occur without any trauma?" Steve asked.

"That could occur without any trauma or at least any recognizable trauma."

"Something trivial?"

"Something trivial could cause you to continue to bleed into the subdural hematoma blood clot." He explained that if a child had a serious old injury on the brain, a much lesser injury could kill her.

"But that trivial event would have to be more than a slight event?"

"More than a slight injury, yes. Yes, trivial injury would not cause you to die if you were in that kind of condition."

This was almost going too well. The doctor's commentary on Melissa's fragile condition, combined with Melissa's fall Friday morning before Mary picked her up, provided more reasonable doubt.

Steve handed him a picture of Melissa's Cookie Monster chair.

"If a child fell from that chair and struck her head on a padded recliner afterwards, and appeared to be playful and eating and everything, would you say that that fall caused the recent injuries that you observed, in your opinion?"

"No. You'd have to have a much more substantial fall, a much more forceful impact than you could get from falling off of that chair, even with the earlier injuries."

*Rats.* He should have left that alone. Steve walked back to the counsel table and consulted his notes, chiding himself for that last exchange. Before that last comment, Steve could almost smell acquittal. Rather than end the doctor's cross-examination on a blunder, Steve pressed on.

He asked about the process doctors used to establish the age of injuries. Did they work together and compare notes, and did they do that in this case?

# CHAPTER 8

"We would like the findings to hang together," Schelper said. "But if the eye doctor comes up with some time interval of injury that is five to seven days, and I have one that is six to nine days, and the other guy has one that's six to ten days, we all know that those injuries all came from the same incident. We are not talking about three totally different injuries. So you conference and see if you can't come to a consensus understanding of a time interval that is compatible with all of the injuries that are of about the same age."

Steve raised his eyebrows. "And you do so without compromising your own view on the things you have seen?"

"You have to do that, or it wouldn't be honest. You'd be fudging. So, you wind up with maybe a bigger time interval than the time interval of the other person, because they say, 'I can't get any more accurate than this to this, and my time interval fits inside there.' Well, that's fine with me. But I would not cheat and say, 'Well, I really think it is four days, but if you guys think it is six days, I will change mine and say it is six days.' If we really had significantly different time intervals, then we would come back and say, 'We had a skull fracture this time, and then we had a thrombus at a different time, and then we had a necrosis at a different time.' If we could not make reasonable sense out of that and put it in a single time interval, then we would wind up having to conclude that those are all separate-timed injuries."

On the surface this consensus process sounded reasonable enough, but it exposed a hidden flaw. Scientific knowledge was only part of the equation. Some parts were subjective. Personal integrity determined how much a pathologist was willing to bend those subjective parts to fit a particular theory.

Timing was crucial to Mary's case, and Steve sensed timing was less exact than the doctors liked to admit. But Schelper had no agenda. He simply reported his scientific findings.

Next the prosecutor would call witnesses whose clear agenda was to stamp out child abuse. Convictions helped their cause. Would their thirst for conviction blind them to the uncertainties of the case? Would they bend their opinions to form a consensus that led to that conviction?

Dr. Randell Alexander stepped up to the witness stand next. He was the first to testify of the three Steve had come to think of as the "child abuse SWAT team from Iowa City." He looked to be slightly older than Bennett but sported a matching mustache.

Since Steve had already deposed Alexander, he knew what was coming. Alexander had done extensive research on child abuse, published the results in medical journals, and gave lectures on child abuse to medical and law students. In fact, he and Dr. Smith would be giving a session soon in San Diego at one of the premier child abuse conferences.

As Alexander was sworn in, Steve leaned over to Mary. "Here comes the doll shaker."

They knew from Dr. Alexander's testimony in other cases that his practice was to violently shake a baby doll in front of the jury, demonstrating for them what he believed to be the mechanism of injury to the baby.

When Wilder-Tomlinson asked Alexander his opinion about the cause of death, he said he believed it was shaken baby syndrome complicated by previous injuries. There were two episodes of violent shaking. She asked him to demonstrate and handed him a pillow.

Steve leaned toward Mary. "He must have forgotten his doll." Steve tried to keep the tone light, hoping to calm Mary.

Alexander clutched the pillow like he would a toddler, under the arms. "There is the practical matter, that there is only so long you can shake some child at arm's length that weighs a certain amount of pounds." He moved the pillow slowly out and back, extending his arms and retracting them as he spoke. "You wear out. And physically, this isn't anything you are going to do for minutes. It just can't happen. We do know from again our study of using sandbags and things that you can do about two or three shakes a second. So that once you get going, a fair number of shakes could be delivered in just several seconds."

With that, he unleashed all his demonstrative fury on the pillow, thrashing it back and forth in a violent blur. His short brown hair flopped over his forehead. The horror of imagining a real child in the place of the pillow brought dead silence to the courtroom. Steve and Mary tried not to react.

Wilder-Tomlinson broke the silence, "So, these are not, as you demonstrated–not the type of shake that would be shaking to resuscitate a child, to bring a child back. It is violent, forceful head jerking?"

"Right." Alexander handed back the pillow and fingered his hair back into place. "If Melissa had been shaken that way, she would have a concussion, probably knocked out. Vomiting, altered consciousness, perhaps. Not able to move very well. They would happen at least within a minute or two of the shaking. She could be unconscious and have respiratory arrest."

Alexander said Melissa wouldn't have been able to eat after a shaking that was violent enough to cause this severe injury. He said it would have to be four or five shakes to get the kind of retinal injury Melissa had. The retinal hemorrhages were key since, Alexander said, 75 to 90 percent of babies who had been violently shaken had them. In cases where infants were known to have head injuries alone without shaking, none of them had this injury.

Alexander was trying to set retinal bleeding as a marker for shaking. For a simple shaken baby syndrome injury, the child had to have retinal hemorrhaging, a subdural hematoma, and no other injury. Of course, Melissa's injuries were much more complex and had led the doctors to add "slammed" to the shaken baby diagnosis. But Melissa had experienced retinal bleeding, and Alexander was using this to try to prove Melissa had been shaken. Some of the jurors were probably trying to imagine Mary shaking Melissa in the way the doctor had just demonstrated.

But Alexander's testimony also helped them. Upon cross-examination, Steve asked Alexander if he had ever seen a child shaken the way he had shaken the pillow. He hadn't. Through his questioning Steve established the fact that shaking a child like Alexander had shaken the pillow sometimes caused bruising on the ribs, broken ribs and limbs, and other bruises. Melissa had none of those injuries. This was a very minor victory. But even though Alexander had testified for the prosecution, they might be able to use his testimony to help Mary.

Alexander had written a paper called "Serial Abuse in Children Who Are Shaken" in 1990 with Smith, Bennett, and some other doctors. He was considered an expert on serial abuse.

"Have you ever studied the pattern that results from a child who's been abused, who then later goes on to become a perpetrator?" Steve was expanding the pool of potential suspects.

The prosecutor objected, but the judge overruled her. Her objection only highlighted the importance of the doctor's answer.

"We see court-ordered cases each week of people who tell us about abuse in their own personal background when they were growing up," Alexander said. "And they are before us—it's because of abuse-related concerns that the court is sending them to us."

# CHAPTER 8

"And that's a pattern that you have seen over the years of your work?" Steve asked.

"Oh, yeah. Definitely."

If Alexander knew how much he was helping them, he might have been less enthusiastic.

# CHAPTER 9

**D**r. Vincent DiMaio was a bulldog on the pant leg of truth. He didn't let go. Lesser dogs relaxed their jaws in the name of political correctness, the catchphrase of the hour, but DiMaio had outlived a dictionary of catchphrases. He relied on solid research and refused to follow the medical crowd.

DiMaio was a witness for the defense, but Judge Baker allowed him to testify out of order during the witnesses for the prosecution, because his schedule would only allow him to testify at this time. He had flown in from Texas especially for this trial.

DiMaio's thin, white hair came with age and lots of experience. He served as the medical examiner and director of the criminal investigation laboratory for Bexar County, Texas. The area included 1.3 million people who lived in San Antonio and the surrounding county. He was a specialist in anatomical, clinical, and forensic pathology.

Even Dr. Bennett respected DiMaio. In his deposition the younger doctor had referred to DiMaio as someone who had served for many more years than he had, and whose experience and training he trusted. But DiMaio didn't chant the SBS mantra as Bennett did.

At the suggestion of Earl Rose, Steve had called DiMaio in September, asking him to review Melissa's case. DiMaio agreed. He was willing to challenge the assumptions of SBS. He would refuse to squeeze facts into a mold that didn't fit. And unless Steve missed his guess, DiMaio wouldn't put the jury to sleep either.

DiMaio told how he had reviewed the autopsy report, microscopic slides of the tissue taken from the report, a brief, a police investigative report, and Melissa's medical records from Marshalltown and the University of Iowa.

Formalities over, Steve said, "Can you tell the jury what, in your opinion, happened to Melissa Mathes?"

DiMaio frowned. "She was murdered. It is very simple. Somebody either slammed the head against a hard, flat surface, either by picking her up and throwing her against the wall or a floor, or grabbing her by her feet or her body and then swinging her like a baseball bat against a hard, flat surface." He demonstrated, slowly swinging an invisible bat.

The jury winced as one. DiMaio's image of a baby being swung like a baseball bat would be too vivid to forget without conscious effort. Steve would save the image for his closing argument. This brutality was the silent killer the state wanted the jury to forget and instead to focus completely on the forty-two minutes Melissa had been with Mary at least six days later.

The doctor explained the medical findings that supported his conclusions. "What happened is that at the time of the impact, some of these cells were killed immediately. That dead tissue was seven to ten days old. Then there are other cells that are dead that don't look that old. What it means is in that seven to ten days, they died. And then gradually, as the week progressed, the wound died. Slowly, one by one, the cells died until she ran out of brain cells."

DiMaio shrugged. "That's a crude way of putting it, but that's what happened. She died as a result of the injury seven to ten days before, when her head was slammed into a flat surface. She got a two-inch skull fracture. Brain cells were killed. Others were severely injured and died over the next couple of days. And she just went along until one cell maybe too many died, and she just stopped breathing."

DiMaio believed that this initial injury was the cause of death. Steve shifted his focus to Mary's forty-two minutes with Melissa that Friday morning.

"Doctor, in your opinion, was there any evidence, from what you examined, of any kind of new or acute trauma?"

"There was no evidence of any acute trauma."

Steve highlighted the doctor's comment with a brief pause. The doctor went on to explain other injuries and why, seven to ten days later, her blood couldn't clot anymore. He explained how all the various new injuries could have come from the old injury.

Steve rolled his shoulders and relaxed his tense muscles. The pressure of Alexander's accusations was gone. Here was a medical expert who explained the autopsy findings in a manner consistent with Mary's innocence. Now Steve needed to show that other suspects should have been investigated.

He asked DiMaio about Melissa's low body weight. DiMaio said the two causes of low weight would be difficulty in absorption and not being fed. He said that nothing in the autopsy report indicated an absorption problem.

Steve stole a glance at the jury. They seemed uneasy with these haunting implications. He could imagine that the eleven women jurors, most of whom were mothers, were disturbed by the image. No one wanted to consider the possibility of an infant not being fed.

Steve asked about other autopsies DiMaio had performed as the Bexar County medical examiner. In the last ten years he'd dealt with about one hundred homicides in Melissa's age group.

"In your practice and in your years of experience," Steve asked, "have you noticed a connection between certain child abuse—slamming heads, things like that–and not feeding a child?"

"Yes."

"Do you see abandonment?"

"You see parents even abandon children. Everybody knows that abused children tend to end up as being abusing parents and ending up with abused children just as a cycle."

"That's a pattern that you have seen in your actual practice?"

"Yes, it is a cycle. Everyone recognizes that."

"Dr. DiMaio, there's been some testimony that Melissa died from shaking. Can you comment on that?"

The doctor pushed his glasses up. He described the studies done on shaken baby syndrome, which had started in the early 1970s. "The problem was that most of these papers were clinical studies. They weren't done by pathologists. Most of those kids didn't die. And you can have skull fractures–you can have bruising of the scalp, injuries to the brain—and you can miss that unless you do an autopsy. Unfortunately, the forensic pathologist, as I said, knows everything in a way, but it is too late." He shrugged.

The jury relaxed a bit. DiMaio's light tone was a welcome break from the tension of the trial.

DiMaio continued. "You can have a four-inch skull fracture and have no bruise on the outside. It looks perfectly normal. You have to have an autopsy to tell."

The doctor paused, shifted back to the original topic. "So, by the mid-1980s, a lot of doubt began to appear. And there is a classic paper that came out around 1987 in which they studied a number of these children. Thirteen of them died, and about half of them showed no evidence of head injury on the outside. When they did the autopsy, they found head injury. Essentially what the paper showed was that in every case of the so-called shaken baby syndrome, when they did the autopsy, they found head injuries. It is the only paper that I know of where they actually did research using dolls, by the way, not babies to see how fast a head would accelerate."

Steve knew the jury would be thinking about Alexander's furious doll shaking.

"Based on their studies," DiMaio said, "they determined that it was impossible for a head to go back and forth with enough velocity to tear blood vessels, to cause subarachnoid hemorrhage, to cause subdural bleeding. And so the forensic pathologists concluded that the shaken baby syndrome was sort of let's-make-everyone-happy syndrome."

Dr. DiMaio turned toward the jury, gesturing to them like a classroom of students. "Instead of telling the parents, 'You slammed the kid's head against the wall,' you say, 'Maybe you shook it too vigorously.'" He spoke the last sentence with a humorous, patronizing tone. "And, you know, I am not going to say I slammed a kid's head." His voice turned comical. "Oh, yeah, sure, I guess I shook the kid too vigorously. That's right. I really didn't mean it."

Several jury members smiled.

"And so gradually what is happening in the last couple of years," he went on, "the shaken baby syndrome is kind of losing respect. Now they are saying it's shaking and throwing a baby. Shaking these kids—it's made everyone feel, well…the parent didn't have to admit to hitting the kid, and the doctor didn't have to believe that the parents could do those things. So everybody kept feeling nice about things."

Steve had been so caught up in the monologue that he had to consult his notes for the next question. "Is this shaken-slammed baby syndrome sort of like a shaking throw?"

# CHAPTER 9

"Yeah, it is the same thing. Slam it, throw it. I know it sounds terrible, but, you know, people aren't nice sometimes." He cocked his head to the side, choosing to keep the tone light in spite of the inevitable nastiness of the subject.

Steve admired the doctor's ability to balance such vivid word pictures with an easy bedside manner that helped the jury process such brutality. "In your practice, in your years of experience, have you seen a child who's died purely from shaking?"

DiMaio said he had seen one, but that child hadn't had the same injuries as Melissa. He had a broken neck, and the mother admitted that she broke it. Melissa didn't have that kind of injury.

Steve continued his line of questioning and DiMaio performed in stellar fashion, lifting language from Melissa's autopsy report, describing and explaining her injuries. Most importantly, he worked through all the injuries, showing how the acute injuries could have come as a direct result of the initial trauma.

Steve smiled to himself as the doctor finished his testimony. Doubt based on reason and common sense from a believable expert witness. Just what they needed. Acquittal was edging closer.

Wilder-Tomlinson made her cross-examination short. "So," she said, "you are saying that this was a homicide, not accidental?"

"Oh, yes, I agree it is a homicide. It was due to the head being slammed against something flat."

"And then you are saying on Friday, for no apparent reason, she just collapsed?"

"No, I think there was an apparent reason." He spoke emphatically and patiently, as a teacher does to a slow student. "The reason is the massive head injury. She died because of the injuries which she received in the incident seven to ten days prior. It just took a little longer for her to die."

DiMaio waited for that to sink in, shrugged. He turned to address the jury. "Some people, you know, you shoot and die in five minutes. And some people you shoot and die two hours later or two days later or two weeks later. They are still dead of the gunshot wound. And this child was dead of the head injury seven to ten days before."

DiMaio's testimony brought frown lines to the prosecutor's forehead. It would take more than a lawyer to intimidate this experienced witness.

As her examination came to a close, she attempted to paint Dr. DiMaio into a corner. "Was Melissa Mathes's condition such that on Friday, the twenty-second of January of this year, she could have passed out, stopped breathing, without any trauma?"

DiMaio folded his hands and leaned across the front of the witness stand. He gave an emphatic one-word answer.

"Yes."

DiMaio stepped down from the witness stand, and Steve threw his legal pad into his bulging briefcase. He could enjoy his lunch today without the knot of tension that had been there on previous days.

DiMaio had been worth the expense for his testimony and travel fees. This expert firmly believed all Melissa's injuries could be traced back to old injuries. The abuse cycle certainly shifted the spotlight of accusation away from Mary and to the person or people responsible for the baby's older injuries. And pointing to other possible suspects was Steve's main strategy in this trial. Anything to raise reasonable doubt.

But Steve wouldn't have rested so easily that day if he'd had more experience dealing with this kind of trial. He had yet to learn one important fact about juries.

# CHAPTER 10

**D**r. Wilbur Smith testified last of all the witnesses for the week. Steve knew for that reason the jurors would remember his testimony more vividly than some of the others. Too bad DiMaio hadn't been able to testify last. He'd done a masterful job of pointing the suspicion away from Mary.

Alexander had begun the day of testimony with a brief history of research done on shaken baby syndrome. As a radiologist, Smith gave a more vivid picture of SBS. "Look at the CT scans of babies that have injuries," he said, "and you compare those to babies who have nontrauma—for example, in an automobile accident. The level of injury we are talking about is comparable to a fall from a second- to third-story window or thirty-five-miles-per-hour, unrestrained automobile accident."

He gave a lengthy description of studies on SBS. Since he was a member of the Committee on Abuse and Neglect, he was asked to look at Melissa's CT scans because there was "a high suspicion of abusive head injury," otherwise known as shaken baby syndrome.

Smith peered over his half-lens glasses. "The fracture was, to my best estimate, seven to ten days old, probably seven to eight days old. If you pressed me for six, I'd say it could be. If you pressed me for four, I'd say it couldn't be. So about right around seven days to ten days old."

Smith said Melissa died of abusive head trauma that had multiple events. There was evidence of a seven- to ten-day-old fracture, no question. There was also evidence of a severe, recent injury. The second injury was the cause of death. Both episodes of injury involved shaking, but the first also included a slam. The second episode probably involved only shaking. He said the old injury couldn't have caused the acute findings.

When Steve got his chance to cross-examine the doctor, he zeroed in on the timing of the more recent injury. In his earliest telephone conversations with the police, when Smith hadn't known the call was being recorded, he said the injury had to have occurred within twenty-four hours of Melissa's 11:13 a.m. seizure. That window of time began almost a whole day before Mary picked Melissa up.

At his deposition Smith had tightened the time frame of the second injury, saying it had to occur within four to five hours of the CT scan which took place about 12:30, shortly after noon. That time frame could extend back to 7:30 that morning, three hours before Mary picked Melissa up.

This time, in his response to the prosecutor, he had said that Melissa could not have eaten, jabbered, or looked happy after the recent injury. She would have been, at her best, semicomatose immediately after the injury. Smith's testimony had changed. The time window now framed Mary.

As Steve began his questioning, he could stay seated no longer. He rose from his chair, picked up his file on Smith, and stood in front of the counsel table. "Is it your testimony today that what you saw on the CT scans and the X rays indicates to you that this injury or this trauma must have been inflicted moments before the onset of symptoms?"

"It is my idea that at the maximum window to the onset of symptoms after this—now by symptoms I mean grogginess and

things like that, not necessarily death or need for support—
would be a matter of minutes to an hour at the outside, yes."

Steve tried to stay calm, but his tone and volume became confrontational, one step short of fightin' words.

"Do you recall making the following statement on the telephone to Lieutenant Buffington?" Steve opened the transcript
of the phone call and began to read the doctor's first statement
about the cerebral edema and how one could be fooled by it.
"Your response..." Steve began to read. "'I am afraid that with
the pattern that I have got, I can't put it any better than twenty-four hours or so. So within twenty-four hours of the time of the
seizure is when the injury occurred by the X rays.'"

Steve allowed enough awkward silence for the jury to consider the contradiction between Smith's current testimony and
the previous police statement. He glared at Smith, pointed the
transcript in his direction. "Did you make those statements?"

Smith switched to defense mode. "I don't recall. I do know
that I was in Texas without the X rays and everything else when
the detective called me. And I emphasized to the detective that
I need the history to narrow this down to get this window close.
And that with the history, I would be able to fix the window."

Steve used the transcript to remind him of the history
Motsinger had given him during the phone call. "You were
talking about the slower onset of the pattern," Steve said, "saying the twenty-four hours, even having that history, was the best
that you could do, noting that you had reviewed the X rays, the
CT scans. You had seen the baby, and you had been there the
Tuesday following Melissa's death and reviewed everything."
Steve held out the transcript again for emphasis. "Are those your
statements?"

Smith seemed completely deflated. He said he didn't recall
and made excuses for not remembering.

Steve glared harder. "So now the maximum window is sixty minutes, and back in January it was twenty-four hours?"

Smith stuck to his story. He said he'd been acting on partial information back then, and now that he had the history and had looked at it carefully, he was comfortable with the sixty-minute interval.

Later Steve came back to the timing issue. "It is possible, isn't it, that Mary Weaver could have had this child–it was happy go lucky when she picked her up–and could have had her for a period of about forty minutes–the baby seemed alert, talkative, awake, and for that child to still be suffering at that present time from an increasing edema that only became apparent later without any trauma from the baby-sitter?"

Finally Dr. Smith conceded. "It is not probable. It is remotely possible."

Steve reached for the deposition transcript. Unlike the police statement, Smith couldn't have claimed a lack of history during the deposition.

He read the pertinent passage from the doctor's sworn statement about the timing of the acute injury. "'On the second episode, well, then the swelling took place after that fairly rapidly because the baby became—went downhill very, very fast and was dead within twenty-four hours essentially. So probably the swelling took place, I would guess, when the injury occurred, within four or five hours of that first CT scan.' Question: 'Four or five hours of the Marshalltown CT scan?' Answer: 'Yes.'"

Steve glanced up at Smith, reading more slowly, emphasizing the words. "Question: 'Can you pinpoint it any better than that?' Answer: 'I don't think I can, no.'"

Steve let the transcript drop to his side while he probed the doctor's eyes. "Did you make that statement?"

"Yes."

"So, at this time you are saying that the injury occurred within four or five hours of the seizure?"

"No. I said the injury occurred within four or five hours of the CT scan, which was at noon. Actually 12:30 roughly, the Marshalltown CT scan."

"And is it your testimony today that the injury occurred within sixty minutes of the seizure?"

"Most likely it occurred right after, as I said before. But the window—I'd give you sixty minutes."

Steve sighed. Smith now spoke with much more certainty about Melissa's death than he had possessed at the deposition. He was sticking to this most recent version of his testimony, but at least Steve felt he had been able to puncture Smith's credibility. It was nearly six o'clock, and the jury was ready to break for the weekend. Would they go home thinking about an injury that happened within sixty minutes of the seizure? Or would they go home thinking Smith's testimony was less than reliable?

Steve had hoped Bennett, the "child abuse SWAT team commander," would be open to change. Instead, Smith had changed not in his objectivity but in his persistent echo of Bennett.

Judge Baker dismissed the jury for the weekend with the standard admonition: They were not to read any accounts of the trial in the newspapers, watch the news on television, or speak to anyone about the case. He would see them again when they returned to their duties Monday morning. Everyone in the courtroom stood as the jury was dismissed. Then the crowd filed out.

Steve packed his briefcase and walked Mary out of the courtroom. He wore the mask of a confident lawyer. "It's been a long week," he said, "but try to put all this out of your mind. Go home to those kids and have a nice weekend."

Mary returned his smile. "I'll make it as normal as I can for them. I want to make some Christmas cookies."

Jim joined them, and they stepped into the dark evening.

Mary wrapped her scarf closer to her ears. "Call if you need to, but I will see you here Monday."

Steve rushed to his car and started the heater. While Steve had never tried to sugarcoat possible outcomes for Mary, he tried to present the optimistic side of things. But privately he had to wonder. What if the jury didn't see Mary's innocence as clearly as he did?

His preoccupation with the case spilled into his home time. At dinner his conversation with Kim quickly faded, and he chewed his food in a daze. Two members of the child abuse SWAT team had testified. What would Bennett add to the case?

A toy tractor woke Steve from his daze. Four-year-old Nic put-putted the tractor close to Steve's plate. "Wanna play farm, Dad?"

Steve sighed. "You'll have to farm by yourself tonight, buddy. I have things to do."

Nic's sad eyes showed that he'd accepted the rebuff a little too quickly. Nic dropped to the floor and put-putted the Allis-Chalmers tractor onto the carpet.

Soon Steve felt Kim's gaze as he pushed food around on his plate, staring aimlessly at the tabletop. He met her eyes.

She squeezed his hand. "What's the matter? Are you worried about the case?"

Kim could read him well. He could open his heart to her. His frayed emotions drank from her steadfast support. "What if the jury doesn't get it? What if we lose?"

Steve studied Nic who was busy plowing furrows in the deep pile of the carpet with his toy plow. "I know I've been preoccupied lately. I picture Nic standing on the church platform with Catherine and John; two shepherds and an angel singing 'Away in a Manger.' I've been pushing Nic away because I only have one chance, a few more days, to fight for Mary's innocence. I have a lifetime with Nic, but Catherine and John . . ."

Steve pushed his half-eaten plate of food away. "In Iowa, a life prison sentence is for life. No parole. We turned down the plea bargain. We can't afford to lose. If we do, what will happen to Mary's children?"

Kim's eyes shone with a certainty he couldn't feel. "You've said it before. You do the best you can do, and you leave the results with the Lord. That's all you can do."

Somehow leaving it with the Lord was easier to do when he was representing guilty clients for lesser crimes.

# CHAPTER 11

Monday morning Mary applied a fresh coat of lipstick during the fifteen-minute break, steeling herself for the testimony ahead. The next testimony would strain her already weary emotions.

She had already spent nearly a week reviewing the trauma of Melissa's last days and the intimidating investigation that followed. With each new witness she could feel the side glances of the jury, wondering, suspecting. Could this ordinary housewife have shaken a baby so hard she caused whiplash? Could this baby-sitter have slammed a baby into a hard surface and inflicted multiple injuries that led to death?

Somehow, Mary felt a peace that everything would work out okay. Steve seemed to be optimistic. At times she actually felt she would go to prison. She felt God had prepared her for this with the promise in Jeremiah that God would bring her out of "captivity." Prison must be that captivity. She could accept that. Other times she was confused. Maybe this trial was her captivity, and the whole ordeal would soon be over.

But even though she knew God was in control, reliving painful memories drained her emotionally.

With court called to order, Tessia Mathes stepped up to the witness stand. Her right hand trembled as she was sworn in. She sat in the witness chair, visibly uncomfortable, fidgeting with a crumpled tissue. The young mother with the short, dark blonde hair and glasses looked absolutely fragile. Mary reminded herself, however, that little, short people could pull off the fragile look far more easily than tall, sturdily built people like herself.

Still Mary couldn't help feeling compassion for the young mother. Eleven months ago someone had brutally inflicted a lethal blow on Tessia's baby. Now she was forced to testify in a murder trial before twelve jurors, a judge, the one accused of killing her baby, and a packed gallery.

Ms. Wilder-Tomlinson assumed a gentle tone with the young mother. She adjusted the microphone for Tessia so she could be heard more easily and asked her general questions about her job and where she lived, allowing her time to compose herself for the intrusive questions that were sure to come.

"Have you ever testified in court before?" the prosecutor asked.

"No."

"Are you a little nervous?"

"Real nervous."

This would be difficult for Tessia, but the prosecution had called her as a witness. Steve said the prosecution was using Brad and Tessia partly because they were grieving parents, but the state also wanted to establish that Melissa was "fine" when Mary picked her up that fateful Friday morning.

Mary couldn't understand why the police hadn't thoroughly investigated all of the people who had been with Melissa during the various times she could have been injured. Someone had tried to kill Melissa.

Mary had toyed with the idea that Melissa could have died from some horrible accident, that no one had intentionally hurt her, but if, against all odds, this was true, why wasn't she taken to the doctor after she was injured? Someone was covering something up and allowing Mary to take the blame. The true killer wasn't even being investigated. This sweet little girl had been murdered eleven months ago, and justice might never be done.

Wilder-Tomlinson established the fact that Tessia was twenty-four years old, worked as a supervisor at Hardee's, had nine brothers and sisters, and had been married five years.

"Prior to January twenty-second, 1993," the prosecutor asked, "did you have any concerns that the defendant was abusing Melissa?"

Mary braced herself for the well-worn story.

"Yes, I did. Melissa had come home one day with some real deep scratches on her face. I had taken her to the doctor. She had an anal tear with that."

"Do you remember when this was?"

"In September I took her to the doctor, and the doctor said if we were concerned to find another baby-sitter. She wouldn't necessarily call it abuse. Brad and Brad's mom convinced me that I was just being overprotective, because I was abused as a child. And when I would take Melissa to Mary's house, when we'd pull in the driveway, Melissa would start crying. And she would cry when I took her in the house. She wouldn't stop crying. As soon as I walked out of the door, she would stop crying, but I never gave it much thought."

"You thought it was just the separation from you?"

"Yes."

Sometimes Melissa would cling to Tessia when she was first dropped off, but once she saw the kids, she would light up and be ready to play. Mary glanced at the eleven women on the jury. Would they realize that children commonly cry when they are separated from their mothers? By Tessia's logic, most baby-sitters would look suspicious.

The prosecutor continued her questioning. "Now, you just stated that you were abused as a child. Can you tell us what type of abuse this was?"

Tessia cleared her throat, stared at her lap. "Sexual abuse."

"And have you sought and completed counseling on this?"

Tessia's voice shook. "Yes."

Mary dabbed at her own eyes. When she agreed to baby-sit for Brad and Tessia, she knew the young mother had a rough life, but she'd had no idea how hard it was. If the abuse wasn't humiliating enough, now Tessia had to tell a courtroom full of people about it.

"When my abuser got arrested," Tessia went on, "we went for counseling for a little bit. And then, before I was pregnant with Melissa, I had started going. And then I found out I was pregnant, and I went through the whole time I was pregnant. And probably about two or three times after Melissa was born, I went."

"Why did you seek out counseling?"

"I didn't know how correct parents were. I didn't want Melissa to be raised the way I was raised."

"You thought the abuse that you had received was normal up to this point, up to when you reported it, and your abuser got into trouble. Never as a child—you didn't think about that, correct?"

"Well, you really didn't have a chance to think about it. You were told that they wouldn't believe you, that you would be the one in trouble; or he'd hurt you."

The prosecutor glanced at her notes.

"Did you continue to notice bruises on Melissa?"

"A couple of times, yes."

Tessia said she didn't report anything else to the doctor. Every bruise had an explanation. When she noticed a bruise, she would call Mary and ask what happened. She talked about a large bruise that she had seen in October. She hadn't seen it before she dropped Melissa off at Mary's, but it was there that evening. Tessia called Mary about it, and Mary said she hadn't seen it. Melissa had fallen on the rung of a rocking chair at home that morning, and Tessia assumed Melissa must have gotten the bruise then. She could think of no other explanation for it.

Mary remembered that scene very differently, but she hid her emotions. Mary had seen the bruise first and asked Tessia about it. Tessia had given her the rocking chair story, but it seemed strange to Mary that Melissa could hurt herself that way when she was only crawling at the time, not really pulling herself up to furniture.

Mary was glad she had kept a careful log of her days with Melissa. She had always written down details about how much Melissa ate, dirty diapers, naps, and things like that to give to Tessia so the mother would know what had happened during the day. When she began to notice bruises and scratches, Mary also began keeping a careful log of her own. She did this for her own protection, but she couldn't have known then the grave risk any adult faced being alone with a baby at the time of death or fatal incident.

Mary had tried to establish honest communication with the parents from the beginning. The day after Tessia took Melissa to Dr. Grauerholz with her suspicions, Tessia told Mary what she had done. Mary had assured Tessia that she wanted her to be honest with her if she ever thought something was wrong. But Mary let Tessia know that if she saw anything suspicious, she would report it too. When this "rocking chair bruise" showed up a few weeks later, Mary pointed it out to Tessia. Mary told her then that if she saw anything else like that, they would have to do something. But there were no problems after that.

# CHAPTER 11

Now, snapshots of past events and scraps of conversation flipped through Mary's mind as the prosecutor prepared to focus the jury's attention on Melissa's last week of life. Wilder-Tomlinson started with the Monday before Melissa's death and asked Tessia about the baby's final week.

That Monday night Melissa had vomited profusely and gasped for air. Tessia called the doctor's office, and the on-call doctor said the symptoms sounded like the flu.

Tuesday Melissa was still sick and vomiting, so Tessia took her to Dr. Grauerholz. The doctor said she probably had the flu. She put her on Pedialyte. Tessia gave the baby a tablespoon every ten or twenty minutes and tried to get Melissa to keep that down. Melissa kept vomiting and couldn't even keep one tablespoon down.

Wednesday Tessia took her back to the doctor and got the same diagnosis.

Thursday she returned to the doctor. That morning Melissa wasn't playful; she just lay there and wouldn't move. She threw up at the doctor's office but only the one time on Thursday, and then she seemed a bit better. After the doctor's office, she started playing, got a bit of color back, started laughing and crawling around and walking around furniture, playing, jabbering. She took a nap and started drinking half Pedialyte and half formula, finished a bottle, and wanted more. That night Tessia fed her bananas.

"When or how was it decided that she could go back to the baby-sitter?"

"Well, Thursday morning, I had decided that she was doing better. You know, she wasn't vomiting as much, and she started playing a little bit. I decided that I would go back to work Friday."

"Did you talk it over with the defendant?"

"I had talked to Mary all week long, telling her how Melissa was doing. And she would tell me that she didn't mind a sick

97

baby, that I could bring her out there. And I said I'd rather be home with her."

"But she was improving enough that you thought you could take her back?"

"Yes."

Mary forced herself not to visibly shake her head and object to the story. She remembered things differently. Mary had asked Tessia if she was sure she didn't want to stay home with Melissa one more day, coming up to the weekend, to give Melissa that extra bit of time to get better. Mary had actually felt quite reluctant to bring a baby with flu into her home for a day and infect her own kids, but Tessia had been cooped up with a sick baby all week, and she seemed eager to get back to work.

The prosecutor asked Tessia about Brad's mom coming over that Thursday night, the night before Melissa's seizure and subsequent death. Wilder-Tomlinson handed Tessia Exhibit 25, a photo, and asked if she recognized it.

Tessia said she took the picture Thursday night when Brad's mom came over.

"And does that picture fairly and accurately show what it is meant to show?"

"Yes. We were trying to get the Kool-Aid smile she had on her face."

The prosecutor took the photo from Tessia and passed it around. In the photo Melissa sat in her high chair, drinking Kool-Aid. The grin on her face was highlighted by a bright red Kool-Aid smile that matched the curve of the cup. It was the prosecution's attempt to show Melissa as a healthy little girl, who was recovered from her illness earlier in the week and her previous injury. This Kool-Aid smile insinuated that Melissa would be with them today if Mary hadn't inflicted a fatal injury the next day. But that day in court no one sensed the secret of the picture that would only be revealed years later.

Under questioning Tessia went on to tell about the Friday morning that Melissa had her seizure. Early that morning Melissa sat in her chair and watched TV.

The prosecutor handed her Exhibit 16 and Exhibit 17, and asked Tessia if she recognized them. They were photos of Melissa's Cookie Monster chair and the recliner in their house. Tessia had snapped the photos herself.

"Now," Wilder-Tomlinson said, "you said she fell and hit her head on the recliner?"

"She bumped her head on the recliner."

"How did Melissa react?"

"She cried, and I picked her up. And she cried just a couple of seconds and sat back down in the chair."

"Did you see any sign of injury?"

"No."

"About how long before the defendant picked her up was that?"

"Probably an hour to an hour and a half."

"And all this time, Melissa was playing and crawling around and getting into things?"

Tessia said she was. Mary had picked her up at 10:20, and Melissa seemed fine then. The next thing Tessia heard about Melissa was when Mary called her at Hardee's to tell her Melissa had quit breathing.

The prosecutor specifically asked Tessia whether Mary came to the hospital or ever called her there. Tessia said she hadn't.

Mary wanted to object. Tessia had either forgotten about the calls Mary made or was trying to make Mary look like she didn't care about Melissa.

Wilder-Tomlinson had worked her way to the bottom of her pages of notes and was just summing up. She asked Tessia point-blank, "Did you do anything to cause any of the injuries that were listed?"

"No."

"Do you know how Melissa received any of those injuries?"

"No."

The session broke for lunch. When the courtroom was mostly empty, Steve discussed the high points of the morning's witnesses with Mary, then focused on Tessia's testimony.

Steve eyed Mary with compassion. "Remember, your side of the story will come out next. The jury will see the discrepancies in Tessia's testimony."

"I know." Mary left for lunch with Jim and her dad and a couple of supporters who were there for the trial. She knew Steve would spend most of his lunch hour in his office three blocks away, preparing to question the grieving mother who, in a more thorough investigation, would have been on the list of suspects.

After lunch Steve started his cross-examination by putting a large mock-up of a calendar for January 1993 on an easel beside the witness stand. He had marked out the ten days before Melissa's death. Tessia agreed that Melissa was with Mary Wednesday, January 13, through Friday, January 15; and came home with no apparent injuries. On Saturday, seven days before Melissa died, the baby was at home with Brad and Tessia during the day. That evening they went to the casino and left Melissa with Tessia's sisters in Conrad.

Steve pinned Tessia down with his eyes like an entomologist studying a rare insect. "Did you shake Melissa that morning?"

"No."

"Did Brad?"

# CHAPTER 11

"No."

"Did somebody else?" Steve asked.

Tessia twisted her tissue into a screw, stared at her lap, refused to meet Steve's eyes. "What do you mean, did somebody else? Somebody did sometime."

"Do you disagree with the doctors that something happened to her in the seven- to ten-day time frame?"

"I don't know. I'm not a doctor."

"You understand the doctors are saying that she got her skull cracked open, fractured, on some day in that seven- to ten-day time frame. Is that right?"

"Yes."

"Do you disagree with that?"

Tessia paused to consider her answer. Perhaps she was thinking through the ramifications of her next statement. Finally she met Steve's eyes. "I think it happened Monday."

"What's the basis for that disagreement?"

"She wasn't sick until Monday."

Steve returned to day seven. He asked Tessia who was in the apartment with Melissa when they went to pick her up Saturday night after the casino.

Tessia's sister, Sally, and her daughter were there. Another sister, Cindy, was also there, and Tessia thought Cindy's boyfriend, Brian, was there too.

"When you got in the car, Melissa was crying, wasn't she?"

Tessia shook her head before Steve even finished his question. "No."

He asked her if Melissa was acting like her head hurt, acting like she had a new personality, acting tender.

Another emphatic no.

She admitted that Melissa was fussy and tired, but they weren't worried about her. Keith and Becky, Brad's parents, commented about the baby being fussy. The group went to his folks' place after they picked up Melissa.

Steve stood, adjusting his tone to an even more confrontational one. "You are aware that your mother-in-law, Becky, went to the police and told them about how Melissa was acting on that night; isn't that right?"

"Yes."

"And you are aware that it is her conclusion, Keith's conclusion, Brian's conclusion that Melissa was hurt on Saturday night, right?"

"No."

Steve raised his eyebrows, probed her eyes even deeper. "You are not aware of that?"

"I know that's what…" Tessia studied her lap a minute, breaking contact with the penetrating eyes. "Would you ask the question again?"

Steve continued to press the issue. "Well, you are aware that that's their opinion, isn't it? Isn't that the case?"

She raised her head and spoke directly. "It was their speculation."

Speculation. Tessia echoed Brad now. Her words sounded suspicious to Steve, like they had been coached.

"Who were Melissa's other caretakers on that day, Saturday, the sixteenth?"

Tessia said she had taken care of Melissa. So had Brad and her sister.

Steve glanced down at his notes, shifted his line of questioning. "Did anyone ever indicate to you that the autopsy would be changed to show a five-day time frame for these injuries?"

"That it could be changed."

"Who said that?"

"Maybe Motsinger. I don't remember for sure. And the doctors told me that."

"Does it surprise you that the autopsy has not been changed?"

"No."

"Have you ever indicated to anyone that you fear or were concerned for Melissa's safety when she was left with Brad?"

"No."

Tessia had confided to Mary that she wasn't comfortable leaving Melissa with Brad, so Mary felt her words were a contradiction to that earlier statement.

Steve checked his notes for the next question.

He picked up a copy of Tessia's deposition from August 27, 1993, and turned to a marked page. "Do you recall stating at that time that she had fallen and hit her head an hour before Mary came?"

"Yes."

"You stated earlier that you were in counseling for the things that had occurred to you during your childhood, because you didn't know how correct parents were. What do you mean by that?"

The certainty left her voice. "Well, my parents were abusive, and I didn't want to be abusive."

"Do you now know how correct parents are?"

"I would say I do."

"Now, you have accused Mary of abusing Melissa in the past, right?"

"Yes."

"How many times have you done that?"

"Just that one. I didn't really accuse her. I just asked her about it."

"About what?"

"About the scratches and the anal tear."

Steve clenched his fists. Mary could sense his anger in his direct tone and his refusal to back down. "You didn't accuse her about that? Do you recall telling her that the doctor told you there is no way Melissa could have caused those bruises herself?"

"Yes."

"That's not what the doctor said, though, is it?"

Her lip quivered. "Yes, it is."

Steve's voice raised a notch. "So, are you saying that Dr. Grauerholz lied to these people?"

Tessia's voice dropped until she could hardly be heard. "What I am saying...That's not the way I understood when she talked to me."

"What did you understand her to say?"

"That she could not do that herself."

Steve paged through the doctor's notes slowly. "Have you looked at the doctor's notes?"

"Yes."

"Then you know that the notes indicated that these were innocent scratches on her face?"

"She told me I was being overprotective."

Steve slapped the doctor's notes down on the table and pointed to the entries in question. "Well, what's the truth, Tessia? Did she tell you that these scratches could not be caused by your daughter, or did she tell you these were innocent scratches?"

Tessia shifted in her seat. "She told me they could not be caused by Melissa."

Steve wasn't about to let this go. "So, she lied to this jury?"

Tessia stared at her fingernails, glanced at the doctor's records, paused to consider her words. "I don't know what she told the jury. I understood it as Melissa couldn't do that herself."

Tessia started to dig a verbal tunnel out of the corner she had backed herself into. She went on to say that she wasn't saying Mary abused her child but that maybe Mary's kids might have done something to Melissa.

Mary studied the jurors. Some of them leaned forward or cocked their heads to one side, trying to follow Tessia's outrageous statements.

Steve scanned the medical records and shifted from the scratches and anal tear of September 1992 to the bruise in the first part of October. "You also accused Mary about some bruises later that Melissa had received on her leg."

Tessia said she only asked Mary about the bruise.

Mary hoped the jury could follow Steve's line of logic. Tessia had trusted Mary enough to leave Melissa in her care, all the while accusing her of abusing the child. When Tessia asked her pediatrician about potential abuse, she misunderstood when the doctor assured her of the innocent nature of Melissa's minor scratches. Yet she continued to leave Melissa with Mary.

Steve picked up the statement she had made to police on January 24, 1993, and turned to the marked page. He referred to the part in which Tessia said Melissa had fallen on the rocker and cried for five to ten minutes.

Tessia said she didn't recall saying that.

Steve's eyes challenged her. He paused, read from the police statement. "Tessia Mathes: 'It has been so long ago. We just passed them off as baby bruises. We did ask about the big bruise. I do recall she fell on the rocking chair that morning. She cried for probably five to ten minutes. At the time, I took her pants off to make sure that there were no bones sticking out, or anything. And I didn't see a bruise, but sometimes bruises don't show up. I hit myself, and then a week later I notice there is a bruise.'"

Steve looked up. "Do you remember that exchange with Mr. Motsinger?"

"Kind of."

"Do you remember being concerned as to whether Melissa had broken her leg?"

"Yes."

"And you actually took her pants off to check to see if any bones were sticking out of her skin?"

"Yes."

"And that's how bad she was crying, right?"

She twisted her tissue until pieces tore off. "I don't remember."

Steve went on to ask her about the many times Melissa fell down and bumped her head as she was beginning to learn how to walk. Tessia admitted Melissa had hit her head on the coffee table a few times until they moved it.

He asked her about Melissa's falling out of the Cookie Monster chair and hitting the recliner on the morning of her seizure.

Tessia wasn't sure where Melissa hit her head. Melissa cried. Tessia checked for scratches and cuts.

"Where on her head did she hit?" Steve asked.

"I think the side."

"You think. Didn't you see her?"

"I don't remember for sure. I would say the side of her head. She fell sideways, hitting the side of her head."

"So, you saw her fall, but you didn't see her head hit anything?"

"No."

"Did it hit something?"

"It hit the chair."

"Did it hit the footrest?"

"I don't know where it hit on the chair."

"Did she cry then?"

"Yes."

"And you got up to see if she had any scratches or cuts?"

"Yes."

"Why did you look for cuts or scratches?"

"Because she fell."

# CHAPTER 11

"She hit a padded surface?"

"That doesn't mean..." She studied her lap some more but found no answer. "I didn't know what she hit for sure."

Steve raised his voice only slightly. He never even left his table. But his pointed questions had Tessia twisting her tissue into knots and tears pooling in her eyes. The deeper Tessia got into her testimony, the more confused and unsure her answers became.

Tessia may or may not have hurt her child, but she was certainly accusing Mary. She had to know more than she was telling. She had to know Mary was innocent. Mary wished Tessia would tell the truth. Then perhaps the killer would be found, and Tessia could find healing from her pain, fear, and guilt.

Mary sneaked peeks at the jury to gauge their reactions. Would they be able to see all the contradictions in Tessia's testimony when compared to the testimonies of others?

Steve's last question was the one he had been waiting to ask for weeks. He stepped in front of the counsel table and waited for the young mother to meet his eyes. "Tessia, in the three to four weeks prior to Melissa's death, did you ask anyone about how much it would cost to buy a cemetery plot?"

Her reply was simple.

"No."

But her eyes filled with worry.

# CHAPTER 12

After lunch Dr. Thomas Bennett burst into the courtroom with all the enthusiasm of a small boy home from school. He crossed the empty room in a few long strides and greeted Steve and Mary like old friends. Odd. Mary's defense witnesses didn't even greet him like this, Steve thought, so why this from the "commander of the child abuse SWAT team," whose mission was to put Mary behind bars?

Steve and Mary had chosen this quiet time between sessions to prepare for the next witness's testimony. That witness, Dr. Bennett, chatted about his drive to Marshalltown, the courtroom decor, the weather, the trial. Steve finally had to cut him off. "You'll have to excuse me. I'm working."

Bennett got the hint and wandered away from the counsel table, and Steve returned to his notes. Was this simple friendliness, or was Bennett trying to get him off-balance before he took the stand?

Twenty minutes later the judge and jury returned, along with the gallery of Mary's supporters and a few newspaper reporters. The prosecutor called Dr. Bennett to the stand. As state medical examiner, Bennett, like an experienced actor who had rehearsed his testimony in many cases, was clearly comfortable airing his degrees and specialties in medicine.

His testimony in the case soon shifted to the history of the diagnosis of SBS.

"Shaken baby syndrome is a term that was coined several years ago, but it was used to describe a pattern of injuries found where there was a subdural hemorrhage around the brain, retinal hemorrhages, and no other external findings to explain them. As we investigated these cases, more and more that term has now been expanded to what we use, the term 'shaken/slammed baby syndrome,' implying that there is a shaking episode where it's like cracking a whip or a whiplash-type motion. In addition there is an impact, so it's like a composite. You have a shaking, a back and forth motion, and then impact, which is the slamming part."

The jurors listened to Bennett's lengthy, detailed answers with a mixture of interest and boredom. After a long history of SBS cases and research, Wilder-Tomlinson finally directed Bennett to narrow in on Melissa's case. "Have you formed an opinion as to the cause of Melissa's death?"

Bennett leaned forward, warming to his subject matter. "Yes, I have."

"What is that opinion?"

"In my opinion, Melissa died directly as a result of what we call the shaken/slammed baby syndrome, an injury that occurred on January twenty-second, 1993, just prior to her collapse and the emergency phone call made, the 9-1-1 phone call at 11:13 a.m., within minutes prior to that collapse and what has been described as the seizure and the vomiting and so forth."

"Let's start with the timing. You had said that you believed it happened just before she collapsed?"

"Yes."

That made Mary the killer.

"Can you give us an idea of the force? You're not talking about resuscitative shaking, but—"

"That's right. This isn't something like simply shaking some-one to wake them up or simply someone who falls off a couch onto a carpeted floor or someone even, for that matter, that falls from ten feet onto a floor. The comparison is made that the amount of force that is produced on that child is roughly sim-ilar to what an adult would experience when being shaken by an eight-hundred-pound gorilla—tremendous force, back-and-forth shaking force, above and beyond anything reasonable or proper at all."

Steve wished he knew where Bennett got his scientific data for this. Had they lined up fifty eight-hundred-pound gorillas, enticed them to shake adult humans, then measured the force? Bennett had moved from research to opinion and then to pure fiction.

Steve knew Bennett's comment about the eight-hundred-pound gorilla must have wounded Mary. It was a cruel jab at the extra weight Mary carried. As if someone with a few extra pounds was more likely to abuse children or was capable of doing more harm than a person of average weight. Steve glanced at a few of the jurors who were equally overweight and wondered if they felt the cruelty as well.

Upon cross-examination, Bennett said he disagreed with the seven- to ten-day time frame. He thought five to seven days would be more accurate.

Steve raised an eyebrow at the comment. "You think they just missed the boat in saying this is a seven- to ten-day-old set of injuries?"

Bennett stroked his mustache. "When you look at injuries such as these, there is always the objective part and the subjective part. The objective part is documenting what you see factually. Then comes in the subjective part, where you render an opinion. The subjective part always comes from our frame of reference. I think they were incorrect. In my opinion the ruling of seven to ten days is incorrect. The changes are consistent with five days of age also."

Bennett was a strong, charismatic witness, and his testimony was the last for the prosecution. He could weave the facts of a case with subjective opinions, add a gorilla or two, and create a colorful story. Under oath, his testimony danced on the edges of truth. It kept the jury awake, but sometimes juries trusted medical experts to know more than they could know.

So far the various doctors who testified had proclaimed the old injuries to be seven days old, seven to ten days old, and now five days old. The acute injuries had been dated from within twenty-four hours or four or five hours of the CT scan or one hour of the 9-1-1 call. Other doctors saw no acute injury at all.

Doctors needed to realize that in some cases, like Mary's, they couldn't know all the facts. The X rays, CT scans, and autopsies could only drive them so far. If they wanted to go farther, they had to hitch a ride with opinions. Opinions could convict a child abuser or frame an innocent person.

But perhaps that was the point. Uncertainty couldn't convict. If they were going to win the war on child abuse and rack up more convictions, uncertainty was their greatest enemy. Sometimes they might have to push past the edges of proven fact into likely opinion, or they would lose this war. As these doctors compared notes, some of their objectivity could lose its sharp edge. Strongly stated opinions could sound like facts to juries weary of listening to hour after hour of scholarly testimony. When the testimony became hard to understand, they would trust the opinions of the experts.

So far the three doctors were convinced Mary was guilty simply because she had been with Melissa when the baby quit breathing. Ignoring severe older injuries, they were convinced the acute injury killed her. At the very least Melissa had to have been violently shaken within sixty minutes of her seizure, even if Smith had to narrow his time frame from twenty-four hours down to one hour to make it so.

But the other doctors who testified for the prosecution hadn't actually hurt Mary's cause. Steve felt Thomas ruled out direct trauma, the "slam" Bennett accused Mary of committing, because he found no outer signs of injury. Grauerholz had repeatedly examined the baby during the final week and completely missed the skull fracture. This evidence reinforced the fact that Melissa could have appeared normal Friday morning in spite of a severe injury. Schelper had admitted that some parts of the dating of the injury were subjective. The EMT workers' worst accusation was that Mary had been too calm. The prosecution had failed to present the testimony of one person who could say Mary had a temper problem or had ever acted in a violent manner.

With the testimony for the prosecution finished, the defense could begin tomorrow morning with the surprise testimony of Kim Smuck.

As the following court day began, Kim walked through the courtroom doors, passed closely enough to touch Tessia Mathes, who was seated in the front row of the gallery, and approached the witness stand. Kim was sworn in and seated. The routine questions revealed she worked at the cemetery.

"Have you met Tessia Mathes?" Steve asked.

"Yes, I have."

"Please tell the jury how you met Tessia."

"She took my order for lunch one day when I went to Hardee's. She asked about my smock."

"Your smock?"

"Yes, my work smock." She pointed to her shoulder. "It says Riverside Cemetery on it."

"Continue."

"She asked, 'Do you work at the cemetery?' and I said, 'Yes.' Then she asked me how much it would cost to bury somebody."

"How did you respond to her?"

"I told her that the grave spaces were two hundred to eight hundred dollars, depending on where they were located in the cemetery."

"What happened then?"

"I said, 'Why do you ask?' thinking a family member must be ill, or a sick relative, that sort of thing."

"How did she answer you?"

"She said something like, 'Oh, I was just curious.' Then she took my order."

"When did this event take place?"

"It was right around Christmastime 1992."

"And did you see Tessia again?"

"Yes. Nearly a month later, Tessia walked into my office. She wanted to buy a grave space for her daughter, who had just died."

Steve heard a jury member gasp. He turned just enough to see the prosecutor's eyes widen and her hand freeze over a pen she had just dropped on the table. Wilder-Tomlinson recovered quickly, picked up the pen, and scribbled calmly on a legal tablet as if she had expected this lightning bolt to strike.

Steve hid a smile, turned back to the witness. "Is that typical behavior for a mother who has just lost a child?"

"No, not at all. Most often, the family will just send someone else to take care of this. A mother who has lost a child is grieving too much. They're just beside themselves."

Several jurors jotted a note to themselves. Tessia began rocking back and forth in her chair. wringing her hands.

Steve turned to Judge Baker. "No further questions, Your Honor."

# CHAPTER 13

As Kim Smuck stepped down, whispers exploded across the public gallery. Wilder-Tomlinson pulled a deposition from her briefcase with the detachment of a law student who had attended a lecture for one hour too many. Only the pinched firmness of her lips hinted at exasperation at learning this vital information so late in the trial.

Steve glanced outside the glass doors to see Dr. Rose, the patient teacher who guarded the boundary between scientific fact and medical opinion. When other doctors had declared Mary guilty, Earl Rose reviewed the autopsy with an objective eye. He was the first to lay out a scientific and defensible theory about the death that harmonized with Mary's memory of the events that last tragic day. Rose had given them their first taste of hope that they could win the case.

Rose met Steve's eyes and nodded. He was ready.

The judge called for the next witness, and Rose entered the courtroom. Steve relaxed as the gray-haired man stepped confidently up to the witness chair. Rose wouldn't entertain the jury like Bennett had, but he would tell the truth and stick with the science. He would give careful answers and never claim to know more than he could.

Steve began by establishing Rose's extensive credentials. Then he asked, "Do you have an opinion as to Melissa's cause of death?"

"Yes. It is my opinion that she died of complications resulting from a head injury." He went through findings he considered to be the traumatic indications that led to her death.

"From your review of Melissa's records, is it conclusive or open in your mind as to whether Melissa's injuries would have required new trauma on Friday, just prior to her seizure?"

"No. They can be spontaneous, and, of course, they can recur from trauma as well, minor trauma or major trauma. But there is no requirement, in my opinion, that there be new trauma."

"And in your opinion then, the initiating event is a rebleed into the subdural hematoma that we have heard about?"

"It is a rebleed from the tiny capillaries that are forming in there, which are quite fragile, and they would bleed quite easily, yes."

Dr. Rose led the jury into a journey through the world of the brain, gesturing with large hands. He talked about the subdural hematoma that had begun bleeding a week or two before the baby's death. These blood clots could repair themselves, but they could also rebleed spontaneously. He went on to discuss retinal hemorrhages in the eye, the swelling of the brain, and all the various injuries Melissa had suffered.

After about half an hour, Steve turned the witness over to the prosecutor for cross-examination. As Wilder-Tomlinson started her questions, Steve whispered to Mary, "She won't rattle Dr. Rose. Truth and science stand up to the harshest cross-examination."

Wilder-Tomlinson proved this to be true. First she tried to question his credentials.

When she asked him how much he charged for consultation, examination, and testimony, he smiled. "Oh, you know that. It is one hundred twenty dollars an hour. You know that because of the deposition. You haven't paid yet, by the way."

The prosecution crossed her arms. "I would bet the defendant hasn't paid either."

She moved from injury to injury, but she couldn't get Rose to change his conclusions, which were drawn from careful science rather than emotion. At one point she tried to challenge him about the microscopics of twenty cc's of blood. "Do you remember giving a deposition in this matter, Doctor?" she said.

"Yes. In November."

"The one that you haven't been paid for yet?" she teased.

"Yes, that's the one, but I am not going to sue."

Wilder-Tomlinson smiled. "Okay. That's good."

Steve figured the jury appreciated the humor. Wilder-Tomlinson had scored some points for that, but she couldn't get Rose to change his testimony. When she raised her voice, the doctor answered with politeness and firmness. The prosecutor moved from topic to topic, from one autopsy finding to the next, trying to force Dr. Rose to make concessions regarding the diagnosis of shaken baby syndrome, but her efforts were fruitless.

Steve asked more questions on redirect examination. At the end he said, "As a last question or last topic, these terms 'shaken baby,' 'shaken-slammed baby,' 'battered child'—are these terms that you use in describing findings made in a pathology lab?"

"No, I do not. I use 'traumatic injury.'"

"Why don't you use those terms?"

"I think those terms carry meanings, subjective meanings as well. And they invade the province of the deciders of the fact on this." He gestured toward the jury, those deciders of the fact, recognizing the important position they held. "I prefer to use 'traumatized injury.'"

Steve checked his notes long enough for the jurors to absorb the last answer. The labels "shaken baby syndrome" or "shaken-slammed baby" assumed a baby had been shaken or slammed. A pathologist couldn't determine whether a baby had been shaken or slammed from the injuries alone. That was for the jury to decide.

"No further questions, Your Honor."

Wilder-Tomlinson stood up and eyed Rose. "You are not saying by your last answer that there is no such thing as a type of child abuse called 'shaken baby,' correct?"

"No. I think there is an injury to the child that can result from shaking the baby. Yes, I do."

He went on to say that retinal hemorrhages, subdural bleeding, subarachnoid bleeding, and brain edema could be caused by shaking, but a skull fracture couldn't.

"And is it also true, Dr. Rose, that you may see these, the injuries that we have described to the brain, without outside signs of injury?"

"Yes, you can."

"No further questions, Your Honor."

The prosecution was downplaying the significance of the fact that the emergency room doctors had seen no outward signs of injury, but Steve hoped the jury caught the significance of Rose's testimony. This was scientific evidence that Melissa may not have received any new injuries the Friday of her seizure. She could have already been suffering from the fatal injuries when Mary picked her up that Friday and still appeared healthy. The seizure could have been caused solely by the cumulative effect of the seven- to ten-day-old injuries. And if there was reasonable doubt about Mary's guilt, the jury must return a not-guilty verdict.

Dr. Ruth Ramsey's testimony added weight to Rose's idea that Melissa's sudden seizure could have come with no new injury. As head of neuroradiology at the University of Chicago, secretary of the American Radiological Society, and author of the massive textbook Neuroradiology, Ramsey was an expert in the vital task of imaging the human brain. Her blonde hair was pulled back in a bun, and her cashmere sweater and natural elegance hinted at a higher level of professionalism than was usual for the central Iowa courtroom.

Ramsey had examined Melissa's two CT scans, which had been taken four hours apart. She enumerated the injuries that were apparent on the two sets of scans. Comparing scans allowed her to see the progression of an injury or lack of it, which could give clues to the cause of injury. Steve had seen the scans and the two sets looked the same to him. He asked her to describe the differences in Melissa's scans.

"The main difference," she said, "is that there is a loss of gray-white distinction as you examine the second set of images, and that is consistent with a hypoxic event."

"What do you mean, 'a hypoxic event'?"

"Hypoxia—without oxygen. It means simply that this little girl's brain suffered a lack of oxygen. The injury that is clear on these CT scans is consistent with what we see when a child falls into a swimming pool and drowns."

"Is there any indication of a blow to the head?"

"No. Not on the scans."

Steve turned the witness over to the prosecution, satisfied that the jury could see that Melissa's death could have been caused by her older injuries.

With the medical testimony finally finished, Steve turned to the character witnesses. The state's theory of the case was that Mary Weaver, an otherwise typical housewife, suddenly and without warning murdered an eleven-month-old baby. Steve called a long list of character witnesses to show that such an act was completely out of character for Mary.

# CHAPTER 13

Some of them shared baby-sitting times with Mary. Some knew her through her children's preschool or Christian women's club. All testified that even in stressful situations, Mary was patient with children, never violent. Some had talked to Mary after Melissa's seizure and told how upset Mary was by it, that she was crying. A church nursery worker explained that Melissa never seemed to be afraid of Mary. The state had failed to present the testimony of even one person to testify that Mary was violent or impatient. The testimony of these witnesses harmonized in one voice that said Mary would never hurt a child.

✿ ✿ ✿

Wednesday morning Mary set the milk on the table for breakfast, then began restacking the fridge to make room for the frozen turkey. Today she would defrost the Christmas turkey, wrap a few presents, and testify in her own murder trial.

She had never testified in a trial before and certainly never dreamed she'd testify in her own.

Most of the time she believed she would be acquitted. Five doctors still seemed to think she was guilty, but Steve had countered with three equally qualified doctors who didn't. They believed the evidence didn't necessarily show that any new trauma had occurred. In the sight of the court, however, she was innocent until proven guilty. In the sight of God she was truly innocent. How could she lose?

Still, the jury hadn't begun deliberations, and Judge Baker had yet to bang his gavel and pronounce her "not guilty." Mary decided that if Catherine and John could experience stage fright at their recent performance in the church Christmas program, she shouldn't feel guilty about some frayed nerves before her testimony. Today Mary would end seven days of testimony with her own.

119

Steve's advice had been simple. "Tell the truth." He had considered rehearsing her testimony with her beforehand. This basic trial technique was designed to inspire confidence in a witness. But in the end he decided not to.

"If we practice, your testimony will sound like we rehearsed it," Steve said. "We want it to sound like what it will be, a natural retelling of what actually happened. More than anything, your testimony needs to have the 'ring of truth.' We can't lose that."

Mary drove to the courthouse, reminding herself over and over, "The truth will set you free." Telling the truth was easy. Nothing to remember but the facts.

After she finished her testimony, Steve and the prosecution would present their closing arguments and rebuttals. The jury could start deliberations tomorrow. If things went really well and the case was clear to the jury, they could—just possibly—bring a not-guilty verdict by Friday night, Christmas Eve. It would be just like God to give her acquittal as a glorious Christmas present. Closure at last!

But Mary had to remind herself that juries didn't usually decide that quickly. If the verdict wasn't settled by Christmas, she would still make the holiday special for their family. And she hadn't even given her testimony yet.

Steve began Mary's testimony with basic questions. "What is your name? Where do you live? How many children do you have?" These questions gave Mary a chance to get comfortable with her own voice, to loosen up a little as he had instructed her to do. She kept her eyes trained on Steve until she recognized he was giving her little cues.

"Can you tell the jury…," he hinted several times. Soon she turned toward the jury and began to talk to them as if she were sitting on the porch talking to friends.

# CHAPTER 13

Steve asked about the six months Mary had baby-sat for Melissa. Mary was able to give her own interpretation of the testimony of others. The anal tear and bruise. The final Monday when Melissa was a bit fussy and spitting up. Her phone calls with Tessia. Tessia's eagerness to get back to work.

"Mary, you have heard a lot of testimony about the events of January twenty-second," Steve said. "Take us back through the events of that last day you shared with Melissa."

Mary just walked through the day. Running errands, going to the grocery store, then picking up Melissa from her home. Getting into the van, stopping by the library, driving home, carrying Melissa into the house. Taking the snowsuit off, setting the baby on the counter in her car seat. Putting groceries away, feeding Melissa.

Finally she came to the moments before Melissa passed out. She had told this story so many times, yet reliving it now brought fresh pain. "I saw that it was time to go and pick up my kids, so I walked into the living room and knelt down on the carpet. I laid Melissa down and put her legs into her snowsuit. Then I reached back behind her shoulders and head and helped her sit up into a sitting position." Mary sniffed, dabbed a handkerchief to her eyes. "And as I did that, her eyes rolled—they went back in her head—and she quit breathing."

From the sound of it, everyone in the courtroom had quit breathing too. A few women jurors blinked back some tears.

Steve broke the silence. "What did you do then?"

"I picked her up and called 9-1-1. They helped me with instructions–clearing her mouth of food, clearing her airway. Then helping her breathe until the ambulance arrived."

"So you were standing with the phone propped up to your ear, holding Melissa, and trying to do CPR?"

"Yes. I had the phone on my shoulder. I think I set it down to do what they told me from time to time. Then I would come back to the phone."

"By the way, you heard the dispatcher say you sounded 'too calm.' Did you feel calm, Mary?"

Mary's eyes widened. "I was terrified! No, I was definitely not calm."

"What happened then?"

Mary described hearing the siren and going outside to flag down the police officer, of his attempts to revive Melissa and the attempts of the EMT staff. She spoke about worried phone calls to Tessia and fears for the baby's welfare.

"When did you learn that Melissa had died?" Steve asked.

"The next day Lieutenant Buffington called me to the police department to ask about what had happened. I told him about that morning, and when I finished, he told me that Melissa had died."

"How did you react to that news?"

Mary shook her head. "I couldn't believe it. I thought the paramedics and doctors had saved her life. I just couldn't believe Melissa was gone."

"Mary, you have heard the opinions of the state's doctors."

"Yes."

"You've heard them say that they think you traumatized Melissa. Let me ask you, did you hurt Melissa?"

Mary shook her head over and over. "No."

"Did you slam her head on the counter?"

"Never."

"Did you shake her like Dr. Alexander demonstrated?"

"Oh, no."

"Did you hurt her in any manner?"

"No." Mary addressed the jury. "All I did was try to save her life. I loved Melissa."

"No further questions, Your Honor."

Mary sighed. Now the hard part. The prosecution would try her hardest to trip Mary up. If Mary showed uncertainty, Wilder-Tomlinson would take advantage of that. Mary thought about how confrontational Steve had become with Tessia when her answers didn't add up. But the jury had maintained good eye contact with Mary and seemed to be on her side.

The prosecutor had little to question Mary about. She made the point that Mary had fed Melissa, that Melissa had been vomiting. "Also on the 9-1-1 tape the lady instructs you to make sure to position her so she won't vomit or swallow the vomit. Correct?"

"That's correct."

"And yet you laid her on the floor on her back and left her to go and greet the ambulance personnel? You left her on her back in the kitchen on the floor?"

Mary cleared her throat. Tell the truth—even now, with your freedom hanging by a thin thread. "Yes, I did."

The prosecutor went on to point out that Mary had admitted shaking Melissa to Motsinger. Mary agreed she had. She demonstrated shaking the baby gently and calling her name.

But the cross-examination didn't last long. As Steve had said, "When you tell the truth, there's not much to cross-examine."

Mary watched Steve flip through his legal pad of questions. He seemed to be considering whether he should question her again. If he did, he would give the prosecution another chance to trip her up. After a few minutes, he met the judge's eyes.

"No further questions, Your Honor."

Mary stepped down, relieved to be finished with her testimony.

When the court adjourned, Mary greeted a full gallery of friends and family who had shown up to support her. They assured her that she'd done a great job testifying and promised to keep praying.

By the time she reached the car, she felt too exhausted to move. Thankfully Jim was there, as always, to drive her home. His quiet support for her meant so much.

Mary refused to second-guess her testimony the same way she had refused to second-guess her decision not to plea-bargain or to use a friend as a lawyer, even though he lacked the experience of others. She had told the truth. She would leave it with God. She was innocent. God was in control.

Names of other apparently innocent adults who had been convicted of murder in similar incidents flashed in her mind. Just as quickly she dismissed them. Mary refused to muddy her faith with situations involving other people and God. What God did in their lives was between them and God.

If the trial went as she expected, her name would be totally cleared in a few days. But if it didn't, she couldn't imagine the alternative.

Certainly a good God wouldn't allow her to be sent to prison. For life. Without parole.

# CHAPTER 14

Thursday afternoon Steve sloshed three blocks through the city slush in his four-buckle overshoes. He was ready. He had spent the entire noon hour in his office, preparing to deliver the most important closing arguments of his life. Mary's freedom depended on his ability to persuade the jury of reasonable doubt.

Snatches of Christmas carols sifted through doors of the shops he passed. He hummed his own reply:

> Then pealed the bells more loud and deep:
> "God is not dead: nor doth He sleep;
> The wrong shall fail, the right prevail,
> With peace on earth, goodwill to men."

The trial had gone well. Mary was innocent. God exercised providential control over the jury's decision. Steve could almost smell acquittal like hot pumpkin pie straight from the oven. If the jury decided quickly, the Brenneckes and the Weavers could rest easily during their family Christmas celebrations. A good resolution to his biggest case ever would be an awesome Christmas present.

Once the court resumed and the judge asked for closing arguments, Wilder-Tomlinson stood with confidence. She told the jury that Melissa died as a result of violent shaking by Mary Weaver. Five doctors, whose fields varied from neurology to forensic pathology, had testified that the baby's brain was injured just hours prior to an autopsy performed on January 23. Doctors had testified that Melissa couldn't have been a happy, jabbering, talking, eating, just-fine baby one minute and then lapse into her seizure soon after. Mary's testimony wasn't consistent with the injuries. Mary had shown indifference toward the baby by not going to the hospital to explain what had occurred. The defense was unable to dispute that a recent injury showed up in the autopsy.

When the defense's turn came, Steve stepped forward with more confidence than nerves. Perhaps it was just plain pride.

The murder case against Mary Weaver was an unusual one, Steve told the jury. Other than the defendant, there were no witnesses to the scene where Melissa had succumbed to her injuries. The case against Mary consisted almost entirely of medical evidence. The controversy wasn't about the findings of the autopsy but about what those findings meant.

The state's evidence consisted of a self-contradictory medical case, shored up by the forceful opinions of medical experts, who had discounted any findings that contradicted their theories. They ignored Melissa's older, life-threatening injuries. Since some of the doctors insisted that Melissa was healthy when Mary picked her up, they needed a lethal blow to explain her death.

Perhaps the most important pieces of evidence were observed before the autopsy. Dr. Thomas, the state's own witness, had searched in vain for any sign of injury when Melissa was brought into the emergency room. Dr. Ramsey had testified that the injury shown by the CT scans was simply hypoxia. The baby had quit breathing, a fact that agreed completely with Mary's testimony. There was no goose-egg, no freshly-broken bones, no contusion, no cuts or bruising to support the state's contention that a brutal murder occurred while Melissa was in Mary's care. Dr. DiMaio had seen no evidence of new trauma. Dr. Rose said Melissa's death could have been caused by a re-bleed of an old injury.

But Steve's main strategy was to show that other people should have been suspects. Others could have killed Melissa. Melissa was abused, not by Mary but by the person who inflicted fatal injuries seven to ten days prior to her death.

"Only one person here has shown evidence of premeditating murder," he said. "It is the mother who inquired about grave sites and two pay periods later lost a child to violent injury."

Several people had opportunity to inflict Melissa's injuries, but the investigators hadn't suspected anyone but Mary. The state hadn't proven beyond reasonable doubt that Melissa's injuries were inflicted during the forty-two minutes she was with Mary. Someone else had to have inflicted the previous severe injuries. The evidence pointed to that "silent killer," the seven- to ten-day-old injury which was advancing toward death.

In the end the jury must realize that this whole case was built on medical opinions, which could be used to support either side. This was hardly evidence required for conviction, proof beyond a reasonable doubt.

Steve finished his argument. The state gave its rebuttal. The judge instructed the jury, and the wait began. With the jury already in deliberations on Thursday, Steve and Mary prayed they would come to a not-guilty verdict before Christmas.

On the day of Christmas Eve Steve lay on the floor with Nic, building castles out of large, wooden building blocks, but his mind was in the jury chambers. His mind hadn't rested for weeks. He'd exhausted all his energy trying to remember every word of every testimony, yet even now he couldn't shut it out. He knew

Mary also hovered close to the phone while she baked pies and wrapped presents.

Late that afternoon Steve called Mary. "We should be encouraged that the jury is taking such a good look at things and not coming to a snap decision," he said. He was a lawyer. Spinning an optimistic slant to proceedings was part of his job description.

The jury retired for the holiday. The eleven women probably rushed home to do last-minute baking. The Brennecke and Weaver families celebrated as normal, but Steve couldn't resist giving a few comments about the case to his lawyer father. With all its flaws, the American legal system was still the best in the world. Tessia's testimony was inconsistent and anxious. Mary's testimony was unshakable. Doctors couldn't agree. Reasonable doubt. More pie, Dad?

At church on the day after Christmas, Steve and Mary were constantly circled and questioned. Each optimistic comment exposed the uncertainty of an unfinished trial.

Monday the jurors were back in deliberations. Tuesday Steve received word that the jury was having trouble coming to a unanimous verdict. The judge sent them back to the jury room to try again. Wednesday Steve's phone rang again.

The jury was unable to reach a verdict.

A hung jury was infinitely better than a guilty verdict, but now they would have to go through the whole ordeal all over again. Steve dreaded calling Mary. This would buy her a few more months with her kids, but the uncertainty of an undecided verdict would shadow her every move. If the case was obviously unclear to this jury, what would the outcome be in her next trial?

# CHAPTER 15

In his office Steve pulled the list from a folder of notes from Mary's trial. What had gone wrong? Mary was supposed to be acquitted, totally done with her murder trial by now. Instead she began 1994 as a murder suspect.

He studied the list of jurors and their contact information from the clerk's office.

These twelve people were the only ones who could help him understand the jurors' mind-set. Maybe they could help him fix his mistakes so he could represent Mary in a way that would bring acquittal. Then this mother of two small children could return to her family for good.

Steve forced himself to dial the first number on the list. He would attempt to set up interviews with the jurors. They were under no obligation to speak to him. Most of them probably wanted to put the Weaver trial behind them and never look back. But each one who agreed would give Steve a better understanding of how the next jury might think.

He called the nurse. The homemaker. The businessman. Others. Reaching them all took hours, but several agreed to an interview.

During the next few days he tried to coax information out of each juror. Some were only willing to give a brief phone interview. When they were willing, Steve arranged to meet them face-to-face. As he talked to them on their front porches, he could read their body language and understand them better. Though a majority had voted against Mary, he reminded himself that they would likely tell him what he wanted to hear instead of what he needed to know. Still, polling the jurors gave him valuable information.

Evidently eight of the jurors had believed Mary was guilty of the murder charges, and nine believed the endangerment charges. No one understood the doctors. They felt they had needed a crash course in medicine to understand much of the testimony. Made sense. Steve had spent many hours researching anatomy books to bring himself up to speed on the medical issues so he could understand the medical experts. No wonder the jury hadn't understood them. In fact, the judge had told them not to do research on their own—their decision must rise only from their common sense and the evidence presented in the courtroom. This essentially left them in the dark.

The jury also struggled with information overload. The trial had piled on more than the average juror could possibly absorb. Several were irritated by the rule that required them to sit silently and observe the entire trial. They were never allowed to ask a witness a question simply to clarify his or her point. When uncertain about a point of tedious medical testimony, they remained in the dark, hoping someone would ask the question that was on their minds.

One woman felt certain Mary was not guilty—not because of the doctors' testimony, but because of Kim Smuck's. She had worked hard to get the rest of the jurors to change their decisions without success. Steve was just glad four jurors didn't bow to the pressure of the majority and vote for a guilty verdict.

Steve also found that presumption of innocence was hard to apply. The simple fact that Mary had been arrested and was sitting in court as a suspect made her look guilty. On the other hand, Steve learned that juries don't want to believe a mother would kill her own child. The whole concept is just repugnant. If a jury had to decide who had killed a child, a mother or a baby-sitter, believing the baby-sitter did it was easier. Of course, others could have done it too, but it didn't sound like the jury had considered other suspects.

All the facts had come out in the trial, but a majority of the jurors still believed Mary was guilty. That fact activated warning lights and buzzers all across the control panel of his lawyer's gut instincts.

Warnings were good. God had used the mistrial to warn Steve that he needed a different approach. In a few months they'd have to start all over again with a new trial. The next one had to go better. He had to figure out what had gone wrong in the first trial so he could fix it in the second.

Steve began to wonder if a trial to the court would better serve Mary's interests. Then the judge would sit both as fact-finder and as the judge of the law. The judge could interact with the witnesses when the testimony became too difficult to follow.

Still Steve had to consider his advice to Mary carefully. A jury trial required a unanimous verdict. The right to a jury trial had just saved Mary from a murder conviction and life in prison. On the other hand, some of the jurors disconnected during the trial and gave over their function of juror to the medical experts. Since a judge had more education than the average juror, he might be able to better understand the medical witnesses. When he didn't understand, he could ask questions.

Steve spent days analyzing the trial and the jury polls. He prayed. He weighed the alternatives. He discussed the issue with Kim until his brain ached from exhaustion. Yet he knew Mary would want to know the results of the polls. She'd ask for good advice from her lawyer, and he'd better be prepared to give it.

Finally Steve poured himself a cup of coffee, sat in his office chair, and made the call. When Mary answered, he described his interview with each juror and noted his or her impressions. As he discussed juror after juror, the themes of difficulty in understanding and information overload became clear.

Steve ticked off the last point on his notes and took a deep breath. Was there a gentle way to drop his bombshell? He couldn't think of one, so he kept babbling. "So when faced with the overwhelming task of assessing all that medical evidence, they opted for simpler measures. They counted the doctors who testified for the state and the ones who testified for you and went with the majority. That became their measure of guilt and innocence. More than one juror asked me, 'Why would a doctor lie?' Polling the jurors has shown me that the next trial is going to be a very difficult, uphill battle."

The other end of the line became so quiet, Steve began to wonder if they had been disconnected. Mary must have sensed the ticking bomb on his end of the line. "What do you think we should do?"

Steve sipped cold coffee and weighed his words one last time before lobbing the bomb her direction. "I think you need to consider waiving the jury, so that the next case is tried by the judge. The judge would then determine whether you are guilty according to the evidence, and if at any point he is confused, he can stop the witness and ask questions to clear things up."

Mary promised to consider the trial by judge. Steve knew she would pray about it and talk to Jim. In the end his advice would weigh more heavily than anyone else's. Lawyers bore heavy responsibility at times like these.

# CHAPTER 15

Steve was advising Mary to give up one of her constitutional rights. He just hoped it was the right decision.

✡ ✡ ✡

Mary ran her fingers over the underlined Bible verses. "I know the thoughts that I think toward you...thoughts of peace and not of evil, to give you a future and a hope...I will bring you back from your captivity."

What did these verses mean for her? She pushed her Bible toward the center of her kitchen table and rested her head in her hands.

"God, I don't understand. I thought for sure I would be acquitted. The trial went so well. We put everything we had on the table. The facts came out clearly. Why couldn't the jury see the truth? And if this jury couldn't see that I'm not guilty, what will the next jury do?"

She reached forward, resting her hand on the Jeremiah promises she had first read months ago. They had convinced her that she would go "into captivity." Maybe that captivity for her was eventual prison, but she was confused. The trial had been stressful. Maybe that was supposed to be her calamity. Maybe she'd be acquitted at the next trial.

Her mind teeter-tottered back and forth between the possibilities. Judge or jury? Acquittal or conviction? Thinking about another trial was hard enough, but what would happen to her family if she had to go to prison? John was used to being with his mom all day long. Who would dress Catherine and do her hair? Could Jim handle two anxious kids at home with a wife in prison?

Mary knew she would be all right, no matter what happened, but how would her family cope? Her wheelchair-bound mother wasn't in the best health. How would this affect them?

If the jury was overwhelmed by all the evidence and couldn't understand the medical experts, maybe a judge could sort through the evidence more easily, give it a more objective look. Steve thought so. Jim agreed. Mary wasn't sure, but she trusted Steve.

Just as the jurors had trusted the opinion of the majority of doctors, Mary was now risking her future to the opinion of her lawyer. She hoped this outcome would be better.

# CHAPTER 16

Steve thanked God for second chances. The hung jury was disappointing but not final. Steve decided it could be God's way of warning them that the medical testimony crucial to this case was too complicated for a jury to follow.

His legal colleagues had assured him that Judge Peterson was a good, fair judge. Steve watched this good, fair judge question Mary as she waived her right to a trial by jury.

"You realize then," Judge Peterson said, "what you are asking is that one person make the decision about guilt or innocence as opposed to twelve people, which would be people within the community that have been selected through a process of jury selection?"

Mary nodded. "Yes, I understand."

"And this is your own decision to move to waive the jury trial? No one has put you under any coercion or threats to make you feel you have no choice but to waive the jury trial?"

"That's right."

Steve hadn't coerced her, just advised her, but she wouldn't have chosen this decision apart from his advice.

The judge concluded that Mary's waiver was voluntary, and the case began, as it had in the first trial, with the 9-1-1 operator. Now it was one judge and a packed gallery that heard Mary's urgent voice. "I need an ambulance! I have a baby that's stopped breathing!"

Mary would have to relive the seizure that led to Melissa's death all over again. And the accusations, suspicions, questions, outright lies. At least this trial couldn't end with a hung jury. As difficult as this was, Steve knew the case well by now. Mary had assured him, "You did a good job on the first trial. We've done it once. We can do it again."

Support for Mary extended well beyond the packed public gallery. Many Christians were praying for the trial. All of these things gave reason to hope that Mary would be acquitted. Another few weeks, and Mary could be a free woman with no threat of prison hanging over her.

The first trial had allowed Steve to literally "practice law" and fine-tune his legal strategy for this second trial, but this advantage came at a cost. While he knew the state's battle plan, they also knew his. Ms. Tomlinson (who had now de-hyphenated her surname) was prepared to counter any moves Steve made before he made them.

The 9-1-1 responders described the tragic scene again. Mary had been too calm, the house was too clean, and the baby was not breathing. Dr. Thomas testified that he had examined the baby in the ER and found no outward, visible signs of injury. The Iowa City doctors gave their version of the last hours of Melissa's life and the autopsy along with their opinions about the cause of death.

During the first trial, the mere hint of Kim Smuck's startling revelation had caught Tessia like a bunny in the headlights. Even Tomlinson's lawyerly façade had cracked for a moment as Kim testified to the mother's inquiry about a grave space. This time Tessia knew what was coming and was ready for the question. When Steve asked Tessia if, in the three to four weeks prior to

Melissa's death, she had inquired about the price of a grave, she simply answered, "No."

Kim Smuck's testimony would come later, but Tomlinson had been given months to plan her own strategy for handling it when the time came.

Drs. Smith, Alexander, and Bennett brought the courtroom into the grisly world of child abuse. Again they expounded the mechanics of shaking a child to death: how the snapping of the head back and forth left a pattern of injuries, some of which were found in Melissa. They spoke with one voice, now even more united than in the first trial. Again these doctors seem to play down Melissa's older injuries, believing Mary had to have inflicted the fatal injury during the forty-two minutes just prior to the seizure.

Steve couldn't believe Judge Peterson would buy this unlikely scenario when the alleged death blow left no mark visible to the ER doctor just after the seizure. But Judge Peterson scribbled notes from their testimony with great interest.

Since they had been through all the testimony before, Tomlinson could anticipate the testimony of the defense's witnesses and counter it before it was even presented.

The first part of the trial didn't go well, but Steve felt he could present a strong case in Mary's defense. He started with a long parade of character witnesses. If Judge Peterson could truly see what kind of person Mary was, he would have to see how unlikely it was that she killed Melissa.

Steve called Dick Ritter, Mary's boss for sixteen years; people Mary had baby-sat for; and people who had worked with her in their church youth group or the nursery of her women's club. He called the teacher of her kids' preschool. These were people who knew Mary well and had watched her patience under pressure.

During the first trial the character witnesses were able to give full testimony with specific examples of how Mary showed patience even in stressful situations. But Judge Peterson's thirst for new information seemed entirely quenched.

With almost every one of the ten character witnesses, Tomlinson objected to at least one thing right away: "Irrelevant" or "Hearsay." The judge usually sustained her objections, and Steve had to cut his questions short under Judge Peterson's stricter implementation of the rules of evidence.

The average testimony of a character witness lasted about five minutes. Witnesses were allowed to say whether Mary was patient under stress but not allowed to give specific incidents that showed that patience. They were allowed to testify that Mary had a reputation of nonviolence in the community but little else. Witnesses became confused about what they could and couldn't say. In the end Steve could merely ask witnesses their names, how they knew Mary, and what her reputation was for violence in the community.

Sustained objections and subtle nuances of body language all pointed like road signs to a guilty verdict. Steve tried to remain optimistic for Mary's sake, but his lawyer's gut feeling churned with impending doom.

After Kim Smuck was sworn in, Steve's gut feelings only got worse. Kim gave her name and place of employment at the cemetery. She told how she had seen Tessia at Hardee's during her lunch break about a week before Christmas of 1992.

"And what happened there at Hardee's?" Steve asked.

Tomlinson broke in. "Your Honor, I'm going to object as to relevance."

Judge Peterson told Steve he was going to have to make the relevance clear.

Steve nodded and turned back to Kim Smuck. "Did you have a conversation with Tessia Mathes at that time in Hardee's in December of 1992?"

# CHAPTER 16

"Yes, I did."

"And what was the substance and contents of the conversation?"

"Objection," Tomlinson snapped. "Your Honor, hearsay."

The judge's routine response showed no emotion. "Sustained."

This began a ten-minute discussion between Steve, the judge, and the prosecutor about whether Kim's testimony should be allowed. Tomlinson argued that only Kim and Tessia had heard the Hardee's discussion and that Tessia had denied it. The state had never taken Kim's deposition. Kim had never reported the discussion to a police officer. With nothing to back it up, it was only hearsay.

Steve promised to corroborate the statements with testimony from Kim's supervisor, whom she had told about the conversation. Tessia had denied making the statement, and he wanted to offer Kim's testimony as impeachment of her testimony. Tessia had been the sole caretaker of Melissa from Tuesday to Friday. She had reported that Melissa wasn't injured during that time. The trustworthiness of her testimony was a key element of his defense.

Judge Peterson drummed his fingers. "So are you saying if she made some statement, which she denies, to a person at Hardee's a month prior that may have been incorrect, it is relevant determination as to whether or not she's telling the truth on other factors in these proceedings?"

Steve felt the legal ground slip away from him, like sand in an outgoing tide. "Her reliability in general is an issue, and that is my—"

"The objection is sustained." Judge Peterson spoke with a finality that shot down Kim Smuck's entire testimony.

Steve asked for a recess to gather his thoughts. How could Kim Smuck's testimony be irrelevant to Mary's defense when it pointed to another suspect? Why would Judge Peterson exclude it from the record when he could give it the weight it was entitled to? Peterson didn't have to worry about swaying a jury with it. If he found it wasn't worthy of merit, he could treat it that way as a fact finder. Steve began to think about the unthinkable. He needed to record reasons for an appeal.

After the break, Steve made another attempt to show legal grounds for the judge to hear Kim's testimony. The judge countered with a long explanation of why he wouldn't allow it. These efforts to block Kim's testimony took more time than it would have taken her to testify. In Mary's first trial Judge Baker had accepted Kim's testimony, but Judge Peterson suddenly seemed ready to end the case and render a verdict.

Steve pressed on with their other witnesses.

Dr. DiMaio testified again about the unreliability of the shaken baby syndrome diagnosis with witty statements and the tenacity of a bulldog.

Dr. Rose, the wise teacher, taught the judge about Melissa's injuries.

Dr. Ramsey had grown more comfortable in the courtroom since the first trial. Her clear explanations demonstrated her expertise as a radiologist.

But Judge Peterson stared at the ceiling during testimony and drummed his fingers as if this trial were an ugly chore he wanted to end. Steve's initial optimism dipped lower every day. He couldn't shake a feeling of doom as he approached the last day of testimony, the eighth day of the trial. He had saved his strongest witness for last. Mary had spoken out clearly and consistently during the first trial. She never wavered from the truth, so she didn't have to worry about keeping her stories straight.

# CHAPTER 16

He knew he could trust her to do a good job on the stand again. But would her words be enough to change the mind of Judge Peterson?

✿ ✿ ✿

The next morning Mary checked her crocuses on the way to the car. Only the first spiky leaves pushed through the frozen dirt. They refused to show the slightest purple tinge of a blossom. The unusually bitter winter had slowed their reawakening. Mary told herself it didn't matter. It had nothing to do with her trial, but lately she had been grasping for any sign of hope.

She slipped into the car seat beside Jim and began to prepare her heart for the day ahead. Today she would testify in her own murder trial. She had done it once. She could do it again. The truth would set her free.

And yet.

Recently she had been rethinking her promise from God about bringing her out of captivity. She had spent months trying to figure out what captivity meant for her. During the first trial she was generally optimistic about the outcome. This second trial had a completely different feel to it. From the beginning Judge Peterson's body language hinted that he had already decided she was guilty. She tried to convince herself that she was reading him wrong, but it wasn't working. His disinterest in the character witnesses shouted, "The baby-sitter did it!"

She turned up the car heater a notch. She had waited for more than two months for this second trial, hoping to clear her name. Every day she trusted that God was in control, but sometimes she worried what that control would mean for her.

That afternoon Mary stepped up to the witness stand as the last witness for the defense.

Again she swore to tell the truth. Nothing new here. From her first interview with Buffington, she had simply told the truth. During her testimony she relived those awful moments when Melissa quit breathing: giving CPR, calling 9-1-1, holding a phone and a baby while trying to breathe life back into her. She had flagged down a police officer in a move that would simultaneously save a life and raise suspicion.

She related her interview with Buffington. The police didn't read her rights to her, but that didn't matter. She wanted to help them find out what happened to Melissa. She described Melissa's seizure to the detective. Then he suddenly announced the baby's death.

"I couldn't believe it," Mary said. "I was very upset. I...I...I didn't want to..." Mary swiped at her eyes and tried to regain control of her emotions. "I just can't tell you how I felt. I was very emotional. I cried. I didn't expect that she would have died. I thought she had just been sick, and I thought once she got to Iowa City, they would be able to cure her. They would be able to help her."

Steve moved on to Motsinger's angry questions. The skull fracture had surprised her because she would have expected a head with a skull fracture to be broken open or bruised. She had asked, "What do you mean by a skull fracture?"

The detective's reply: "You tell me."

"I can't tell you because I don't understand what you mean."

Motsinger found her statement suspicious, but Mary had just been trying to make sense of things.

Steve asked about the detective's demeanor at his second interview.

"He was very angry," Mary said. "Very upset. He told me that he had been getting reports from Iowa City, and he told me that what I had told him could not possibly have been the truth. And he said that I was not telling him the truth, and he wanted to know what the truth was."

"What did you do in response to that?"

Mary said she explained what happened to Melissa.

"How did that interview conclude?"

"It was a very violent interview. He was very angry, very upset, very loud. He just, 'I don't believe you; you're a liar.' You know, just very, very angry."

The bruises and scratches were all discussed again. Mary testified that she felt Tessia had accused her of abusing Melissa. The anal tear even suggested sexual abuse.

Steve ended his examination with questions about Mary's contact with Brad and Tessia after the funeral. Mary had phoned them several times, first at the Iowa City hospital. Tessia had denied this during the first trial, but this time Mary had her phone bill to prove it. Brad stopped by Mary's house once to talk about Melissa's death and how they were coping. Tomlinson objected to the line of questioning twice. The second time Judge Peterson sustained the objection, and Mary could merely testify that she missed Melissa and had never shaken, hit, or hurt her.

On cross-examination Tomlinson asked, as she had in the first trial, about leaving Melissa on her back when she went to greet the ambulance personnel.

Mary admitted that she had, without commenting on how she had consciously tilted the baby's head to one side in case she vomited.

The cross-examination didn't last long, and Mary stepped down. One more day, and the trial would be over. The judge would decide, and her emotions could get off this roller coaster of painful memories. Her future was in the hands of Judge Peterson—and God.

# CHAPTER 17

Steve scanned his notes one last time. After his closing arguments and the prosecutor's arguments, the trial would end. One more chance to argue for Mary's innocence. He wished he could escape the emotional cloud of doom that hung over this trial, threatening to rain down a guilty verdict. But the judge's decisions, rulings, and solemn looks did not predict sunshine.

He could be wrong. God could surprise them, but if Mary was acquitted it would be the greatest surprise of his career so far.

The afternoon recess ended. The courtroom was full once again as closing arguments were presented to the judge. Because the state bears the burden of proof, Tomlinson argued first. She reviewed the evidence with a broad stroke, describing the end of Melissa's life, then narrowed her focus to Mary's role in Melissa's death. She walked through the days, arguing that on Monday when Melissa had left Mary's care, she wasn't acting like herself. She began vomiting and remained sick for the next few days. When Melissa finally revived and began to act like herself again, she returned to Mary's care. When Mary called 9-1-1, it was really too late to save Melissa. The medical experts testified that Mary must have violently shaken and slammed Melissa, causing her death. Tomlinson asked the judge to find her guilty on both charges: first-degree murder and child endangerment.

# CHAPTER 17

The judge then turned to the defense, and Steve began his most passionate closing argument.

He emphasized the fact that the medical experts couldn't agree on what happened to Melissa. Their one point of agreement was the seven- to ten-day-old traumatic incident. The doctors couldn't agree on the only real issue at stake here, whether the state had proven beyond a reasonable doubt that Mary Weaver had inflicted any injury on the child.

No one had offered any evidence to say Mary beat the child, slammed her head down or shook her. Police hadn't made any effort to find out about the seven- to ten-day-old injury. Mary fully cooperated with the detectives to figure out what had happened to Melissa until it became abusive to do so any longer. No one had given any proof of premeditation from Mary, nor any motivation or plan to kill Melissa.

Steve asked Judge Peterson to return a not-guilty verdict on the count of first-degree murder as well as child endangerment.

Tomlinson followed with her brief rebuttal closing argument. She said she believed the judge, after considering all the evidence, would be convinced beyond a reasonable doubt that Mary intentionally injured and killed Melissa by a violent shaking that caused the baby to quit breathing. The prosecutor believed that this kind of conduct inferred malice and child endangerment, and asked the judge to find Mary guilty on both counts.

As Tomlinson spoke her final words, Steve felt exhaustion cover him like a lead overcoat. The trial that had started with such optimism now hovered beneath storm clouds of impending gloom. Judge Peterson wore an emotionless mask, but his eyes bore the weight of the decision only he could make.

Then the wait began.

Steve tried to concentrate on other cases, but as he returned calls and drafted pleadings and letters, he couldn't help thinking about Mary's case. Would the judge decide to acquit or convict? Snippets of remembered testimony interrupted his work with second guesses about how he handled the case.

Steve and Kim were also preparing to move. The old mansion they had bought in Grinnell had seemed like a good idea at the time, but they soon discovered that it needed far more renovation than they would be able to do on it. As the year passed, they realized they didn't want to live on a busy street corner anyway. Now they had sold it and bought a house in the country.

Steve tried to set aside his worries as he packed boxes with Kim. She was a constant cheerleader in spite of the fact that Steve's busyness had left her to do most of the packing. "Don't worry about the case," she said. "Things will turn out fine." Steve wished he could share her confidence.

While the snow in the yard melted around the edges, Steve built castles from large wooden blocks with Nic. He wondered if Mary was spending her last days with her kids.

Days passed without word of a verdict, and Steve reminded himself that judges bear a full case load. He pictured Judge Peterson reviewing his notes, perhaps calling on his court reporter to review specific testimony as he finalized his decision and drafted his opinion. At home and in his office Steve stayed close to the phone, listening for the ring with a mixture of anticipation and fear.

One moment Steve felt sure that truth would prevail and Mary would be acquitted. The next he worried about the judge's stern face. Was the expression simply a reflection of the gravity of a child murder case and all the evidence he must weigh, or did he believe Mary was guilty?

After a quiet dinner one evening, Kim dismissed Nic to go play, then turned to Steve. "You're worrying."

He tried to smile. "How'd you know?"

"You didn't clean up your plate, and you haven't said a word."

"Sorry."

"Hon, you'll be fine. There is a doubt about this case, right? Isn't that all you need?"

"Yes, a reasonable doubt. Or a doubt based on reason, and we have plenty of that."

"Well then? Isn't it a matter of trusting God with this?"

"Yes, but you didn't see Judge Peterson's face."

"Maybe he's weighed down by all the evidence. The other lawyers said he was a good judge, didn't they? You had good reasons to waive the jury."

'I know." Steve frown softened. "I don't envy him the task. I have to remember that God can turn his heart in the right direction."

"Right." Kim rose from her chair and hugged his shoulders.

The encouraging words lifted his spirits temporarily, but he couldn't keep from fearing the worst. Why was it taking so long? What would happen to Mary's family if she was sent to prison? How would it feel to have an innocent mother led away in handcuffs because he had somehow failed in his representation of her?

As the wait grew into a week and more, Steve felt so uncertain about the verdict that he started considering how he would appeal the case if they lost.

Ten days after the trial ended, the office phone at Steve's elbow jangled, startling his already frayed nerves into attention. The bailiff requested their presence in court. The judge had reached a verdict.

Steve willed optimism into his voice and called Kim, then dialed Mary. The time had come for God to work a miracle—or for a huge injustice to begin.

# Edges of Truth

✿ ✿ ✿

Friday afternoon Mary left the courtroom with the energy of an eighty-year-old camp counselor at the end of summer. She and Jim picked up the kids and a pizza on the way home. Listening to childish chatter unraveled her already frayed nerves, but she couldn't bear to shut them out either. Catherine and John had enjoyed new adventures every day at the sitter's while Daddy and Mommy were away. They had no idea that their days at the sitter's meant Mommy might go to prison and not come home for a long time.

By suppertime they had received no word from the courthouse. That meant they wouldn't get the judge's decision until after the weekend, but they didn't complain. A quick decision could be a snap decision. A bad one.

Sunday morning before church, Mary brushed Catherine's long, platinum-blonde hair.

The five-year-old tried to control her urge to squirm. "Mommy, can you make two little braids on top and use my new purple hair clips?"

Mary put on her Stern Mommy mask. "I suppose I could do that"–she winked–"for my favorite daughter."

Next Sunday would she be brushing Catherine's hair or wearing an orange prison jumpsuit? Who would fix Catherine's hair if she wasn't around? Jim's mechanic hands made lopsided ponytails.

Monday they still hadn't heard from the judge, so Mary started working on routine housework. Routine was good. It gave her something to do, made life run normally instead of spinning out of control. Mary was good at routine, doing the next thing. Mothers across the world kept their houses running this way.

# CHAPTER 17

Mary vacuumed the carpet, cleaned out the fridge, stocked up on groceries. The jobs needed to be done anyway, whether she went to prison or not, but uncertainty colored every task. She didn't know whether she should buy the big jar of peanut butter now so Jim wouldn't have to or wait for a sale. A week from now, who would fix John's favorite meal or bake his favorite cookie? Mary couldn't picture Jim baking cookies.

God could do a miracle here, but would he? In the Old Testament God allowed Joseph to be unfairly put in prison for two years. Maybe God was preparing her for prison too. Not for life. Judge Peterson could issue a life sentence if he wanted, but she felt sure God wouldn't make her serve one. Maybe she would go to prison for two years like Joseph did. Mary knew a two-year sentence in a murder trial made no sense at all, but she couldn't entirely shake the feeling either.

The second weekend slowly arrived with no further word from the judge. Mary's family went to a birthday party for a member of their extended family. Mary tried to keep attention centered on the birthday boy. She didn't want her presence to darken the occasion. Most of the adults there, however, knew her situation. Some had even sat in the gallery during the trial. The pity in their eyes told her they had also noticed the negative vibrations coming from Judge Peterson, but their comments showed that they, like Mary, hadn't given up hope.

"If the judge was really sure you were guilty, he would have decided by now," one person said. "He would have given the verdict before the weekend."

"Right," another agreed. "If he really thought you were a killer, he wouldn't want you to run free all this time. He'd be afraid you would run away to escape prison."

"Maybe he thought you were guilty at first," another suggested, "but he's taking so long to decide because he can't be sure. He's a judge. He knows he can't convict when there's reasonable doubt."

Mary held the hopeful comments close to her heart. She wished Judge Peterson would decide and get it over with—unless he was going to convict her. Then this would be her last weekend with her family. Her last weekend in church.

Her church family continued to pray faithfully for her. Other friends and a host of strangers did too. Maybe God would show himself strong by using the judge's lips to declare her "not guilty." After all, the media had made it clear that she was a practicing Christian who attended church and several other Christian groups. If she were convicted, people would start eyeing all Christians with suspicion.

Another Monday came. Another court day, nineteen days from the beginning of the trial, ten days after the end. What was taking so long? She calmed her nerves with the assurance that the longer the judge took, the better her chances were of being acquitted.

Tuesday her phone rang. Steve.

The judge had reached a verdict.

Courthouse. What time?

Call her friends. Call the prayer chain.

What should she wear? The media would be there. Oh, who cared? Her family was what mattered.

God would reveal her future in one sentence by Judge Peterson—today!

At the courthouse she trembled with anticipation as she sat beside Steve at the counsel table. Constantly she checked the doorknob on the front wall where the judge would enter. Friends, media, and strangers packed the gallery. Sixty, seventy, eighty of them. Some were standing.

Several in the gallery bowed their heads. A few lips moved silently. Praying friends. Praying strangers. She could feel God's spirit in the courtroom.

# CHAPTER 17

Steve met her eyes, tried to smile, stared at the counsel table. His eyes weren't closed, but Mary knew he was praying. One knee vibrated with nervous energy. At her first trial he'd seemed so calm, but his quiet confidence was gone now.

The doorknob at the front of the courtroom turned.

Whispers hushed.

Judge Peterson stepped up to the bench.

# CHAPTER 18

Whispers died suddenly as the packed courtroom of people rose to their feet. Mary tried to read Judge Peterson's face as he entered the courtroom, adjusted his flowing robe, and sat. He pounded his gavel, needlessly since the air bristled with silence. The judge's stony face did not promise a happy ending.

Judge Peterson cleared his throat and studied his paper. "I have reached a verdict. I find the defendant guilty of murder in the first degree and child endangerment…"

The judge went on, but Mary heard none of it. Steve reached over and squeezed her hand.

When the judge finished reading Mary leaned toward Steve.

"What's going to happen to my family?" Jim would have to be both father and mother to John and Catherine. Since her mom was in a wheelchair, Mary would rarely be able to see her. With God's help Mary knew she would get through it, but the real victims were her family.

Her tear-filled eyes met those of her lawyer. Steve had become a close friend. He would blame himself for this. She grieved for him.

She had to pull herself together, to thank the supporters who now packed the courtroom. Day after day they had come from

# CHAPTER 18

Marshalltown, Steamboat Rock, Dubuque. One man even came from Texas. They followed the trial with interest and gave constant emotional support. She prayed that God would give her words to comfort her supporters.

Mary turned to address this group, who lingered just past the rail in emotional, hugging, weeping knots.

"It's going to be all right," she said. "Joseph was accused falsely and sent to prison. The apostle Paul and Daniel were too. God used them in prison. God will take care of me too."

She leaned into the public gallery to hug some of her supporters, and the bailiff didn't stop her. She could feel God's presence here, with so many supporters who were believers. God wasn't done working. She was sure of it. He would get the victory yet.

Forty-five minutes must have passed before the bailiff snapped handcuffs on her and led her away. She couldn't imagine what her new life was going to be like, but she couldn't help notice the bailiff's unusual kindness in allowing her extra time with friends and family. The bottom had fallen out of her world, but God was still in control.

A female deputy delivered Mary to her new "home" and unlocked the handcuffs, belly chain, and ankle shackles. She would stay in this cell in the Benton County Jail until sentencing, then move to the Oakdale prison for evaluation and finally move to the Mitchellville prison to live out her life sentence until God delivered her. And he would–wouldn't he? Steve would appeal. He had to. Mary was innocent. Surely God wouldn't let her case end like this.

The Benton County Jail was new and clean. She had one other cell mate, a pleasant gal who immediately told Mary she thought Mary's verdict was bogus. She had watched the case with interest on the news and especially disliked one of the lady newscasters who had covered Mary's case.

The first family visit was heartbreaking. She had to talk to her children and husband by phone and gaze at them through thick glass. What did her children think when they visited their mommy and she couldn't even touch them? The visit didn't last long.

Every night Mary was locked into her inner cell, but during the day she could sit and watch TV in the outer cell. Mary and her cell mate were allowed to walk around a big activity yard for about an hour every day. Past the brick buildings, she could see trees budding and beginning to flower. Spring brought hope after a cold Iowa winter.

Mary realized this was a new season of life for her as well. As much as she hated being separated from her family, God had purpose in this new season. Each season came to an end, and this one would too.

In her free time Mary sat on her bunk with her Bible open and considered anew the promise she felt God had given her from Jeremiah. She would go into captivity, but she would come out again. Before the second trial, she had felt her "captivity" might be that uncertain time of waiting for the trial, the hung jury, then more waiting and a second trial. From Melissa's death until the guilty verdict, fourteen months had passed. Fourteen months of roller coaster hopes and fears seemed like captivity. But that couldn't have been her captivity, because here she was in prison.

Maybe God would use the appeal process to deliver her. Until then she would search for God's blessing in this new season of life. She would ask Steve to talk to the judge about getting contact visits with her family. Steve would appeal her case. God would not let her live out a life sentence for a crime she didn't commit. This could not last forever.

# CHAPTER 18

In a few days Mary was escorted to the visiting room. Her lawyer had come for a visit. But Steve's face wasn't reassuring. He looked like he'd just been given his own life sentence. Mary considered what it must be like to choose a legal career, give your best to represent an innocent friend, and watch the legal system convict her of first-degree murder. People who told lawyer jokes ought to see the burden her lawyer carried now.

☆ ☆ ☆

## APRIL 1994

Steve sat alone in his office, reviewing notes for the inevitable worst-case scenario to come. The sentencing was merely a formality. Nothing he could say would deter Judge Peterson from imposing the mandatory life sentence for anyone convicted in Iowa of first-degree murder. The judge would have no judicial discretion. The law gave him none. Only the death sentence could be more final.

The phone rang. Steve stared at it, hoping the call would be about anything other than Mary's case. After three rings he reached for the receiver. "Steve Brennecke here."

An unfamiliar woman's voice answered. "Hello. I'm Robin McElroy. You don't know me, but you just represented Mary Weaver, right? I think I know something you ought to be aware of."

Steve listened with growing interest. He moved the phone to his other ear, reached for a legal pad, and began scratching notes. "Could you repeat that?"

"Yes. I saw Tessia at church shortly after Melissa died. I told her I was sorry for her loss, and she said she knew Mary Weaver hadn't hurt Melissa. She said she was putting the baby's snowsuit on before Mary picked her up, and Melissa hit her head really hard on the coffee table. Tessia knew Melissa was hurt because she cried and cried."

"When did Tessia say this to you?"

"It was Sunday, Valentine's day last year."

Steve scribbled the date. "It was also during the time of the investigation, before they charged Mary with this."

"Do you think that's important?"

"Yes. It could be very important." Tessia had been trying to explain Melissa's death even before the police charged Mary with Melissa's death. "Why do you think Tessia told you this?"

"I don't know. I just told her I was sorry for her loss, and that's how she responded. I was glad to hear her say that the death was just an accident. I didn't realize it was important until I heard that Tessia didn't mention it at the trial. I thought she would."

"Are you willing to sign an affidavit under oath, stating what you just told me?"

"Sure, if it will help."

He hung up the phone and grabbed the Iowa Rules of Criminal Procedure with renewed vigor. He paged through the rules. "Aha. Motion for new trial. Just what we need."

Steve's motion for a new trial hit the newspaper, stirring the already divided opinion of the people of Marshalltown. The news stirred up people who had followed the trial in the local newspaper, the *Times-Republican*, and were already outraged by Mary's conviction.

Mistry Lovig read the news and also called Steve. Mistry didn't know Mrs. McElroy. She had worked at Hardee's with Tessia. Within three or four weeks after the death, while Tessia was still off work, Brad and Tessia had come into the restaurant. Tessia told her that she was putting Melissa's snowsuit on when the baby hit her head on the coffee table. When Mistry heard

# CHAPTER 18

Melissa had died of shaken baby syndrome, she thought the story wasn't important. But when she read that Tessia had testified differently at the trial, she realized Melissa could have died from the injury. She was also willing to sign an affidavit, alleging Tessia had told her this.

Steve felt Mrs. McElroy and Mistry's statements gave them legal grounds for a new trial. Their testimony was newly discovered evidence that couldn't, with reasonable diligence, have been discovered before trial, and he believed this evidence probably would make a material difference in the outcome of the trial. The points were simple enough, but would Judge Peterson buy them? In spite of all the evidence to the contrary, he had just declared Mary guilty beyond a reasonable doubt.

At the hearing for a new trial, Steve submitted the affidavits to the court, and he and Ms. Tomlinson argued the cardinal points of the motion. But on May 4, Judge Peterson ruled against them and denied Mary's motion and the new trial that went with it. Steve's legal tactics had delayed Mary's sentencing, but the outcome would be the same. He would appeal the verdict again, but would it do any good?

That night Steve and Kim ate their dinner in silence. Steve felt like an ancient car stalled in the desert out of gas at five miles past nowhere. Somehow the spark of hope that had fizzled so quickly made the case seem even more hopeless. He had exhausted his legal strategies as well as his professional and emotional energy.

A ringing phone broke the silence. Kim answered it, then handed it to Steve. "Your dad."

Steve pushed his half-filled plate to the center of the table and held the phone to his ear. "Hi, Dad."

Concern colored the older lawyer's voice. "I heard about Judge Peterson's ruling. How are you doing, Steve? This news must have hit you pretty hard."

"You can say that again."

"And Mary?"

"She's doing well"—Steve sighed—"considering the fact she's about to be sentenced to life in prison without parole."

Condolences over, his dad's voice sparked with the newfound energy of a US Navy SEAL on a mission. "Are you ready to file an appeal?"

Steve leaned back in his chair, crossed his ankles, took a deep breath. "Dad, I'm drained. Totally empty. I'm no appellate lawyer—you know that. I need to find her someone who is capable of straightening this out."

"Who do you have in mind?"

"I don't know. I need Superman."

"I've got an idea. You ask around and make your list of the top-ten appellate lawyers in Iowa, and I'll do the same. We'll talk in a few days and compare notes."

Steve agreed. Rising to his dad's level of enthusiasm wouldn't be easy, but he knew he needed to do it. Steve managed to "uh-huh" his way through several more minutes of father-son chatter, when his dad's voice shifted into yet a higher gear.

"One more thing. A whole lot of people care a great deal about Mary. From the front of the courtroom, you may not have noticed. But I could look out my office window and see them coming and going every day, all day long, during the trial. You couldn't even find a parking spot. What if we get her friends together and organize a support group?"

Steve couldn't match his dad's enthusiasm, but he managed a polite reply. "Sounds good."

When you're stalled on a road five miles past nowhere, you don't turn down a ride to civilization. His dad's offer was nice, but after two trials and a guilty verdict, Steve couldn't believe a few sentimental friends would make much difference.

# CHAPTER 19

## MAY 8, 1994

It was Sunday, the day she was allowed to visit with her family for half an hour. Mary walked as fast as she was allowed down concrete hallways to the exercise yard of the Marshalltown County Jail. She had arrived a few days earlier and was waiting in this jail for her sentencing on Tuesday. Since she was the only female in the jail, she had spent several days in solitary confinement. At this point she would welcome conversation with a total stranger.

As the heavy metal door clanged open, two little people rushed up and grabbed her legs. "Happy Mother's Day, Mommy."

Mary squatted down and hugged her precious children tightly. *Thank you, Lord,* she prayed, *that the judge has granted us contact visits.* The glass partition separated them no longer. The holiday would be hard enough without that.

"I made you a Mother's Day card, Mommy." Catherine pouted. "But Daddy said I couldn't bring it."

County jail regulations didn't allow her family to bring her anything. She could only receive cards that had been mailed in and inspected.

"I'm sorry you couldn't bring them, but my best Mother's Day present is hugging the two of you." Mary squeezed each of her kids and kissed their foreheads. "Stand back and let me look at you."

She smoothed Catherine's baby-soft hair. The girl's blonde bangs hung over her eyes, and her socks slouched around her ankles. Mary ran her hands through John's fine red hair. His shoes were on the wrong feet, but she wouldn't insult Jim by adjusting. He was doing the best he could.

Mary blinked hard and gulped down extra moisture, over-flow from tears that were not allowed to fall. "Look at you two. You're growing up so fast." Too fast. Each year she was in prison, she would miss precious stages of their childhood.

Jim sighed. He gathered two basketballs from the edges of the exercise yard and handed them to the kids to play with. Catherine and John were soon playing as if it was entirely normal for preschoolers to play basketball in a prison exercise yard.

Mary and Jim sat on opposite sides of a metal table that was bolted to the ground. This visit wouldn't last long. She must make her time count.

Mary breathed deeply of air that was only slightly less stuffy than her cell. "How was church?"

Jim avoided her eyes. "Mother's Day would have been a good day to skip."

"I suppose they recognized all the mothers—the oldest, the one with the most kids." She attempted a smile. "No prize for mothers in prison wearing orange jumpsuits?"

"None. By the way, happy Mother's Day. How are you holding up?"

Mary wiped her eyes with an orange sleeve. "I thought moving to Marshalltown might make me feel closer to my family. But now I'm only blocks away from you, and it might as well be a million miles. It makes it even harder, if that's possible."

# CHAPTER 19

Jim pulled a hanky from his back pocket and blew his nose. "Sorry."

"It's not your fault."

"I know, but I worry about you."

"I'll be all right, Jim. Really I will. I'm an adult. I can get through this. I have God to help me."

Jim bristled at the mention of God. Finally he met her eyes, challenging, not comforting. "Where was God when you were convicted for first-degree murder? Tuesday Judge Peterson reads his sentence, and we know what's coming. In Iowa first-degree murder is always life in prison, no parole."

A heavy cloud blocked out the last bits of sunshine that had filtered into the cramped exercise yard. Mary lifted her chin, shook off the darkness. "The judge can sentence me to life in prison, but God's not through with me yet. He's going to get me out of prison. I know it."

Jim's voice rose in frustration. "How can you say that? You've had two trials—by judge and by jury. All the evidence came out, but they just couldn't see your innocence."

"But Robin McElroy and Mistry Lovig stepped forward right after the trial with what Tessia told them, and they don't even know me."

"What good does that do you if it's not admissible in court?"

"Steve's going to keep trying. He still thinks their evidence may get us a new trial yet."

"I'd like to believe it'll make a difference, but, well…" Jim stared at the dark clouds, left his comment unfinished. Mary had to admit to herself that finding new evidence fourteen months after Melissa's death wouldn't be easy.

Mary grieved for Jim. He carried a heavy burden these days, and he didn't have God to help him. She hoped her conviction wouldn't drive him farther from God and salvation. She had to keep their hopes alive.

"We can't give up, Jim. Friday, when the deputy sheriff from Benton County drove me here in the squad car, God showed me that my case isn't impossible. I was led, as usual, handcuffed and shackled, out to the car and locked into the back seat. Then, all the way here, the deputy complained about the verdict, assuring me that she knew I didn't kill Melissa. She went on and on about how the courts made a big mistake, that she was sure I'd be getting out of prison. You won't believe this, but she even stopped at a gas station and bought me a Snickers bar and a Diet Coke. She unlocked my handcuffs and let me eat without them."

"You've just been convicted of murder, and you're excited by a Snickers bar and a Diet Coke?"

"It shows she believes in me, Jim. Other people in the legal system will be able to recognize that a mistake has been made too. You can't imagine how much her kindness meant to me. After the grueling interrogation with Agent Motsinger"–Mary shook her head–"I was more afraid of him than anyone in my entire life. So the deputy sheriff's kindness almost restores my faith in the legal system. Isn't God good to give me that glimpse of hope?"

Jim stood up, knocking his chair sideways. He stared at the walls of the confined exercise yard. "Excuse me if I can't trust a God who allowed my wife to be convicted of murder and is about to be given a life sentence."

Mary watched Catherine dribble the ball with a staccato beat. John tried to dribble but only managed a couple of irregular bounces at a time. The legal situation didn't look good. Mary believed God would someday get her out of prison, but what would her family do in the meantime? Jim was a good father, but now he'd have to do the job of both parents, keep the house running, and work as well. On top of all that, he had to pay hundreds of thousands of dollars of her legal bills.

## CHAPTER 19

Mary brushed her tears away and moved to play with Catherine and John. They rolled the balls back and forth on the concrete. Jim set John on his shoulders and let him try shooting baskets. When her eyes could no longer hold back the flood of tears, Mary hunched over the table and sobbed openly. Jim reached to touch her shoulder, a feeble attempt at comfort.

She could mark this Mother's Day down as the hardest day of her life.

And yet.

The half-hour visitation time stretched to several hours before the guards asked her family to leave. This simple kindness by the guards assured her that God was lurking in the shadows. She just wished he would step out of the shadows and give them their life back.

# CHAPTER 20

## MAY 9, 1994

Steve sat at the counsel table, feeling as helpless as a hand-cuffed engineer watching two brakeless trains speeding toward each other on the same track. Mary's sentence was so inevitable that even God couldn't change it. Okay, theoretically he could, but Steve knew he wouldn't. Iowa's law in this regard was as strong as the laws of nature. A conviction of first-degree murder equaled life in prison. Period.

In a few minutes Mary would appear at the front of the court-room for sentencing. He had committed his entire career to this legal system. But what kind of legal system could get a verdict so wrong, be so unjust, and then perpetuate the injustice by ripping a mother away from her children for life? What was he thinking of when he advised her to give up her right to a jury trial? If even one juror had believed she wasn't guilty, she wouldn't have been convicted, at least not at that time. From now on he would never advise a client to give up his or her right to a jury trial. His lack of judgment had landed Mary in jail. His prison bars were invisible, but he felt their cold shadows nonetheless.

He pulled Mary's file from his briefcase and scanned his notes as if he could change the unchangeable . At least the activity kept his hands busy, took his mind from probing eyes of supporters, who studied him with confusion, anger—even pity. And lawyers didn't get much pity.

Loud whispers stirred the gallery packed with media, Mary's supporters, and Melissa's grieving parents.

"Mary!"

"She's here."

Mary entered the courtroom through a door near the front. She was wearing handcuffs and was dressed in an orange Marshall County Jail jumpsuit. Her face flushed as she stepped to the counsel table.

"God bless you, Mary."

"We're praying for you."

Mary called out greetings to her supporters, some by name, half-smiling in spite of the inevitable coming sentence.

The deputy unlocked Mary's cuffs for the proceedings. Ms. Tomlinson slipped into her place at the prosecutor's counsel table. The crowd settled into their seats. They grew quiet when Judge Peterson entered the courtroom.

Judge Peterson called the court to order and began to rattle off the routine phrases that preceded every sentence issued by the court.

Steve tried to concentrate on the judge's words. If only he could change it all, but it was too late. Only God could help Mary now, and he didn't seem to be trying. Steve could sense the certain life sentence approaching in slow motion like two trains on a collision course.

He pulled himself back to the droning judicial words and steeled himself for final impact.

"Life in prison without parole."

*Bam!* The inescapable sentence slammed into Steve like a physical blow. The crowd murmured over the judge's remaining words. Some began to shout out to Mary.

Judge Peterson finished, closed his book, and exited behind the bench, away from a gallery packed mostly with supporters who opposed his sentence.

Mary met Jim and the kids at the rail. The kids had come for the final good-bye.

John hugged her legs and stared up at her with wet eyes. "Are you going to come home now, Mommy?"

Mary sniffed. "Not yet, John. Mommy's got to be away a while longer, but you can come visit me."

A little longer—like for the rest of her life.

They hugged and wept. Steve gulped down sobs and blinked away tears. Open weeping filled the gallery. No physical train wreck could have produced more tears than the sight of John and Catherine hugging their mom like frightened refugees.

The deputy shuffled close to the rail and cleared his throat. He held out the handcuffs. "Sorry, ma'am," he said. "Regulations."

Mary's sentence had just begun. He failed, so she went to prison. How fair was that?

✿ ✿ ✿

The next night Steve sat in Chris and Lisa Murphy's crowded living room. Compassion demanded his presence, while his heart called him a hypocrite. Steve couldn't visualize this support group as any more than a heartwarming exercise in futility. He was alive enough to keep his chair warm, but if his brain had a gauge, it would have registered empty. While he was mostly dead, however, his attorney father came alive.

One day after sentencing, Al Brennecke stood before the passionate group, agenda in hand, ready to do battle. Twenty-seven people packed the room because they believed Mary was innocent, and they wanted to see her unjust sentence reversed and her name cleared. Most of these people had filled seats in the gallery during both trials. A few had held placards and protested peacefully outside the courthouse during her sentencing. They believed they could make a difference.

Steve had given his heart and soul to defending Mary through two trials. He couldn't make a difference. What good could a few desperate friends do?

Steve watched his father wave a clipboard and champion this hopeless cause. This tax-and-probate lawyer spoke with a strong voice like the apostle Peter on the day of Pentecost. From the beginning he set the tone for the meeting, channeling all the anger, disbelief, fear, desperation, and confusion into a positive direction.

"The purpose of this support group," Al said, "is to see justice done. Mary did not receive justice, Melissa did not receive justice, and the citizens of Marshall County did not receive justice."

Al pulled a page from a ream of paper fresh from the copier. Bold, black letters spelled out, "Was justice done?" across the yellow sheet. "We want to post these signs in car windows all across Marshalltown," he said. "We want people to ask themselves, 'Justice for whom?' That will get people talking about Mary's case and keep it alive so the court system can't ignore it."

*Justice.* That lofty legal term Steve had given his entire legal career to defend. Justice hid like a coward in the shadows now, intimidated by the strong assumptions of experts.

"Mary has been sentenced to life in prison," Al said, "but the case is far from closed in my mind. They will appeal this case. God can turn this around to see that justice is done."

God could, but would he? Why didn't he just give Mary a not-guilty verdict in the first place?

"In the meantime Mary and her family will need support in many ways." The older Brennecke consulted his clipboard. "First of all, we need to pray for Mary and her family and all the adjustments they need to make. We can also support her by writing letters."

Marge Wolfe spoke up. She knew Mary from a Christian club they both belonged to. "Mary's going to get discouraged in prison. Let's make sure Mary gets a letter every day."

Nancy Pins, a church friend, suggested they break the month into three ten-day segments. Everyone could agree to write Mary three times a month, on a day assigned alphabetically by last name.

Everyone agreed to that. They also talked about writing letters to the governor and attorney general to ask them to reopen the investigation into Melissa's death.

Al listened as the excitement built, then brought the comments and ideas together in one united voice. "We can support Mary by talking about her case, but we need to keep that talk positive. Ephesians 4:29 says, 'Let no unwholesome word proceed from your mouth.' We need to guard our conversations and resist any negative talk against Judge Peterson, Ms. Tomlinson, or the Marshalltown Police Department."

Steve couldn't argue with that. They may or may not be able to help the case, but careless words could do more harm than good.

"We need to focus on certain facts." Al glanced at his clipboard and enumerated some facts they needed to keep in mind.

1. We don't know who killed Melissa.
2. The seven- to ten-day-old skull fracture is still unexplained.
3. The most experienced doctors stated Melissa died of old injuries.
4. Mary is a wonderful person, not a criminal.
5. Mary only had Melissa in her care for forty-two minutes that morning.

One of the men waved his hand. "Could you put that in writing?"

"Nancy Pins will be sending around a newsletter with all the information you need to know, including these points. She'll include addresses of people you might want to write to. It can't hurt to get Mary's name mentioned over and over again before the appeal. Let's help each other remain positive in outlook and attitude. We also want to have a petition drive on Memorial Day to request that the investigation be reopened. Who will volunteer to help us?"

Nearly every hand went up.

Al surveyed the room, estimating the number of volunteers. "Thanks. We'll need all the help we can get to canvass Marshalltown streets. We'd like to collect ten thousand signatures to send to the county attorney, the attorney general, and the governor."

Several people offered helpful suggestions.

"We could all wear yellow ribbons when we do the petition drive–you know, to say we welcome Mary home from prison."

"We ought to wear yellow ribbons every day until Mary is released."

Steve imagined some very tattered ribbons pinned to the pajamas of very old Iowans.

"Hey, why don't we have a 'Buck Night' when we do the canvassing? If people sign the petition, we can ask them if they want to donate a buck towards Mary's legal fees."

"Great idea." Al jotted a note on his clipboard. "That's our next topic. Mary has substantial legal fees of over one hundred thousand dollars, and throughout the appeals process, legal expenses will continue to accrue. We have already collected six thousand dollars. What else can we do to raise money to help this family?"

Hands went up all over. Garage sales, car washes, auctions, dinners. They even talked about marching in the Oktemberfest Grand Parade.

Steve donned the noncommittal mask of a practiced lawyer as the ideas buzzed around him, but his inner skeptic was shouting. An innocent person has been sentenced to life in prison, and we're talking car washes and parades? Might as well put a Band-Aid on a severed jugular vein.

The skeptic kept silent because one spark of hope deep within him wondered if these crazy ideas could make a difference.

✼ ✼ ✼

Several weeks later Steve forced himself to drive toward the Oakdale prison for "the pep talk." He felt like the father of the slowest runner in class the night before the fifty-yard dash. "Do your best. You never know, you might win. But if you don't win…"

He would pursue every legal procedure he could think of, knowing the odds were stacked against them. What else could he do?

He had visited her in the Benton County jail. Now the state had moved her to the classification unit in Oakdale for evaluation to determine the appropriate prison facility for her to live in. It was time to prepare Mary for the arduous appeals process.

He just hoped Mary didn't ask why a righteous God would allow her to be convicted of a crime she didn't commit. He had worn a hole in his own faith trying to make sense of that.

As a lawyer, he was supposed to be trained to deal with tragedy. He had read the standard advice somewhere. "Do the next thing. You may not understand the reasons why, but just do the next thing. God will make sense of it in the end."

# CHAPTER 20

Steve wondered if the author of those words issued a guarantee. All he knew was that today, doing the next thing was visiting Mary, holding out the feeble hope he had, being a friend as well as a lawyer.

Steve turned at the sign for Oakdale, a tiny Iowa town best known for the Iowa Medical and Classification Center. Somehow "Oakdale" sounded more like a Grant Wood painting than what it was—the second-to-last stop on the train to nowhere for a lifer.

Would Mary blame him for putting her in prison? If only she would. She could say, "Steve it's your fault. You messed up, and I have to pay for it." Then he could defend himself, but she didn't have the decency to blame him. It would be easier if she did.

He pulled into the parking lot and walked toward the building entrance, aware that multiple cameras were tracking every movement. He passed through the metal detectors and followed protocol for entry: identification verification, purpose of visit, visitor list check. The jailer pushed a release button, and the electronic bolt clicked open so he could push the heavy steel door and enter. Then he waited in the visitor room for a prison guard to notify Mary that her lawyer had arrived.

Several inmates visited with guests around metal tables and chairs. Guards watched from a polite distance. It wasn't much like home, but it beat the county jail. There Steve was forced to nearly yell at Mary through a slot in the metal door. Here inmates were able to have relaxed conversation with approved visitors.

When Mary arrived, they exchanged greetings, then sat and leaned across a table to discuss her situation. Steve was still searching for words when Mary spoke. "How are you?"

Steve blinked hard. "Me? How am I? I should be asking you that."

Mary smiled, though the smile was a bit crooked. "Well, I'm in the hands of God, so I'm fine."

"But you're in jail for a crime you didn't commit."

"I know. But don't you think this is somehow what God wants for me?"

Steve rolled his shoulders, working out the kinks and pulling his spiritual socks up. "Well, I didn't come to speak of his sovereignty, but if you insist. I guess if God is sovereign, then this occurrence, even this injustice, is within his plan—for now."

"For now." Mary smiled. "I like that. Because I still want to get out of here."

"Good. We want to get you out of here. We need to file an appeal, but remember, appeals take time—lots of time."

"How long?"

"Eighteen months to two years."

Mary stared past the window bars, out into the distance. Steve could imagine her calculating how old her kids would be when she got out of here—if her appeal worked, which was highly unlikely.

"And you need a new attorney."

Mary stared at him "I don't want another attorney. You did a good job. We've already worked through two trials together. We can do a third."

Steve had counted on her objection. "Think of it like this. If you have a heart problem, you might like your family doctor, but you need a cardiologist. Appellate law is a specialty, and you need an expert in it, someone who can look at this with fresh eyes."

Mary frowned. "Are you sure? I'm satisfied with you."

"Thanks for the confidence, but Mary…" Steve sighed, searching for words to explain the awkward situation he was in. "Your appellate attorney will need the freedom to look at everything

I did during the case, every decision, and see whether you had adequate representation. I'm not flawless. Your appeal may need to include a claim of ineffective assistance of counsel, and they need me out of the way to pursue that on your behalf."

"This wasn't your fault, Steve."

So whose fault was it? "That's not important. We need to do whatever we can to get you out of here."

Mary glanced at a wall calendar as if making mental calculations. "Do you really think it will take two years?"

"Yes, that's a realistic time frame. The schedule is extended because you are on the supreme court's calendar—or the court of appeals' calendar, whichever one hears your case."

"You mean, I won't know who will hear my appeal?"

"In Iowa, all appeals go right to the Iowa Supreme Court. They can either hear the case themselves or direct the case down to the court of appeals for their ruling. If you're not happy with the court of appeals ruling, however, you have the right to ask the supreme court to review anything the court of appeals decides."

Steve explained that both he and his dad had made lists of good appellate attorneys and that Paul Rosenberg had made it to the top of both lists. He suggested she hire him.

Hope shone from Mary's eyes like a survivor on a leaky life raft. Part of Steve wanted to point out the hole in her life raft, but only a bully would do that if the raft had any possibility of getting her to shore safely.

"God is working, isn't he?" Mary ticked off blessings on her fingers. "Paul Rosenberg will help us make a new appeal. People in Marshalltown, Eldora, and Steamboat Rock prayed for us every day during the trials. And the support group has already started writing letters to support my case and raise money to help with expenses."

Steve chose his words carefully. He didn't want to be a dream-squasher, but encouraging hope for something that would probably never happen seemed cruel. "Mary, it's amazing how much support you have among those who know you and know you are innocent. You are also getting a lot of media attention now, but it'll soon move to the back burner. Life goes on for those people—even your close friends."

Mary stared at him as if sensing his pessimism for the first time. The clock ticked loudly. She checked her fingers again as if willing him to see the blessings she had just enumerated.

Steve would have fidgeted in the silence if the guards had left him anything to fidget with. "I just want to encourage you to be realistic. Paul Rosenberg is the best appellate lawyer in Iowa, but this is going to be very, very difficult."

Mary straightened, lifted a resolute chin. "But I'm innocent. God isn't going to leave me here. This is just the present chapter of my life. How can I give up when God isn't finished writing my story yet?"

Steve opened his mouth to correct her, then shut it again. The same events that had caused him to question God were making her faith stronger. He might not understand that, but he wasn't about to argue with it either.

# CHAPTER 21

## TUESDAY, MAY 10, 1994

Mary stepped into the cell block at the Iowa Medical and Classification Center at Oakdale. Her evaluation process was over and this was her next stop on the way to what the state meant to be her final residence. Prison bars clanged behind her. Immediately a short, feisty inmate leaned close to her face.

"Hey, girl. You Mary Weaver?"

"Yes."

Mary glanced around the cell block. Fifty to sixty inmates had been lounging around sturdy tables and chairs. They wore navy jumpsuits that matched her new one. Most of the inmates now left their places to examine the newbie. Mary had survived six weeks alone in a cell at Benton County and several days at the Marshalltown County Jail. No companionship but no people problems either. As a circle of scowling inmates surrounded her, she hoped the movies she'd seen of prison life weren't accurate.

The short woman studied her from head to toe and back again as if wondering how much weight she would lose in prison. "We saw you on TV. Did you kill that baby?"

"N-no, I didn't."

Would they believe her? After all, she was a convicted felon, just like they were. She had just passed three weeks of evaluation like they had. She had exchanged the orange jumpsuit for a navy two-piece, which was much more flattering when you carried a few extra pounds. Passing easy physical, psychological, math, and reading tests had made her one of them. She had been pronounced healthy enough not to pass contagious diseases to other prisoners and mentally capable of handling prison.

A tall, curly-haired woman in her early twenties swaggered close and towered over her. "How can that judge call you guilty? You ain't guilty. If you're guilty, I'm guilty. Okay, I lifted a couple of things from some ritzy shop, but I ain't no murderer. You neither."

A middle-aged woman in prison-issue glasses pushed forward. "The judge says you're guilty—beyond reasonable doubt. So where are his eye witnesses? That's what I want to know. Looks like there's plenty of doubt to me."

"Yeah, girl. What about the skull fracture? TV says she had a two-inch skull fracture before she ever got to your house. Is that true?"

Mary forced herself to stand her ground and not be pushed into the bars behind her. These women might seem confrontational, but at least they seemed to be on her side. She cleared her throat. "That's what the experts say. They didn't all agree on how old the fracture was. It may have been seven days old. All I know is, I didn't give it to her. I never hurt that little girl."

The curly-haired woman planted a hand on one hip. "Course you didn't. TV says you had plenty of character witnesses. Wish I had character witnesses like that at my trial."

"Witnesses don't mean nothing," the short woman argued. "Anybody can say anything." She turned to Mary. "Was it true that the mama banged the baby's head on the coffee table?"

Mary guarded her words. She didn't want to slander Tessia with secondhand knowledge. "She said the baby arched her back and hit the coffee table. At least that's what she told one lady at church and another lady from work. My attorneys are basing my motion for a new trial on that information."

Another voice entered the discussion. "We know. We watch the news. But the judge wouldn't listen, would he?"

Mary faced the newest voice of her strange new fan club. "He ruled it to be hearsay evidence. That makes it inadmissible in court."

Strong opinions buzzed around her.

"That judge don't know nothing. Mama did it. 'Cause what was she doing pricing cemetery plots if she didn't?"

"That's right. That's key evidence, is what I say. How come your lawyer didn't do more with that?"

Mary pictured the genuine pain in Steve's eyes, his grief over losing the case. "My lawyer did everything he could to win the case. He called the cemetery worker as a witness. What more could he do with that?"

"He should have done something. And the judge—he should have jumped all over that."

"You got a raw deal, girl. No justice in your case. We watched it on TV. We knew before we ever laid eyes on you."

Mary didn't know what to say. She had found belief in her innocence from unlikely places, but she hadn't expected this. "Well, thanks for the vote of confidence, but we don't know that the mother hurt the child."

The short lady grunted with impatience. "How can you say that?"

Mary shrugged. "I believe every person has the right to be considered innocent until proven guilty. If I want that for myself, how can I condemn the mother without knowing the facts?"

"Are you for real? People done you wrong, girl. You don't owe them nothing."

That night the warden locked Mary into a cell by herself. They couldn't have this "convicted murderer" risking the lives of the other inmates. Mary couldn't blame the rules. She hadn't hurt Melissa, but she was a convicted felon, in spite of her innocence. God knew the truth.

Mary lay on her bunk in the semidarkness, listening to sleep noises echo off the concrete walls. She breathed deeply, too deeply, then coughed from the impersonal, antiseptic prison scent. At least cleaning supplies smelled better than some other alternatives.

She might as well get used to this prison existence. Soon she would be moving to Mitchellville, and she'd probably be there a while. Steve predicted eighteen months to two years.

As much as anything, Mary missed making her own choices. Strict rules governed every activity, but she could follow rules. Many of the rules were for security, her own safety. She had few possessions besides her Bible, but she could read that anytime and write all the notes she wanted.

And though this was prison, things could be much worse. This cell had much more room to move around than the cell in Benton County. She had been afraid of what the other inmates would be like, but she had to admit they were nice enough to talk to. And if they could see so clearly that she was innocent, wouldn't the appellate court see it too?

Mary wasn't allowed to join the prison Bible study because she was only at Oakdale temporarily for a few more weeks. But she did request a chaplain's visit. In time she was escorted to his small office along one side of the cell block.

Dr. Calvin Yoder was a dignified, older man who had followed her case in the news as the other inmates had. In the beginning he looked past her murder case and asked her personal questions. Did she know Jesus Christ as her personal Savior from sin?

Had she made her peace with God, and was she prepared for eternity? Mary enjoyed telling this gentle man about her salvation experience fifteen years earlier. By the time she finished her story, she could tell this godly man believed she was innocent of the crime for which she was now doing time.

Dr. Yoder soon arranged for his wife to talk to Mary. Mrs. Yoder visited Mary several times, each time leaving her more encouraged than before. On that first visit the silver-haired grandmother shook Mary's hand warmly as soon as Mary entered the chaplain's office. "It's nice to meet you, Mary. Calvin has told me so much about you. He tells me you're a believer."

"I am." Mary smiled crookedly. "But I suppose many inmates claim to be Christians just to help their case."

"Many profess to be Christians." Mrs. Yoder winked. "But sometimes truth rings out clearer than others. Calvin says you have a fine testimony, and we can see God working on your behalf."

The two huddled close together in Dr. Yoder's small, book-lined office. Compassion shone from Mrs. Yoder's eyes as Mary shared her family concerns. They rejoiced together about the ways God had encouraged Mary in prison and raised up a support group for her cause.

Mrs. Yoder's work-worn hand squeezed Mary's. "We don't understand why God allowed you to be convicted, but God is still in control. He will help you through this time, even use this time for good, if you allow him to. Calvin and I believe that in time they will reverse your sentence. But right now, God has allowed you to be locked in prison for a reason. He's got a job for you to do."

"I can pray for people. I'm starting to get letters from my support group too. Some of them have great needs. I can write them notes of encouragement."

"Prayer and letter writing can be a wonderful ministry. But we don't know what else God may do through you. You are living among inmates who are out of reach to most people. These inmates need encouragement. Most of them need salvation. You won't have to preach at them. You live with them twenty-four hours a day. They will watch you. They will see what's important to you."

Mary had always thought prison ministries were supposed to be led by people who could go home at night. Could a convicted felon have a prison ministry?

"I need that reminder. I know God has a plan for me in prison. I want to serve him here somehow. Will you pray for me?"

"Of course."

Mrs. Yoder opened her husband's prison Bible and shared several verses with Mary. Mary's spirit drank in this Christian fellowship. She hadn't been to any church or Bible study for months.

That night Mary lay on her bunk, locked securely in, staring into the dimly lit outer cell. God had a job for her to do.

A prison ministry. She pictured Paul and Silas in a Philippian jail. With ankles locked in stocks and backs raw and bleeding from a fresh flogging, they shivered in a stone, cold prison cell. They weren't praying for release but singing praises to God.

Mary had no choice about being in prison, but like Paul and Silas she could choose how she reacted to her new lifestyle. The way she reacted would affect others around her. Every day her reactions would either please God or grieve him, help others see God in her life or turn them away from him. Her reactions would determine how well she survived prison. Right now, at this moment, she would make a good choice.

# CHAPTER 21

*Thank you, Lord, that my cell is warm, that I have a mattress to sleep on. Thank you that I feel safe here, that the other inmates have been friendly and helpful, that no one has been really nasty to me.*

Paul wrote some of the New Testament in prison. Joseph, Jeremiah and Daniel were imprisoned unfairly, but that didn't stop them from serving God. Then there was Jesus. What could possibly be more unfair than a death sentence for God's perfectly righteous Son? Yet Jesus grasped that ultimate unfairness and used it like a tool to construct his crowning achievement— our salvation!

How would God use unfairness in her life? She still yearned to be released from prison and get back to her family, but until she was released, God had given her a prison ministry.

Her cell mate flopped on one side, searching for a more comfortable position on the thin mattress. Mary closed her eyes and listened to other nighttime sounds from nearby cells. In her mind she matched a face to each snore, sniffle, and snort. She turned her heart toward God.

*Lord, you've brought me here. I don't believe it's an accident. As long as I'm here, help me see the people around me with your eyes.*

# CHAPTER 22

As Steve predicted, for four months after her conviction, Mary watched her case cool and move toward the back burner until only the occasional editorial hit the paper. Then one phone call pushed it back to the front burner.

Frank Santiago called Steve from the *Des Moines Register*. Frank had been following Mary's case and felt that the facts just didn't add up. He wanted to know if Mary would be willing to talk to him.

Mary agreed. Since she was serving a life sentence for murder, any review of her case sounded positive. She knew God could use this big-city reporter to shine a spotlight on her case in the media. Maybe that would force the court to reopen her case. Frank Santiago was one more way for God to work.

Frank arranged a meeting while she was still at Oakdale. Mary gave careful thought to what she would say to him. The facts of the case were easy enough. She would just tell the truth. But he would also be digging for Mary's deeper feelings. Would she lash out against the system, place blame, seek revenge? She needed to consider what she would say about these things.

On the day of the meeting, a guard escorted her to the visitor's room. Would she be able to answer all the reporter's questions? Would he twist her words? Could she trust him? She only knew she could trust God. He would accomplish his purposes.

# CHAPTER 22

As Mary entered the prison visitor's room, Frank met her at the door, shook her hand, and introduced himself. He was on the short side of average, middle aged with a full head of dark hair, nicely dressed in business casual attire. Mary picked some lint from her plain navy uniform.

Frank thanked Mary for meeting with him. They chatted for several minutes in the friendly manner of new acquaintances, and Frank asked for permission to tape their interview. Soon they sat across from each other at a metal table.

Frank adjusted a small recorder in front of her. "Mary, I've been following your case very closely, and I believe there's been a miscarriage of justice. Could you tell me, in your own words, what happened during the time you were with Melissa on January twenty-second of last year?"

Mary recounted the forty-two minutes she had spent with Melissa. She had told this story many times, and she presented the basic facts now with minimal emotion.

Frank scribbled notes furiously. He sorted through several pages to find some questions of his own. "So Melissa seemed to be fine when you picked her up, but less than an hour later she was slipping towards death?"

"That's right." As Frank questioned her, Mary relived her interview with Buffington, learning that Melissa had died, and her interview with Motsinger.

"The second interview was different. Detective Motsinger asked me the same questions I answered that morning, but he was angry. He accused me of lying."

Frank waited for her to meet his eyes, challenged her to think clearly. "This second interview took place the day after Melissa first quit breathing, the day she died, before medical evidence had been gathered?"

"Yes." Mary considered the accuracy of her words. "It was the day she died anyway. I don't know what evidence they had gathered."

Frank shook his head. "Believe me, they would be gathering medical evidence for months after she died." Frank jotted some notes, shifted positions. "So if you are innocent, what do you believe happened to Melissa?"

"I don't know. Someone hurt that little girl very badly." Mary shook away the mental image of the limp body she had tried to revive. "I don't know who did it. I could guess, but that wouldn't be fair. Every person deserves to be considered innocent until proven guilty."

"You insist you are innocent, and yet you have been convicted of first-degree murder. Do you feel the legal system has failed you?"

Mary sighed. "So far, yes, but my case isn't over yet. I believe my innocence will be proven in time. Someone inflicted a fatal injury on Melissa about a week before she died, but I'm not that person."

"And you can't prove you aren't that person."

Mary could sit no longer. She stood over the reporter, allowing her voice to raise several notches. "I shouldn't have to prove my innocence! The state is supposed to prove my guilt. Still they seem to think I hurt Melissa, and I can't prove them wrong." She raised her arms in frustration, then dropped them. "It's frustrating. When my case didn't fit the shaken-baby label, they just changed the label to 'shaken/slammed baby syndrome.' Child abuse is a terrible thing, but in the state's zealousness to stamp it out, it seems like they are stamping the shaken-baby label on cases it doesn't fit. I'm probably not the only innocent person condemned by their ill-fitting labels."

# CHAPTER 22

Frank allowed her to pace the floor a few times and regain her composure. "Thank you, Mary. That must be a hard story to tell, but I needed to hear it from you. I just want to expose the truth. I've talked to your lawyer and several people from your support group. Maybe if we get enough media spotlight on your case, the truth will come out."

Mary breathed deeply. "Thank you, Frank. This is one more avenue for the truth to come out, and I'm glad for that. I believe it will in time."

Mary realized she had wandered away from the microphone. She resumed her seat in the metal chair and adjusted the recorder.

Frank leaned back and crossed his legs. "So, Mary, tell me what prison life is like."

Mary relaxed, glad to move past the memory of Melissa's death. "Life has settled down to a normal routine. I have made friends among the staff and inmates."

Frank frowned. "But if you are innocent, what do you have in common with other inmates?"

"Quite a lot actually. We live in the same place, eat the same food, do the same activities. And though I'm innocent of killing Melissa, I'm guilty before God for other wrong things. God has forgiven me for the wrong things I have done, but I'm no better than anyone else. God has been good to give me friends, even here."

Frank guarded his reaction, moved past her "religious" answer. "You have a lot of time on your hands in here. How do you pass time?"

"I do normal daily things—eat, sleep, exercise. I have a Bible, and I read it. I have a prayer list."

Frank's eyebrows shot up. "A prayer list? You mean, you pray for other people?"

"Yes. I'm a Christian, and that's what Christians do." Mary shrugged. "I've got plenty of time. Who has more time than me?"

"But you've been convicted of first-degree murder and sentenced to life in prison. And you pray for other people?"

"Yes."

"Who do you pray for?"

"I hear about people in need, and I get prayer requests from our church bulletin, which is sent to me. I pray for my family, Jim and the kids." Mary pictured the worn list on yellow legal paper. "Monday I pray for my extended family. Tuesday I pray for my lawyers as they prepare my appeal. See, my prayers aren't entirely unselfish. There are financial needs." Mary smiled crookedly. "It costs a lot to be convicted of murder these days. Then, after my conviction, the state sent me a bill for fourteen thousand dollars, including nine thousand dollars for the prosecution's medical experts, whose testimony helped convict me."

Frank shook his head and jotted a note with dollar figures. He scratched bold underlines and exclamation marks beside the numbers.

"The cost of prosecuting me was nothing compared to the cost of defending me," Mary went on. "But my supporters are already starting to raise money for my legal costs. Every little bit helps. So I pray about that. Some people in my church have health needs and other problems in their lives. I'm not the only one with problems."

Frank stared at her as if she were a crossword puzzle in Yiddish. "I can't believe, with the problems you have, you pray for other people."

"Why shouldn't I? There's not much I can do to help in other ways. God has given me this way to help."

Frank doodled on the corner of his paper. "You must have a very strong faith, Mary."

# CHAPTER 22

"No, but I have a very strong God."

"In spite of that, you must find some things hard. After all, this *is* prison."

Mary stared past the bars and the inmates exercising in the colorless courtyard. "I miss my family. My home is a little more than an hour's drive from the prison's wire fence, but it seems much farther. I missed my little boy's fourth birthday in June." Mary cleared her throat and blew her nose hard. "I wanted to be home with him. He'll never turn four again. But Jim visits me every Sunday and brings the kids to visit. Still I long to be home with them."

"What else do you miss?"

"It seems pretty small, but I miss going to a restaurant and ordering what I want to eat. Just getting in a car and going for a ride. Simple pleasures."

The felon and the reporter had huddled over the metal table for hours when Frank asked a question Mary had learned to expect at the end of most interviews. "Mary, you've been very helpful, and I appreciate your time and attitude. Is there one thing you'd like to say to readers out there?"

"Yes. I know that somewhere people know what really happened to Melissa. I don't think that just one or two people know. I think several people know. I just want the truth to come out." Mary poked a tissue at her watery eyes. "But I'm optimistic. I believe in time I'll be released and my name will be cleared because I'm innocent."

Frank turned off the recorder and stuck it in his pocket. Mary's mind was in a daze, and Frank's eyes glazed over too, like he needed time to digest all the information.

Mary returned to her cell and did her own digesting. Frank Santiago was a major reporter for Des Moines' biggest newspaper. He seemed to believe her, seemed to be on her side. But he would continue to do other interviews. He would talk to Brad and Tessia and various medical experts. He might interview Judge Peterson and the police detectives, even the jury from the first trial. Would his article really help her or only make matters worse? She had to smile at the irony. What could be worse than being convicted of murder and sentenced to life in prison?

Mary had trusted the police, and some of them had disappointed her. She had trusted Steve, and he had worked hard to defend her, but his effort had failed. Could she trust this reporter, who would certainly be looking for a sensational story?

In the end she realized she wasn't in the reporter's hands but in the hands of God. He was a God of limitless power and endless love. He was the God who created the vast universe and kept it running. But he was also the God who had allowed her to be falsely convicted of murder and sentenced to life in prison.

# Chapter 23

On day one at the Iowa Correctional Institute for Women at Mitchellville, Mary held her arms straight out to the sides to allow the prison employee, who was in charge of the supply unit, to measure her bust. The worker called out the measurement, wrote it down, and went on to the waist. Did she really need to announce her measurements to all the other inmates?

But privacy was no more an option than the chambray work shirt and jeans she would wear every day in prison.

Choice. It seemed like such a small thing. Even Catherine and John sometimes chose what clothes they wore. But prison by definition was a lack of choice. Having every detail of her life dictated to her was as much a part of prison as the physical iron bars.

Prison meant rules, and she'd better learn Mitchellville's fast. Unlike Oakdale, the state meant this address to be permanent. Here she would hurry to each destination and wait when she got there. She would keep her shirttail tucked in, make her bed, turn in her laundry at the prescribed time, and avoid all physical contact with inmates. She would sign in or out every time she moved outside her cell block, and she would be in place for head count six times a day. The most minor infraction would earn her a ticket and cause her to lose privileges.

She would take an anger management class, because the state had decided convicted murderers needed one, and a parenting class, in spite of the fact that they had sentenced her to life in prison. The state would choose her cell, her food, her job, her companions.

Mary had learned some things from her nearly three months in jail and prison cells, with and without cell mates. Since choices were rare in prison, inmates were especially sensitive about people invading their personal space or cutting into the few choices they had. The rules and iron bars could strip her of outward choices, but unless she let it, the state couldn't build bars strong enough to imprison her mind.

Mary moved from one line to the next to receive her prison uniform. Her mind quickly drifted to her family, who didn't even know she had been moved to Mitchellville. She wished she could tell them where she was, but no phone calls were allowed during orientation.

As she picked up a pile of shirts and jeans, with socks and tennis shoes on top, a middle-aged inmate who was working in the area approached her. "I'm Jennifer. My husband has been in contact with your attorney. I was convicted of child abuse too. My husband has written your attorney to tell him how the child abuse zealots came after me. Does your family know you're here?"

"No. I wish they did. I feel so disconnected when they don't even know where I am."

"I can call my husband tonight, if you want. He can call your family and tell them that you're here and that you're all right."

"You would do that for me?"

"Yes. I've been watching your case. I know you go to church. I'm a Christian, and I want to help."

"Thank you. I would appreciate that so much."

# CHAPTER 23

Mary gave her Jim's phone number and hugged her briefly, unknowingly breaking a prison rule. Mary hadn't learned the "no physical contact rule" yet, but Jennifer didn't refuse the hug. Mary marveled anew about God's provision. God was bringing her fellowship in prison, even among the inmates. Mary would never know if Jennifer was guilty of her crime or not, but Jennifer claimed to be a Christian, and she was showing Mary kindness. Mary could sense God smiling on her.

Once the measurements were finished, they were escorted from the orientation building to the cafeteria.

"Stay on the sidewalk," the guard warned them. "Walk directly to the cafeteria."

The sidewalk skirted one side of the recreation yard, where other inmates were spending yard time. Mary followed the group of new inmates who stuck to the sidewalk, but she stole glances at a group playing volleyball and another group smoking furiously over a Scrabble game.

One of the Scrabble players leaned back and blew out a stream of smoke. She caught Mary's eye. "Are you the new lifer?" she yelled at Mary.

"Yeah, I am." She wanted to add that she expected to get out soon. She was totally innocent and hoped her lawyers would get her acquitted. Like that was an original story in a state prison. Plus she didn't think an explanation that long fit into the "walk directly to the cafeteria" command.

Mary kept following, but inside the door a big, burly guard named Wayne spoke sternly to her. "Mrs. Weaver, when moving from building to building, you're not allowed to talk to inmates who are in the yard."

Mary gasped. "Sorry. I didn't know."

"Now that you know, don't do it again. That inmate knew better. She'll get a ticket for calling out to you."

Mary had broken two rules already without even knowing it. In the days to come she could scream "unfair!" a thousand times a day at the guards and at God, but she had already decided that such behavior would only imprison her spirit as completely as her body. She wouldn't let anger destroy her spirit. The state could imprison her body, but if she made the right choices, her spirit could fly free.

Prison officials decided Mary would work in the kitchen five days a week. She would be paid thirty-eight cents an hour, less than 10 percent of the minimum wage. Outside of prison she wouldn't have chosen this job, these hours, this pay. She had no choice about doing the job, but she could choose to be glad for a job that broke the monotony of prison life and gave her some money in her prison account for stationery and craft supplies.

She missed her home and family but chose to think about how her living conditions had improved from each jail or prison cell to the next. Each day she had a bit of time outside her cell to play volleyball or Scrabble and attend Bible study or do craft classes. Time in her cell allowed her to search out answers from the Bible and pray.

Mary was friendly to everyone, but she became the best friends with those who, like her and Jennifer, had been convicted of child abuse. She had no way of knowing if people who claimed innocence were guilty or not but several seemed to have received particularly harsh sentences. One woman had been given an eight-year sentence for leaving her children with her husband when she knew he could be violent. Another had run into a building to escape her abusive husband, then was sentenced for child endangerment because she had left her kids in the car with him.

During Mary's first year in prison, all three of her cell mates—Kristy, Barbara, and Shelly—claimed to be Christians. One in particular seemed like a godly Christian woman. When the other cell mates found out Mary was a Christian, the four of them began to pray together every time the head count came while they were in their cell. They couldn't hold hands, but they would gather in a circle and pray. Each time they would pray that Mary would get a new trial and justice would be done. They'd pray for one another's families, safekeeping and protection throughout the day, to be able to advance to a higher classification in prison, to honor God, and to be good witnesses.

After two weeks of orientation, Mary could also receive visitors. She could have visits from her immediate family, three extended family members, and two other friends. Several lawyers could visit as well as the prison chaplain and Mary's own pastor, Bobby Shomo. They would have to submit to a criminal background check. If they passed that, they could have a full-contact visit with two brief hugs allowed.

Jim and the kids were her first visitors. They had been approved for visits at Oakdale, and that approval carried over for Mitchellville as well. The visiting room at Mitchellville was well stocked with games, books, and toys, making these family visits more fun. The kids loved the vending machines, too.

Myrna Prage visited Mary every Sunday, and Marge Wolfe visited every Tuesday. Their friendships and the Christian fellowship helped renew her spiritual energy.

Mary's new lawyer, Paul Rosenberg, also visited. In appearance Paul was a darker, slightly older version of Steve. On his first visit Paul made small talk for several minutes before talking about her case. "Well, Mary, the judge ruled against you on your motion for new trial, but that's not unusual. We'll keep working. You've got several things going for you. First of all, according to Steve Brennecke, you're not guilty." He grinned. "Right?"

"Absolutely." She matched his grin.

Laughter shone in Paul's eyes. If he wanted to keep this light, she wouldn't argue. She had laughed plenty of times with Steve in the past, but since her conviction, he seemed burdened, weighed down by the fact that he had lost her case. She grieved for Steve. He would continue to work on her case, but now Paul was in charge of her appeal.

"I also attended one of your support groups," Paul said. "Must have had thirty people there. I've got to tell you, these guys are dynamite! Petitions, editorials, car washes. Do you know they have yellow signs all over Marshalltown that read 'Was justice done?' I've never seen anything like it."

"I'm so thankful for them. They also send me letters. It's great. Best of all, they look after my family. They're going to take Catherine out and buy her school clothes before kindergarten starts."

"That's great. But right now we're going to work on getting you out of here so you can be with your family again. I've got to warn you. It could take a while. But we're going to do our best."

"I know you will. I know Steve blames himself for my conviction, but he actually did a great job defending me. I don't blame him."

"Sure. Steve's a great guy." Paul turned her attention to several legal issues.

At the end of the visit, Mary asked Paul, "How can I pray for you?"

Paul didn't claim the Christian label, but he must have believed in a God out there somewhere because he took her offer of prayer seriously. "Pray for clarity of thought. This case has so many details. We need to stay focused on the big picture and not get distracted by the details."

Mary nodded. "Clarity. I'll pray for that. I know God has a plan for my case. Everything is going to work out all right."

# CHAPTER 23

Paul stared at her as if she were a two-headed lizard. He had evidently not been on the receiving end of comfort from many of his clients, but Mary had received comfort from God, and she needed to pass that on. She didn't know how long it would take, but she was convinced God would set her free one day.

A prison was a desert of discouragement, and Mary soon found another opportunity to dispense hope. After orientation she was able to send a note (called "a kite") to the chaplain to schedule a visit. This lady found out Mary was a Christian and asked her to give her testimony during the Sunday evening Bible study. Mary agreed.

As the night approached, she prayed about what she would say. News traveled fast in prison. Inmates had just watched the slow-speed chase of O. J. Simpson in the white Bronco with ninety-five million other viewers. By now they had talked themselves out on the subject. Interest would jump back to her much-publicized case. Whatever she said in the Bible study would soon be analyzed and circulated around the prison. With the best of intentions, she could easily come across as hypocritical or condescending. She asked God to give her the right words so he would gain glory.

That evening Mary waited in her seat while an area pastor led the worship time in singing "Amazing Grace" and "I'll Fly Away." Her hands lay still on her Bible. Her heart beat normally. God would show her what to say.

When her time came, she faced a group of about fifty inmates. The pastor smiled from the front row. Wayne, the burly guard known for strict enforcement of the rules, frowned from the back corner.

Mary moved her focus to the friendly face of the pastor and began.

"On March twenty-second, 1994, I was convicted of first-degree murder in the death of Melissa Mathes, an eleven-month-old girl I was caring for. Someone hurt Melissa. It wasn't me, but the judge thought I was the one who gave her the fatal injury. Even though I'm now serving a life sentence here, I still believe God is with me. He's in control, and he will bring good from my case. I believe he has planned my future, that he will prosper me, not harm me. He gives me hope."

Mary glanced up from her notes. One inmate's raised eyebrow and folded arms challenged the idea of hope in prison, but everyone was listening.

"I can see God working in my life because he has brought people forward to help with my case. My lawyer, Steve Brennecke, and his wife have been great friends to me, and Steve worked hard to defend me. God caused a reporter to take interest in my case and bring it before the media. God provided me with another attorney, who is well known in the community, to handle my appeal. I believe in time I'll be acquitted. Even though I'm in prison unjustly, I still believe God is faithful."

Mary ignored a shuffling of feet and pressed on, determined to speak for God whatever reaction she got.

"I'm not guilty of killing Melissa Mathes, but I'm still guilty of doing many wrong things. I'm no better than any of you. I've said mean things about people and shown wrong attitudes. Everyone falls short of God's standard. Me too. About fifteen years ago, I went to church with a friend, and I began to understand that I could never be good enough for God. Only Jesus, God's perfect Son, could be good enough. He died on the cross—not because he was guilty, but because I am. I told God I was sorry for my sin, and I trusted God to forgive my sin because Christ had taken my punishment on the cross. Now I know that nothing can separate me from God."

One inmate yawned, but some were still following her.

"Every day in my cell, I pray to God and read the Bible and discover his love for me in a new way. He gives me strength for whatever I have to go through. Whatever happens with my case, I know God loves me and will use my case for my good and the good of others. I miss my family." Mary blinked away some tears but never missed a beat. "But God is with me, and he is enough."

Mary finished her testimony and sat with the others. The pastor spoke, and they sang a few more songs, but Mary sat in a daze. She was done. God would have to take her words and use them as he wanted.

The next day Wayne stood at the door to the dining room, watching the inmates file in. He gave a ticket to one inmate who bumped another in what might not be an accident. He called it personal contact. He glared at another one whose shirt bloused out too much in back until she tucked it in better. Then he called Mary over.

"Mrs. Weaver!"

She met his eyes. He motioned with his head to come closer.

What had she done now? As she stepped closer, she tried to read his face, but he wore his usual granite expression. "Yes, sir?"

"That talk you gave at Bible study last night."

"Yes?"

"I never heard a prisoner speak more eloquently in my life."

Mary blinked. "It was God. I asked him to give me the right words, and he did."

The guard nodded curtly and walked away.

Mary stumbled to one of the long metal tables lined with inmates. She thanked God for her vegetable soup and for using her words. She didn't want to stay in prison forever, but for now God had a reason for her to be here, and she could see him working.

After that Wayne was still very strict with the rules, but his body language communicated a new respect for her. Several inmates also thanked her for her testimony. Inmates were skeptical by nature and quick to point out when logic didn't add up, so Mary knew God had guided her words.

✿ ✿ ✿

## Sunday, August 21, 1994

Mary finished her shift in the kitchen and preceded her escort back to the cell. As she entered the lounge area with tables and chairs, everyone in the area stared at her.

"Here comes the celebrity!" Kristy shouted.

Mary frowned. "What do you mean?"

Shelly held up the *Des Moines Register.* "Not a bad picture, actually."

Mary grabbed the paper. Her image stared back at her from page one—an unsmiling figure in prison-issue glasses leaning on a table. "Questions linger in baby's death," the headlines read. "Some wonder: Was justice done?"

"And that's just the front page," Barbara said. "Your case fills two more full pages."

Mary sat and scanned through the pages. A huge picture of Jim and the kids topped 6A. Brad and Tessia frowned from 7A. Frank Santiago had given accounts of her case, doctors' opinions, legal definitions, and what had happened since her conviction. He had obviously interviewed many people and tried to give a balanced view of the case. He had even recorded details that were inadmissible in court, like the testimony of the cemetery worker, Kim Smuck, and of Mrs. McElroy and Mistry, who had come forward after the second trial.

The other gals peppered Mary's reading with so many questions, she could scarcely read the article. In the end she took the paper to her cell and sat on her bunk to reread it. She relived

# Chapter 23

the emotional roller coaster that had set her stomach churning during both trials. In the end she grinned. She couldn't forget Steve's words. *You are getting a lot of media attention now, but it will soon move to the back burner.*

This was no back-burner article. This moved her case straight into the scorching-hot oven.

# Chapter 24

Through the years Steve had seen some pretty strange things parade down Main Street but never anything like this.

In Marshalltown the Oktemberfest Grand Parade always started with a police escort, complete with flashing beacon and screaming siren. Costumed characters on fairy-tale floats threw candy to children. Brass bands blared Sousa marches. Small school bands played their school fight songs as they marched. Antique farm tractors put-putted, and clowns rode unicycles and walked on stilts. Political parties marched.

In the midst of clowns and acrobats and crepe paper floats, over forty men, women, and children marched behind a four-by-eight-foot sign. It read, "WE BELIEVE IN MARY WEAVER." All wore yellow T-shirts with the same message. Young mothers pushed baby strollers or pulled red wagons. Among them were a couple of workers from the Mitchellville prison and a lady over seventy-five years old. They all waved and chatted as if they were on their way to a picnic.

Nic tugged at his dad's pant leg. "Look, there's John and Catherine!"

Redhead John and blonde Catherine skipped along in T-shirts that read, "I BELIEVE IN MY MOMMY." Some of the crowd around him clapped in support of the Mary Weaver group, and Steve joined them, even if he was Mary's lawyer.

Seventy entries followed the parade route, and the largest group outside of the marching bands was marching in support of a convicted felon, who had been unfairly imprisoned for first-degree murder.

Unheard of. Or very nearly so.

Rain sprinkled Steve's nose. Several in the support group opened umbrellas but hardly even broke their stride. Steve, Kim, and Nic watched from the curbside. As a lawyer he had to be careful not to show disrespect for the court system. If he marched in the parade, people on either side could accuse him of being a sore loser who wouldn't accept the judge's verdict. Everyone knew his family supported Mary, but Steve and Kim had passed the baton to her supporters now. This parade showed the role this group could play.

This Marshalltown-Eldora support group was a brave bunch. They had gathered nearly five thousand names on their petitions and passed out over one thousand "Was justice done?" signs that hung in car and shop windows all over Marshalltown. They organized prayer groups and planned car washes, dinners, auctions. One group crafted wooden trains for auction. Nancy, Lisa, and Marge updated supporters on the tedious appeal process and support efforts through their regular newsletter.

Steve heard more clapping ahead as Mary's supporters kept their pace. No hecklers disturbed the peaceful protest. Mary's supporters didn't need to raise their voices with angry chants. They had already made their point with editorials, petitions, and signs. They were just keeping the interest alive.

Six months had passed since the second trial. Steve had felt sure enthusiasm in Mary's support group would be cooling by now, but her supporters were just warming up. Editorials flooded the papers. Santiago's three-page article alone had generated forty-three letters to the *Des Moines Register*, of which they printed twelve.

The enthusiasm for Mary's case was heartening, but Steve feared Mary and her supporters had unrealistically high hopes. Mary herself seemed to possess the gift of optimism. She refused to consider the fact that their appeals might go nowhere. What would happen to her faith if she never got a new trial?

As a lawyer, Steve couldn't afford to be so naïve. No judge was going to reopen the case without new evidence, and they had none. Robin McElroy and Mistry Lovig's testimony had been declared hearsay and hadn't influenced Judge Peterson to grant her a new trial. Tom McIntyre had volunteered his services as a private investigator, but his search had uncovered nothing. The police considered the case closed. Twenty months after Melissa's death was a little late to be expecting anything new.

Steve dreaded the day when he might have to inform Mary that her simple faith had been rewarded by a lifetime in prison.

Soon Mary's support group completely passed from sight, their quiet voices drowned out by a high school band. Mary's supporters would continue to work for the cause, but in time even they had to lose interest. Many of them were strong Christians now, but what would happen to their faith after ten, twenty, thirty years of watching their jovial friend grow old behind prison bars?

✧ ✧ ✧

Mary sat on her bunk, scanning the pages of the September 26, 1994, *Des Moines Register*. Dr. Bennett's picture caught her eye. "Examiner examined—Questions raised about Iowa's Dr. Bennett." By Frank Santiago, no less. Here was a must read.

# CHAPTER 24

Mary's own name jumped out at her in paragraph five. While researching Mary's case, Frank had dug up some of Dr. Bennett's skeletons. The article highlighted mistakes Dr. Bennett had made while he was the state medical examiner in Mississippi for eighteen months.

The article mentioned that Mary's supporters had criticized Iowa's state medical examiner. Bennett had testified that Melissa died of shaken/slammed baby syndrome due to injuries inflicted while in Mary's care, the article said, but some experts hadn't agreed with him.

Mary skimmed the article to see how the cases in Mississippi related to hers. Bennett had evidently wrongly identified a skull and missed a bullet lodged inside a victim. Then the article told of a four-month-old girl who, according to Bennett's report, had died of shaken baby syndrome. The baby's father had been charged with murder.

She read on. "Bennett said the baby had retinal hemorrhages and bleeding around the brain—the same type of injuries found in Weaver's case. The bleeding, especially the bleeding in the eyes, was an almost certain indicator that the baby had been shaken violently, he said.

"But Dr. Edward Smith, a neuropathologist at the University of Mississippi, disagreed with the shaken-baby analysis…The charges were dropped because of conflicts in the medical testimony and insufficient evidence to show there was a murder."

Mary let the paper fall to her lap. This sounded like Bennett had jumped to an SBS conclusion too quickly even before Melissa died. Her case wasn't isolated. Doctors were rightly motivated to stamp out child abuse, but if they put false weight behind uncertain evidence to get a conviction, they ended up abusing caregivers like her instead.

Had Bennett claimed more certainty than he could prove from the results of the autopsy? Anyone could make mistakes, but not everyone's mistakes sentenced innocent people to life in prison. Perhaps God would use her case to help other innocent people accused of abusing a child.

Paul filed another motion with the court of appeals, and they began the waiting process. Mary knew Paul was doing his best, but reviewing the second trial transcript and drafting the appeal brief took more time than allowed. Both Paul and the state's appellate attorneys asked the court for several time extensions. More time for them, of course, meant more time for Mary in prison.

In November Mary turned forty-three, and Catherine turned six. As Christmas 1994 approached, Mary wished she could be home to make it special for her children. Instead Jim drove the kids to visit Mary's family in Dubuque. Jim and Mary wanted the kids' Christmas to be as normal as possible.

On Christmas Day Marge Wolfe gave up three hours of her family time to spend with Mary in prison. Three hours was a maximum visit, and Marge tried to make it special for Mary. She wasn't allowed to bring a gift, but she brought coins for the vending machine so Mary could have soda and other treats. Mary enjoyed Marge's company and catching up on family news, but the atmosphere in the visitor's room was far from festive. Most of the inmates didn't want their family to visit them on Christmas. Such visits only made the holiday harder. The visitor's room was quieter than usual, almost empty. Mary and Marge searched for blessings to thank the Lord for. But as much as they tried to be optimistic, the "We Wish You a Merry Christmas" feeling they worked to create sometimes modulated into the minor chords of a funeral dirge.

# CHAPTER 24

For most of the winter, Mary worked in the prison kitchen, calculating the costs of meals and delivering breakfast to the inmates who were unable to come to the dining hall. Her job started at 5:15 a.m., and she worked six days a week. She told herself the early wake-up call wasn't all bad. She could pray while she dressed in the quiet cell, and she got first chance to sign up for her phone-call time.

In March Mary started a job she liked even better in the library. With her new job she had to work only twenty-eight hours a week instead of thirty-six in the kitchen. The library supervisor was willing to work around her visiting schedule too. Mary enjoyed her job in the library. During yard time, she became a formidable Scrabble player. She also taught craft classes in sewing, cross-stitch, and crochet.

In April the Iowa Court of Appeals heard the oral arguments for a new trial for Mary. Months passed as Mary and her supporters waited for God to intervene. On dark days, when it seemed the wait would never end, Mary searched the Scriptures and spent time in deep and dependent prayer.

Mary's case began the drawn-out appeal process. Her appeal to the Supreme Court of Iowa was first sent down to the Iowa Court of Appeals for their decision. She waited to see if that decision would open her prison doors.

In time Jim and the kids moved to Eldora to be closer to Jim's job. He had hired several nannies to care for the kids while he worked, but that situation wasn't working well. It was clear that Mary wouldn't be out of prison anytime soon. Living in Eldora would allow Jim to work close to their school and allow them to be in day care when they weren't in school.

In June John turned five. Jim bought party hats and cake and ice cream. He planned a party for John at home, but circumstances prohibited his friends from showing up.

The next day the family arrived for their normal family visit. When Mary entered the room, she dashed to her redhead. "Let me see the birthday boy!" She hugged him a little tighter than usual, hoping the guard would allow it. "Five years old. I think you are growing taller every week."

John wiggled away from her arms. "Nobody came to my birthday party. Daddy says they were busy, but who's too busy for a party?"

Mary stroked his fine hair. "I'm sorry, John. I wish I could've been there but..." Mary wiped her eyes on a sleeve. "Well, I just can't leave here right now. But we're here today. We can have a party here in the visitor's room."

"But we couldn't bring the party stuff. Not even the cake." He glared at a guard. "They won't let us."

"We can play Candy Land."

"I'm tired of Candy Land." John's lower lip protruded. "Why can't you come home, Mommy?"

"Someday I will. Just not now."

Mary sorted through the games, but most were too old for him. She folded party hats from old newspapers. They bounced balls. John showed off his shoe-tying skill which he had learned in prison. After a while he even smiled a bit. But Mary was actually relieved when they left. Making a disappointed five-year-old happy in a prison visitor's room was hard work.

Back in her cell, Mary sat on her bunk and blinked back tears. She knew it was her imagination, but it seemed like all her cell mates were stealing glances at her. It was only a birthday party. He could have another one next year. But it was a big disappointment to a five-year-old who had been anticipating the big day for

# CHAPTER 24

weeks. On the outside Mary would have had many alternatives to make his day brighter, but her prison options were severely limited.

She tried to read her Bible, but tears blurred her vision. She longed to be alone with her grief, but inmates were only alone in one place—the shower. She caught glimpses of the TV show her cell mates were watching in the outer cell, paced the floor, reread the newspaper. She ticked off the hours until the time she had signed up for the shower.

When her scheduled shower time arrived, she held her face in the streaming spray, letting the water mingle with her tears. She wondered how often other inmates cried in the shower.

"Lord, help me," she prayed. "I'm an adult, and with your help I can handle my time in prison. But Lord, please spare my children. Please help John to feel loved, even though his party was such a disappointment and his mommy can't come home."

She bent under the water's flow, shaking with sobs. Her own words from her testimony in chapel last year taunted her. *God is with me, and he is enough.*

Mary allowed the sobs to continue until they were spent, then stood up straight in the water and took a deep breath. "Lord, I know you are with me, and you are enough. You love my family, and you provide for them in many ways. I believe it, but today I have a hard time feeling it. Please help me keep my eyes on you."

# CHAPTER 25

One Tuesday afternoon a guard appeared at the door of Mary's cell. "Mrs. Weaver? You got a visitor."

Mary dropped her book and preceded the guard down the hallway. Who could this be? As she stepped into the visitor's room, Catherine skipped up to her in a pink tutu and leotard.

"Mommy, Mommy, I'm going to my dance recital! Aunt Lisa brought me so you could fix my hair." Catherine jumped around so much Mary could hardly get a hug from her.

Mary smiled her thanks at Lisa Murphy, her niece by marriage and one of Mary's approved visitors. Lisa was a mom herself and had figured out this creative way to include Mary in her daughter's special occasion.

Mary sat beside her daughter and drew her close. "I'd love to fix your hair. Shall we do French braids?"

"Yes, yes, yes, with pink ribbons!" Catherine bounced with every word.

Mary pulled ribbons and elastic bands from the girl's current messy ponytail. The quick hairdo must have been Lisa's way of bringing the items into the prison. Lisa hadn't been able to sneak a comb in as well, but Mary pulled long blonde strands into sections with her fingers.

"Hold still," she reminded her daughter as she started one braid. Mary breathed in the fruity fragrance of the superfine hair as she began to weave the strands. Catherine tried her best to stifle her emotions and imitate a statue, though the occasional wiggle just had to sneak out. Mary painstakingly French braided her daughter's hair into identical braids on either side of her head, then tied perfect pink bows at each end.

Catherine whirled away, shaking her head to feel her new hairdo. "Thank you, Mommy! I can't wait to see myself in the mirror."

Mary surreptitiously wiped tears with one sleeve. "You look beautiful. Can you show me your dance?"

Catherine performed several ballet steps, ending with a lopsided pirouette. Mary clapped loudly. "Good job! Just remember, when you're in that recital today, I'm going to be thinking about you."

Catherine gazed at her with pleading eyes. "I wish you could come to my recital."

Mary blinked some tears from her eyes. "Me too, sweetheart, but Aunt Lisa will take pictures, and I'll study them carefully. Just remember that your mommy is very proud of you!"

Mary gave her daughter a quick, prison-acceptable hug and watched the two walk away. Self-pity whispered, "You're missing her recital and all the other important moments in her life."

Mary lifted her chin. But God allowed me to fix her hair. God gave me that precious moment. God is good.

She thought of other ways God had allowed her to mother her children as well. God had given Mary a prison job, and her wages had been raised from thirty-eight to forty-one cents an hour. So what if it was only ten percent of minimum wage? The job made her time pass more quickly, and she could use the money in the commissary or craft store. Supporters could also add twenty dollars a week to her prison account. The activities directors had been especially kind to use this money to purchase fabric and patterns for her. Mary had been able to sew outfits for the kids, paint T-shirts, and buy presents for them.

Mary returned to her cell, sat on her bunk, opened her Bible, and prayed. *Lord, help me to be thankful for what I have, not to complain about what I don't have.*

A prison sentence made it easy to slide into self-pity. Unfairness could defeat her but only if she let it. Instead she thought about *The Hiding Place*, a prison library book she had recently read. Corrie ten Boom had hidden Jews in Holland during World War II. The Nazis had caught her and thrown her into a bitter cold prison for four months, then a women's extermination camp in Germany. Except for her sister, who was imprisoned with her for a time, Corrie had almost no contact with her family. She and her sister existed in overcrowded, filthy cells with little regard for sanitation and little to eat. They were allowed no exercise or fresh air.

Like Mary, Corrie was unfairly imprisoned, yet Corrie's sister challenged her to focus on what she had. Corrie accepted the challenge. In solitary confinement she hungered for human contact, but she thanked God for an ant that crawled into her cell and provided a bit of company. In one of her prison cells, for one hour a day, she could stretch herself out tall and feel the sun shine on her head and chest. She thanked God for the sunshine. Later, at the extermination camp, she slept piled on a straw-covered platform with many other prisoners, sandwiched between other crowded platforms. Fleas infested the stinking straw, but Corrie even learned to thank God for the fleas. The tiny insects kept the guards away from the overcrowded bunk, where she hid her precious Bible.

Mary closed her eyes to shut out the conversation of the other inmates lounging right outside her cell. Her prison cell was the Ritz-Carlton compared to Corrie's. "Thank you, Lord, that my family is safe and that I can see them every week. Thank you that I have other gals to talk to. You've even given me a roommate who seems to be a true Christian. Thank you that I can feel safe in prison, that other inmates haven't given me trouble, that the guards treat me with respect. Thank you that I have a Bible and can read it openly whenever I want. Thank you that I've grown closer to you in prison."

Mary slipped a family photo from the pages of her Bible. It pictured the four of them, preprison era, at a happier time. She caressed the redheaded toddler in the picture and his blonde sister. The state had stolen her family from her. The first year the state had seized all her possessions. Only now they allowed her to keep a few things of her own. The state could separate her from her home and family, but they couldn't take God away from her, and they couldn't take her away from God. She would focus on him and the things she was allowed to enjoy. Today that meant fixing her daughter's hair for a special occasion.

Other people in her support group also reached out to her family. These folks included the kids on family outings and church activities, took them shopping, and invited the family over for meals. She thanked the Lord for their kindness.

At the end of June Mary had been in the Mitchellville facility for one year. Since she hadn't gotten any tickets, not even for minor infractions, this meant a move to a new cell with only one other cell mate. She could now have her own TV set and cassette tape player in her room.

With the new privileges came a new roommate. Brenda was about ten years older than Mary. Out of the 341 inmates at Mitchellville, Mary considered four or five gals to be real friends. These gals, though also imprisoned for some reason, shared Mary's beliefs and values. Brenda was one of these.

The June 1995 issue of the *American Bar Association Journal* featured an article about Mary's case and her picture. This national coverage of her case encouraged Mary. With each step she felt like she was one step closer to being acquitted and going home.

The support network continued to raise money through garage sales, dinners, and food stands. They continued to pray and keep Mary's case in the public eye by word of mouth. Their mailing list grew to 350 names. She got more mail than any of the other inmates, and approved visitors seldom missed their scheduled time.

In August Catherine and John started first grade and kindergarten. Jim kept managing the house and his business. On weekends he took the kids swimming or golfing. Catherine loved riding in the golf cart, and both kids grew in their golf skills. Every Sunday he would bring the kids to visit Mary.

Maybe God would allow her to be home for Catherine's seventh birthday in November or for Christmas. Being tried and acquitted by Christmas might be too much to hope for, but if they granted her a new trial, she could possibly be released previous to the trial by then. How she prayed that her family wouldn't have to spend another Christmas without her!

Mary worried about Jim. With each visit his shoulders slumped more. Trying to manage the house and his business, and be father and mother to his kids was slowing his step and creating lines across his face. Legal fees were mounting far beyond what the support group could raise. Jim paid a private investigator and the nannies. He never complained about financial hardship for himself, but Mary could sense his anxiety about the kids' future as her case continued to drag on.

While Mary felt God had promised to "bring her out of captivity," Jim didn't believe the promise. As an unbeliever he couldn't feel God's peace and strength. His wife was a convicted felon, sentenced to life in prison. Paul and Steve worked hard to get her yet another trial, but they couldn't guarantee she'd even get another chance at a different verdict. She knew Jim was considering what his life would be like if his wife, the mother of his children, was never released from prison.

Jim faithfully drove the kids to visit every Sunday, but she began to notice a difference in the visits. They centered more and more on her time with the kids while Jim stayed in the background, saying little.

As the months wore on, Mary wondered each day when she would hear news about her appeal. Each day she studied her calendar and wondered, *If they grant me a new trial today, will I get out of prison before Christmas?*

Mary pictured the whole family choosing a Christmas tree. The kids would hang their special ornaments their grandparents had given them each year. Mary would mix gingerbread cookie dough, roll it out, and let the kids cut shapes. She could picture Catherine as a golden-haired angel and John, a bathrobed shepherd, at the church Christmas program.

Then one Friday in late September she was called to the visitor's room to see her appeal lawyer, Paul Rosenberg. She had waited more than five months for her appeal to be granted. Maybe he finally brought good news. She could practically smell the gingerbread now!

# Chapter 26

Paul's sober face screamed "bad news" like the headlines the day after a devastating tornado. The court of appeals had voted 5–1 to uphold her conviction.

The news hit Mary like a physical punch in the gut, knocking all the air out of her. She collapsed into a metal chair in the visitors' room. Paul gave her a moment to recover and breathe normally again. She realized she had painted a rainbow of high hopes in her mind. Now that rainbow had faded. Dark storm clouds scowled over the horizon, forcing her to descend to the dark storm cellar of reality.

Paul sat beside her. "We can't be too surprised at this. Appellate courts usually do back the decisions of the district courts. We knew it would likely have to go to the Iowa Supreme Court before someone would take a serious look at it. We'll keep working."

Mary knew he was right, but she ached somewhere deep inside her where the strongest pain relievers couldn't reach. She had hoped for a miracle. Now Paul had to start the process all over again with the supreme court. How many months would that take? Certainly too many to spend Christmas at home.

Two trials stuffed with the best evidence they could find, excellent medical experts to counter the state's experts, strong character witnesses, and lots of reasonable doubt had ended in a guilty verdict. Robin McElroy and Mistry Lovig's statements had changed nothing. Tom McIntyre's hours of investigation hadn't produced anything substantially new. The best efforts of Steve and Paul had ended in this. The court of appeals had affirmed her conviction, denied her appeal.

Mary scolded herself. This was not the end. The Iowa Supreme Court could still give them a new trial. But Judge Peterson and the court of appeals hadn't granted her a new trial. She had no new evidence. Why would the supreme court rule any differently?

Mary sobbed, and Paul squeezed her hand in a very lawyerly way. Usually this kind of physical contact wasn't allowed, but the guard chose to look the other way. Paul murmured words of consolation, while Mary realized she needed to show the hope she had in Christ.

Mary soaked up the tears on her face and blew her nose on the wet tissue. "I know this is a setback, but I still believe God is in control. He has a plan in all of this. I've got to hold onto the hope and the promise that everything happens for a reason and that God has a purpose here. It's going to be all right." She spoke for herself as much as for Paul. The words allowed her to compose herself.

He stared at her in disbelief. She didn't know if he didn't believe her attitude or didn't believe God would work it out. Maybe both.

"Mary, we do have one glimmer of hope. Rosemary Sackett got it."

"What do you mean?"

"Judge Sackett wrote a dissenting opinion."

"Who is she?"

"She is a judge on the court of appeals. Although she wasn't on the panel of judges who heard our arguments, she felt compelled to write her own opinion. She disagrees strongly with the others and is known for speaking her mind."

"What did she say?"

"She blistered the other judges and pointed out the flaws in the state's case. She said that your guilt or innocence hangs on disputed medical theories about shaken baby syndrome. The theory the state presented left too many questions unanswered. She didn't find substantial evidence in the transcripts to prove you were guilty beyond reasonable doubt. She also noted that Melissa was in her parents' or relatives' care when the massive skull fracture happened. She said that, at the very least, you are entitled to a new trial." He glanced upward. "So someone up there is listening."

Mary knew he was right. When she returned to her cell, she sat on her bunk. She counted the months since her conviction on March 22 of the previous year. Eighteen months. A year and a half in prison, almost that long with no new developments. Where was God's promise she had been counting on?

She pulled her Bible from her shelf and flipped to Jeremiah 29. "For I know the thoughts that I think toward you, says the Lord, thoughts of peace and not of evil, to give you a future and a hope. Then you will call upon Me and go and pray to Me, and I will listen to you. And you will seek Me and find Me, when you search for Me with all your heart. I will be found by you, says the Lord, and I will bring you back from your captivity."

God had originally given these verses to Jeremiah, promising to bring him and the Jewish people back from Babylon. They weren't given directly to her in her prison situation, but God had impressed them on her heart, hadn't he? She had prayed to God and searched for him with all her heart. Never in her life had she had more time to read her Bible than in prison. Never had she needed prayer more. She had worked daily to keep a thankful heart and a forgiving spirit amid separation from her family. Surely she wouldn't have to wait for heaven for any kind of hopeful future. Surely God wouldn't allow her to spend the rest of her life in prison for a crime she didn't commit. She had claimed this promise to Jeremiah as her own. Did she have a right to claim it?

Mary didn't know how many more months or years she would be locked inside these concrete walls. But she would not, could not, believe she would spend the rest of her life in prison. The truth would set her free eventually, even if lies and inaccurate medical opinions seemed to be winning right now. She just didn't understand why Judge Peterson and the majority of jurors believed the experts who had pushed past the edges of truth into opinion yet ignored proven facts like the older injuries. And why did God, who called himself "Truth," allow lies to prevail?

Mary's mind drifted back to when she first arrived at Mitchellville, and gave her testimony. She had spoken with confidence of God's purpose in her case, his love for her, his strength to help her through an unknown future. "God is with me and he is enough," she had said. God was enough for her today, and he would be enough for her tomorrow. She didn't know when she would get out of prison, but somehow she knew she would. She wouldn't allow herself to dwell on the events she was missing in the lives of her children. One day she would be free to go to all their special events again. Until then she would keep trusting God one day at a time.

In spite of the denied appeal, sixty-one supporters marched in the Oktemberfest Parade the next day in Marshalltown. The *Des Moines Register* mentioned them, and Marshalltown's *Times-Republican* put them on the front page. This year even more people marched than the previous year—though considerably fewer than the one hundred they had hoped for. Mary thanked the Lord for their efforts, but how many years could she expect people to march in support of a woman convicted of murder? Their enthusiasm kept her case alive in the media, but what she really needed was new evidence.

When Jim and the kids came to visit her on Sunday, his shoulders slumped more than ever. Catherine and John looked more like mourners at their mom's funeral than visitors at her prison.

Catherine's hug even felt halfhearted. "Mommy, Daddy says you're not coming home for my birthday or even for Christmas. Is that true?"

Mary smoothed her daughter's blonde hair and adjusted a hair clip that was falling out. "That's the way it looks right now. We're going to have to wait a little longer before I can come home."

Catherine's watery eyes pleaded with her. "Why can't you come home now, Mommy? All of my friends get to live with their mommies all the time. Why can't you come live with us again?"

Mary attempted a smile. "I'll come home just as soon as I can. We have to wait until the judge lets me come home. We don't know how soon that will be."

John's lower lip protruded. "I'm tired of daddy's cooking. I liked it better when you lived with us."

Mary squatted down to his five-year-old level. "I did too, John. We're just going to have to keep praying."

"But I did pray—lots of times. Why won't God listen to me?"

"I don't know what God is thinking. I just know that he loves us very much and that he's going to take care of us and do what's best for us."

John turned away from her. "I'm tired of waiting!"

# CHAPTER 26

Jim pulled a Candy Land game off the visitors' shelf and set it up for the kids. They both chose markers and started to play. After a few turns, Jim returned to Mary, who was watching them from a nearby table.

Jim turned his back to the kids and whispered, "You shouldn't raise their hopes like that."

"Like what?" Mary whispered back.

"Telling them you're going to get out of here."

Mary wet her finger and traced a Christmas tree design on the metal table. "I'm going to get out of here. I know it. This news about my conviction being upheld is disappointing, but it's not the end. This is just another step in the process of my release from prison."

Jim clenched his fists into balls. His eyes seized hers, forcing them to meet his. "How can you say that? Today's a year and a half. Did you know that? A year and a half since your conviction, and you're no closer to the outside. Steve and Paul are going to keep trying, but what more can they do? You've already had two trials. All the information came out. No one is finding any new evidence. Maybe it doesn't exist. You've got to face it, Mary. After Paul and Steve try everything they can, you could still be faced with a life sentence."

Jim stood and shuffled to a window. Mary watched him stare out the bars. She could tell he knew his comments stung. He considered them necessary, like iodine on an open wound. She could read it in the way he leaned on the windowsill, shoulders weighed down in despair.

She allowed him a few moments of quiet, then followed him. She set her hand on his shoulder. He shrugged it off. She waited for him to turn to her, gave up waiting. "I know it looks bad now, Jim. With the information we have now, it looks like I could spend my life in prison, but I don't believe I will."

"God's promises again?"

"Yes."

He turned to face her. His voice lowered to a fierce whisper. "Fine. You're the Christian. Keep believing if it helps you. But you can't promise the kids this Christmas. Or next Christmas or any other Christmas. I've been giving them the Mommy's-got-to-go-away-for-a-while excuse for a year and a half. I can't choke it out any more. Teachers at school try to protect them, but people talk. Kids hear things and tell other kids. Catherine and John know that something's wrong. Quit giving them promises you don't know you can keep."

Mary opened her mouth to argue, to offer him hope, but like her court case, she had no evidence to back up her feelings. She searched her brain for hope, but her word search came back empty.

Jim grabbed the Candy Land box and shoved the markers and cards into place. "Time to go," he said, folding the game board.

Confusion spelled out across the young faces, but the two hugged their mom's legs and said good-bye. The guard escorted Mary back to her cell.

She sat on her bunk and stared at the bars. All Jim's despair and the decisions of the courts hovered over her shoulder like angry storm clouds. She wouldn't believe that she'd spend the rest of her life in prison, but today she felt she couldn't stand to spend another minute here. She wanted to cry out to God, but not here, sitting in her cell where her cell mates could steal glances at her. She had to hold herself together until her next scheduled shower.

When her shower time came, Mary turned the water on and saturated her hair with it. She used what was left of her emotional energy to work a little shampoo into a lather and finally fell against the white-tiled shower wall, totally exhausted. Day after day she lived with the reality that her attitudes and reactions affected the people around her. But here in the shower she could cry, and the rushing water would drown out the sounds.

"Lord, I'm losing my family. Jim is struggling. My children are scared. My parents are aging, and I can't help them. I'm missing special occasions that will never be repeated. I can't share my sadness with friends. They have enough of a burden to carry just worrying about me in prison. Lord, sometimes I think I can't stand another minute in prison, wondering when I'll be released. Please, Lord, either send me home to my family or call me home to heaven."

# CHAPTER 27

Steve grabbed onto an electrical wire and pulled with full strength, bracing his feet to add his body weight to the equation. Once it started coming, the wire pulled through and left Steve in a heap on the stripped wooden floor.

When they first moved to the country his family lived downstairs while he finished the upstairs. Now they had moved upstairs, and he was wiring the downstairs. Right now everything was a mess, but once the downstairs was wired and hooked up to receptacles, a simple flick of the switch would light up a whole room. Steve would let Nic flick the first switch, but Steve would bask in the pleasure of one more job done.

He just wished he could see the light of reason in Mary's case. Why had God allowed her to go to prison when she was innocent? He still couldn't make sense of it, so he blocked the futility of their attempts to get Mary a new trial with physical exertion.

But today even pulling wires and hammering nails couldn't make him forget the hopelessness of the situation. After nearly a year and a half, Mary's support groups were still raising funds, helping her family with small tasks, and sending her letters of encouragement. They were still writing letters to the editor, but what good did letters do?

# CHAPTER 27

A recent opinion column suggested that "Mary Weaver's supporters' only goal is to get justice for Mary Weaver." The writer defined their justice as "freedom for Mary Weaver."

Chris Murphy, Lisa's husband, had responded with an editorial.

As a supporter of Mary Weaver, I am not interested in 'my justice' or 'their justice.' Weaver is a victim of bad circumstance. There is not one shred of concrete evidence proving Weaver shook Melissa Mathes to death. Her conviction is founded on the opinion of a few doctors who had based their opinions on certain questionable facts. The only way true justice will be done in this case is to reopen the investigation and find the truth—not our truth or their truth, but the factual truth.

Steve agreed entirely, but after all this time, now nearly three years from Melissa's death, he wondered if further investigation would find anything. Tom McIntyre had found nothing. More recently Bill Kidwell, a private investigator friend of Jim and Marge Wolfe, had begun to search for leads. Nothing.

Steve threaded another wire through the framework. Paul was battling the appeal. If any lawyer could turn this around, Paul could. But even the strongest appeal lawyer needed evidence to work with. People were praying for Mary and her family and her case. Steve prayed too, but privately he couldn't believe it would do any good.

His prayers had turned to doubts and questions. "How could this be right?" he asked God. "Mary is innocent. This jovial Christian lady is innocent, but she is serving a life sentence in prison. She can't even raise her own children. How could this be right?"

The question seeped from his soul with every tug of the wires through tight holes. *How.* Tug. *Could.* Tug. *This.* Tug. *Be right?*

Suddenly the wire gave way and Steve fell to the floor. He threaded the wire into the back of the receptacle.

Kim called to him from the top of the stairs. He had a phone call. *Please, Lord, no more bad news.*

Steve wiped his hands on his jeans and headed upstairs. He picked up the receiver. "Hello?"

"Steve? Bill Kidwell here. Got something to show you. You going to be home?"

"Sure."

"On my way."

Steve hung up the phone. What now? If the excitement in Kidwell's voice was any indication, this was not bad news.

Steve was standing in the driveway twenty minutes later when Kidwell pulled up. Kidwell jumped out of the car, grinning.

The private investigator held out three sheets of paper. "Look what I've got."

Steve scanned three handwritten affidavits. Three older ladies—Flossie Wall, Elaine Kail, and Evelyn Braack—had each written her own account of a conversation they'd had with Tessia shortly after Melissa died. They were in Hardee's having coffee when they saw Tessia. They had heard Melissa died and asked Tessia what happened. Tessia told them she was putting Melissa's snowsuit on when the baby arched her back, hit her head on the coffee table, and was knocked unconscious. Steve stared at the vitally important words.

He glanced up at Kidwell. "Unconscious?"

Kidwell nodded. "Uh-huh."

Steve read on. Two of the three affidavits noted that Tessia had told them Melissa had lost consciousness. Each lady had signed her affidavit, swearing it to be the truth.

Steve shook his head. "This changes everything, Bill. Everything! Where did you get these?"

"These ladies saw Chris Murphy's editorial in the paper last week and decided they needed to say something. They had considered speaking up earlier, but they knew two other ladies had come forward after the second trial with similar testimony, but their testimony was considered hearsay. When they read the editorial, however, they decided their testimony might help to reopen the investigation. They called Chris Murphy. He called me. I got the affidavits. What do you think?"

Steve read the affidavits again, comparing them with earlier statements. Robin McElroy and Mistry Lovig had testified that Tessia said that Melissa hit her head on the coffee table that final morning before Mary picked her up. Tessia had testified that Melissa hit her head on the padded recliner, but she'd insisted that the injury was slight. Now these ladies had reported another statement of Tessia's, which specifically said that the injury had been serious enough to cause Melissa to lose consciousness.

Would this information make a difference in Mary's case? Steve reviewed the requirements for a new trial with the detective.

"No doctor has considered this piece of evidence in forming their opinion of the cause of Melissa's death. And the mother told the police that Melissa hadn't been hurt that morning— that she was fine. This evidence is vital to the outcome of the trial. Bill, this could change the medical case entirely!"

Kidwell leaned against his car, nodded, smiled. "Uh-huh."

✧ ✧ ✧

## NOVEMBER 2, 1995

It was a normal day in prison. Mary worked in the library. She grabbed one of the new books that had come in and became the first to check it out. At her desk just inside the door, she made sure other inmates signed in and out and helped them check out books. She arranged autumn-colored leaves and Indian corn around a Thanksgiving cornucopia.

All day long she guarded a secret. Today was her forty-fourth birthday, her second birthday in prison. If she could choose a place to spend her birthday, prison would come at the very bottom of the list, but with the affidavits from the three ladies came hope that this would be her last birthday in prison. Maybe someone would send a birthday card. She couldn't complain. She was already averaging ten letters a day from her supporters. Most inmates received only one or two a month.

She finished her job and was escorted back to her unit. She had just settled on her bunk with her Bible in her lap when a guard unlocked the door to their unit and called out, "Okay, where's the celebrity?"

Mary glanced up to see what was going on.

"Is the famous Mary Weaver in this unit?"

Mary approached the solemn-faced guard, who knew very well who she was. "Got some mail for me?"

The guard threw an underfilled mailbag onto the table. "Here's the mail for the entire unit of fifty-two people. And here"—the guard hefted another bag, stuffed full—"here is your mail, Mary. I never saw an inmate get so much mail from so many places."

Mary grinned. "I'm just lucky—no, blessed—to have a lot of nice friends."

"You must be. I don't have one hundred fifty friends who would send me a birthday card."

"Who knows? Maybe if you were convicted of first-degree murder, you'd get a lot of cards too."

"I doubt it. By the way, I like the card with the mountain scene on the front."

Mary lugged the bag to her cell, dumped the cards on her bunk, and returned the bag. She felt the eyes of jealous inmates study the pile of cards. Some of the gals never got cards or letters from anyone. She wished she could share some of hers. Maybe she could get Marge to find someone to write to some of the gals.

Mary sat on her bunk and started pulling cards from already opened envelopes. She read greetings from people she barely knew and friends she had lost track of completely. Each card bore evidence of another person who supported her. Many of these people prayed for her. Some wrote letters to the editor or signed petitions for a new trial or taped yellow "Was justice done?" signs to their windows. God was so good to send this encouragement to her prison cell. Mary thanked God for the cards and letters, and added a prayer for the guards who had to check her letters for contraband. These letters, filled with Bible verses and praise to God, could be a way to show them God's goodness.

✵ ✵ ✵

## JANUARY 11, 1996

Steve stood in the back of the courtroom of the district court, hemmed in by one hundred people sitting on benches and standing in the gallery. Cameramen checked viewfinders for good angles. Reporters asked supporters for sound bites. Mary's case had been remanded from the Iowa Supreme Court to the district court. Today's hearing would present testimony by the three ladies so Judge Goode could determine whether the newly discovered evidence warranted a new trial.

Standing at the back of the courtroom allowed Steve to observe the hearing more objectively. He was glad to relinquish his place at the counsel table to an expert appellate lawyer.

Mary's freedom hinged on the statements of three ladies. What could an alleged blow to Melissa's head, strong enough to render her unconscious, mean to the already complex medical conditions that contributed to her death?

Paul Rosenberg sat at the counsel table, reviewing his notes. He brought a fresh viewpoint to the case, and a fresh judge would hear the case. That gave Steve hope.

But the prosecution was also refreshed. Diann Tomlinson was gone, replaced by Douglas Marek from the Iowa Attorney General's office. He would try to block Mary's opportunity for a third trial.

"All rise." The bailiff's clear command brought silence to the courtroom. Judge Allan Goode entered, took the seat of authority, and introduced the hearing on Mary's motion for new trial.

The judge eyed Paul at the counsel table. "Mr. Rosenburg, you may call your first witness."

Paul stood and called Flossie Wall to the stand.

Mrs. Wall stepped to the stand, clearly uncomfortable in the public eye. She took the oath and sat, clutching her handbag like a security blanket. Anyone would be nervous in this situation, but Mrs. Wall was about to testify to a key piece of evidence that could unlock the doors to Mary's prison. The state wasn't about to let that happen without a fight.

Paul established from Mrs. Wall's testimony that she didn't know Mary and wasn't part of her support group. He asked her about the ladies who had met at Hardee's and the conversation with Tessia after Melissa's death. "And what did Tessia tell you happened?"

Marek shot out of his seat. "Objection, Your Honor. Hearsay."

Mrs. Wall looked at Marek, then Paul, then the judge, confused as to whether she was supposed to answer the question or not.

Marek rested his fingers on what appeared to be copies of the affidavits. "I expect that much of her testimony will involve hearsay, and I would ask that my objection be allowed to stand."

Hearsay. Steve could hear the arguments coming. *Tessia denies saying these things to the ladies. This evidence shouldn't be admissible. Case closed.* Just like Judge Peterson had closed the books on Robin McElroy and Mistry Lovig.

But these statements were out-of-court statements used to prove the truth of the matter asserted: that, according to Tessia, Melissa had hit her head and become unconscious before Mary picked her up. Would the judge allow them to be admitted into evidence?

Steve leaned forward, waiting for Judge Goode's reply. The crowd in the gallery barely breathed until Judge Goode spoke. "Since the admissibility of the evidence is one of the disputed issues that the court is required to rule on, the court will take the objection under advisement, and the state may have a standing objection to any statements made to this witness by others for purposes of this hearing."

He turned to Mrs. Wall. "You may answer, ma'am. Do you recall the question?"

She didn't.

Steve breathed again. Judge Goode realized that the admissibility of this testimony was key to the case, and he was keeping an open mind.

Elaine Kail and Evelyn Braack shared their testimony after Mrs. Wall. Each lady appeared shy in the limelight, but all three were certain about what Tessia had told them. Marek's cross-examination couldn't shake them. Like a man in quicksand, the more he attacked, the deeper he sank.

After their testimony the focus of the hearing shifted from this newly discovered evidence to the impact of that evidence.

Would a blow to Melissa's head, which caused her to lose consciousness, have an impact on the medical analysis of the cause and manner of her death?

Dr. Rose took the stand and spoke of the tender nature of her wounds that were seven to ten days old and in the process of healing. His testimony showed that Melissa continued in a critical condition throughout that last week of her life.

Next Dr. Brian Blackbourne, the county medical examiner from San Diego, a new doctor for the defense, testified that, from a forensic/medical standpoint, this new testimony was significant in determining the cause of Melissa's death. Melissa's seven- to ten-day-old injuries would have increased the severity of a subsequent injury, such as a blow to the head from striking the coffee table. She wouldn't have responded like a healthy child.

Steve watched Paul build a case for retrial brick by brick like a skilled craftsman. Judge Goode remained attentive, jotting notes throughout the process.

Then the state called Drs. Smith, Schelper, Alexander, and Bennett. Their testimony was shorter than in the trials, but they disagreed with Rose and Blackbourne on a few points and said they didn't believe the testimony of these ladies would change the outcome of the trial.

Judge Goode adjourned the hearing at 1:30. Then Mary and her supporters found themselves waiting for another judicial ruling, hoping again that their prayers would be answered.

The judge could give Mary a new trial. Steve and Paul discussed the rule of evidence concerning hearsay testimony. "Hearsay" was the term for testimony in which the witness repeats someone else's statement from outside the courtroom. The rule was meant to screen out unreliable testimony, since hearsay could be a back door for unsworn statements that were uttered beyond the reach of cross-examination.

# CHAPTER 27

As with most rules, there were exceptions that allowed such statements to be admitted into evidence. The judge had to decide if the testimony from these three ladies fit one of those exceptions.

Steve and Paul analyzed the situation. They agreed that the only exception that might allow this testimony in court was the last one, the "catchall" exception. The testimony of the ladies was reliable. They had no ulterior motive to testify. Their testimony also served to impeach Tessia's testimony, when she insisted Melissa wasn't injured before Mary picked her up.

But Steve couldn't forget that Robin McElroy and Mistry Lovig's evidence had been declared inadmissible at a similar hearing in the same courtroom.

# CHAPTER 28

Steve parked by the curb in front of the courthouse and grabbed his briefcase. He needed to file a deed following a real estate closing. Mundane tasks like this paid the bills. At least these lesser tasks distracted him, if only temporarily, from the relentless question that hovered on the edges of every task, every conversation, every thought. Would Judge Goode grant them a new trial? And three weeks—what was taking him so long?

Delay was good. That's what he told clients when they yearned for a quick ruling. He tried to convince himself of the logic now.

The hearsay issue was controversial, and Judge Goode was probably reinforcing his ruling with extra research. From his own days as a law clerk, Steve could picture Judge Goode's clerk pulling cases off the shelves that held decisions on the hearsay rule. The clerk would brief those cases, comparing and contrasting the various rulings that might impact Goode's decision. The ruling would be tightened, revised, and polished before it was made public. If delay meant extra research, that was a good sign.

Or did delay mean Judge Goode was having difficulty coming to a decision?

Maybe the decision was delayed simply because the judge was too busy to rule on things more quickly.

# CHAPTER 28

Every day Steve debated the matter in his head. His brain grew weary, but educated guesses brought him no closer to knowing what only time could reveal.

The clock in the courthouse tower chimed as he stepped from the slushy street onto the bare sidewalk. Eleven o'clock. Steve's glance at the huge clock brought his attention to the bronze statue of Lady Justice. She perched on the roof line in front of the clock. Was it his imagination, or was the statue smirking?

"Hey, Lady Justice, where were you during our first two trials when we needed you?" He whispered the words out loud before he realized it. He glanced both directions to make sure no one had caught him talking to himself. Inside him a strange voice echoed, *Hey, God, where were you when we needed you?*

Steve shook off the inner voice, gripped his briefcase more tightly, and hurried into the courthouse.

Like Judge Goode, God was taking his time, but they just might get their new trial. That would give Steve an opportunity to correct his mistakes that had sentenced an innocent client to life in prison. Maybe soon life would be right again.

Judge Goode had to do more than allow the new testimony to be admissible in court. To grant a new trial he also had to declare that be believed their evidence would change the outcome of the trial. That would send a signal that the science underlying the conviction was also weak.

No matter which decision Goode made, he had to know his ruling was destined for immediate appeal. Between Mary's lawyers and the prosecution, the ruling would thrill one side and upset the other. In legal circles, someone was always unhappy, and rulings were seldom final.

Steve sighed. Why had he ever considered becoming a criminal lawyer? All he could do now was wait. Wait for the judge to decide the ruling. Wait for it to be delivered to the clerk of court.

Wait for it to be sent to them as well as to the prosecution. The press would pick it up first in their daily review of new rulings. But when would the judge decide?

He finished his courthouse business and raced through the cold wind, counting on speed to drown out the relentless whisper. *New trial or not? When will we find out?*

As Steve entered his office, his secretary waved wildly. She wedged the phone between her shoulder and ear and held out a handful of phone memos. On the top memo she had scrawled, "MARY GETS NEW TRIAL!!!"

He grabbed the memos and raced into his office, slamming the door. He flew to his desk, flipped through the notes. Nancy Pins. Lisa Murphy. More supporters. Kim. His dad. All had called with the news. Steve grabbed the phone and punched Paul Rosenberg's number. He waited for the secretary to answer, then for the call to be transferred, then for Paul, who didn't answer until the third ring. What was taking him so long?

"Paul, have you heard? New trial granted!"

"Yes! Great news."

Paul had confirmed it. Mary really was getting a new trial. Steve started pacing as far as the phone cord would allow. "Congratulations."

"Sure. Time to get busy. Marek will appeal."

"They'll lose." Steve pictured Mary already celebrating in prison. "We can get Mary out of prison while they appeal, right? Goode has granted her a new trial, so you'd think she should be free until then."

"Yeah. She should get out soon. First, we need to look at Goode's ruling. Have you seen it yet?"

Paul was strategizing, and Steve hadn't even sat down yet. "Not yet. I just returned to a handful of phone call memos

234

about a new trial. But if Goode believes this will change the outcome of the case, I can't wait to begin this third trial."

"I'm going to get a copy of the ruling faxed here and then call Marek. We need to talk this through."

"Yeah. Guess I've got to let it sink in first." Steve paced the length of his desk several times. "I was expecting this, but I still can hardly believe it. You watch an innocent client go to prison and...wow... Mary must be so excited. I just...I can't wait for the day Mary walks out of prison. Too bad those ladies didn't come forward earlier."

"Maybe."

"Maybe?" Steve's pacing came to a halt. "What do you mean, maybe? If they had spoken up sooner, Mary might not have had to spend two years in prison."

"Maybe not. I've been thinking about that. Don't you think Judge Peterson would've swept their affidavits in with your other two affidavits? That he would've treated all five ladies as one and denied your motion for new trial?"

Steve twisted the phone cord to spiral around his finger, untwisted it, retwisted it. "I never thought about it that way, but of course. Why wouldn't he?"

"Then Mary would never have received a new trial."

Steve couldn't answer. His mind was too busy ricocheting from one possibility to the next.

Paul gave up waiting for him. "The timing of the whole thing is completely providential. Otherwise Mary would be a lifer in prison with no hope."

Steve searched for words. "So the delay...her years of prison... were necessary?"

"In a sense they were. Yes."

No. Surely not. Yet there was no other way around it. "So Mary did providential prison time?"

"Absolutely. There's no other way she would have gotten a third trial."

Steve collapsed into his office chair. Paul was a streetwise attorney with no theological background, yet he had thunked the bull's-eye of the providential dealings of God. Who was teaching whom here?

Steve scribbled on a legal pad. "1. letter, 2. ladies, 3. Kidwell, 4. Goode." He tried to absorb a reality he had totally missed. "Then the timing wasn't off kilter, late. It was perfect. Mary gets a second chance because the ladies didn't think it would do them any good to come forward until they saw the editorial. At that precise time Kidwell 'just happened' to be in town to charm them into signing affidavits. The case fell to Judge Goode, who was more open to Mary's innocence than Judge Peterson. The editorial, the ladies' response, the detective, and a new judge all had to meet at the same time to make it work." Steve shook his head. "Wow. I always heard 'God works in mysterious ways.'"

Paul laughed. "Don't forget us. I'd like to think we factor into the equation too."

They finished the conversation. Steve hung onto the receiver until the beeping dial tone reminded him to hang up. Moments ago he wanted to dance around the room and shout, "Mary gets a new trial!" Instead he closed his eyes, afraid to move for fear this elusive truth would escape. He could hear Judge Peterson giving that unjust verdict. *I find the defendant guilty of murder in the first degree and child endangerment.* He could feel Mary squeeze his fingers and hear the heartbreak in her words. *What's going to happen to my family?*

At that moment, at the close of the second trial, his young career and his understanding of God's righteous dealings in the world had crashed into the rock wall of reality. Steve's best work had produced his worst nightmare. His failure had sentenced an innocent client to life in prison. God hadn't prevented the unfair verdict. Steve had resigned himself to the reality that Mary would die of old age in prison.

Until today.

Now, with a single ruling, Judge Goode had unlocked Mary's handcuffs and opened her prison doors. She would still have to stand trial again, but she would be presumed innocent again and get another jury trial. Another judge would preside, one who had shown he would weigh difficult evidence carefully.

Until today God had seemingly turned a deaf ear to the years of prayers by hundreds of people. Until today God appeared to observe the tragedy with his hands in his pockets. Today one ruling changed everything. Today Steve could finally see the fingerprints of God.

Steve pictured a near-future scene. Mary would walk out of the Mitchellville prison to meet her family and supporters. Steve could imagine Catherine hanging onto her mom's arm and John jumping up and down with joy. As the picture formed in his mind, a smile grew across his face. Years of tension drained from knotted shoulders. Part of him still wanted to jump and shout and call everyone he knew.

But first he needed to bow his heart in worship. At this moment he was a doubting disciple who had run to a recently filled tomb—and found it empty.

# CHAPTER 29

Wayne, the biggest and sternest guard, searched the patch of winter sky outside the barred window for a glimpse of the powerful rotors clattering overhead.

"I don't care if they are media choppers; they make me nervous. Don't they realize this is a prison? We're a bit finicky when it comes to security."

A female guard opened the door of the outer cell to Mary's unit. "I've never seen anything like it. Dozens of supporters and three news channels—all waiting for a convicted murderer to walk out the gate."

Wayne entered the cell and grinned at Mary. "Ain't easy having a celebrity on our hands."

Mary grabbed the pile of clothing from her bunk and glanced at the inmates crowded around her inner cell. "Well, good-bye, everyone. I'm going home!"

Home. She hadn't been acquitted. She was still under arrest, but bond had been posted, and her current status was as if the first two trials had never happened. Today she would be released from prison, welcomed by friends and family, and returned to the life she had left behind.

# CHAPTER 29

Good-byes and well-wishes echoed across the cell blocks. This had been her home, the last of a series of cells that had confined her for two days less than two years. She preceded Wayne down the corridor, practically skipping. She couldn't restrain a big grin.

Past the cell block, Wayne leaned close. "Don't listen to those who call you a convicted murderer. You may be convicted, but you're no murderer. I've worked at this prison twenty years, and you are only the second person I've felt was convicted wrongly."

Wayne's tough exterior warned inmates not to mess with the rules. But occasional glimpses of softness peeked through, especially for inmates who were trying to follow the rules.

Mary passed Julie Johnson and the guard who escorted her. She was probably heading for her job in the library. Julie waved. "Good-bye, Mary. See you in heaven."

Mary kept on walking. She wasn't supposed to greet inmates between destinations in the prison, but she felt sure today would be an exception to the sacredly guarded rules.

"Right, Julie," Mary called over her shoulder. "I'll be praying for you." Mary knew she would see Julie again. Though Julie admitted to killing her husband during a fit of rage, her humble dependence on God had convinced Mary she was now a true believer.

Mary entered the visiting room and deposited the pile of prison-issue clothing on a table by a female guard. "It's all there, right down to the underwear." Today she wore a red cardigan she had knitted and a knit top she had ordered. These had been stored until today, the day of her release.

The guard sorted through the clothing, counting each piece. She initialed some paperwork and handed the papers to Mary to sign. "Good luck, Mary. Hope we don't see you again."

"Thanks. I'm not coming back. I know it."

"Your supporters are waiting to celebrate with you, but reporters and cameramen are waiting with them. I hope you're prepared for that."

Mary nodded. She would never forget this day. Neither would others. Out of a whirlwind of excitement and mixed emotions, she must choose her words carefully. Cameras would record every move while she embraced and thanked family and supporters.

By now Mary had faced reporters many times. They would be baiting her, watching for signs of anger and bitterness against Melissa's family and the legal system. God had given her many opportunities to speak out in the media about her trust in him. Wrong words today could convince unbelievers of the hypocrisy of Christians in general. But God had given her five and a half weeks since the final decision to retry her case to think about what she would say. She didn't work to devise clever answers because God would help her know what to say. But she did need to prepare her heart. The Bible said that the mouth speaks out of the abundance of the heart, so if her heart was right, the answers would be right too.

"Mommy, Mommy!"

Mary turned to see her blondie, Catherine, and redheaded John run into the room with Mylar "Welcome Home!" balloons and a bouquet of flowers. Jim followed close behind with Lisa Murphy.

John bounced with energy. "Lots of people are waiting outside! We're taking you home today."

Mary accepted the bouquet from Catherine. "I know. Isn't it great? God is so good to us."

Jim squeezed her arm. "How does it feel to be a free woman?"

"I'm not completely free. I still can't leave Hardin and Marshall Counties. I've got to check in with my parole officer daily. I can't contact Brad and Tessia." Mary threw her head back and laughed. "But after two years of being told where to sleep, what to eat, when I could use the telephone—yes, that sounds like freedom. I can't wait to get home!"

"Before that, you've got a lot of friends waiting to greet you." Jim's eyes clouded with warning. "Reporters, too."

Mary took a deep breath. "Of course. I can't wait to see everyone."

She signed the last of her paperwork.

The flowers could have been dandelions and knapweed for all Mary cared, but she sniffed their sweet perfume for her daughter's sake and gave her a big hug. "Catherine, the flowers are beautiful. Can you take care of them for me?"

"Sure, Mommy."

She hugged her son. "And John, can you hold the balloons while we visit with all our friends? Aunt Lisa can help you look after them."

Quality time alone with her family would have to wait. Mary met Jim's eyes. "Ready?"

"More than ready to get you out of here."

Mary scooted out the door with her arms around both of her kids. The prison was locked down for the occasion, probably for security as well as to protect the privacy of the inmates from all the TV cameras. But someone had spotted her from a window. "Good luck, Mary!"

Cheers from other inmates joined the first, and she could hear others clapping. Last night's news had announced that she would be released today, so it was no secret.

"Go, Mary! We believe in you."

Mary had never imagined that the other inmates would be cheering for her at her release, but the clapping and cheering rose to a crescendo. Mary hoped her release would give other inmates hope when they saw how good and faithful God was.

Guards followed them out, smiling broadly but keeping a careful eye on the choppers overhead. Then they turned the corner, exited the gates, and were met by an emotional crowd.

Mary's dad hugged her first, squeezing tightly and patting her back repeatedly. Then others cut in, hugging, crying like an upside-down funeral. Jim and Marge Wolfe were there as well as Nancy Pins and dozens of other supporters. Words of encouragement came from every direction.

"I'm so glad you're coming home."

"I love you, Mary. I'm so happy. What a glorious day!"

Mary hugged Myrna Prage. "I knew you'd be here. You've always been there."

A reporter stuck a microphone through the crowd. "How does it feel to be able to hug your kids?"

Mary's watery eyes shifted to the reporter. "I've lived for this moment, to be home with the kids. Tonight when they go to bed, even though they've grown, they're not the babies they were when I left, but I'll rock them to sleep tonight."

Catherine bounced up and down beside her. "We're going to have a big supper."

Mary hugged her daughter again, focused complete attention on her. "All right! I hope it's pizza and ice cream. How about you?"

Another reporter stuck his mic toward her. "Does it feel like it's over?"

*Lord, help me know how to balance reporters' questions with friends who want to greet me.*

"It's in the back of my mind, but I'm just going to enjoy each day the Lord has blessed me with. Excuse me." Mary hugged several more friends. The chopper's powerful rotors upended hairdos and parka hoods like a giant leaf blower. But Mary felt warm, surrounded by a cocoon of friends and loved ones.

The mic jostled for position again. "What do you think about the dozens of supporters who have shown up for your release?"

Mary smiled into the camera. "It's wonderful to have them out here and see them. They've done a lot of work for me these past three years. I appreciate them being here this morning, and I'm glad to be with my family and my friends."

She continued to hug various friends and supporters and give short replies to their comments. Several carried bouquets of flowers. One wore her yellow "I BELIEVE IN MARY WEAVER" T-shirt under her winter coat. She flashed it for a cameraman.

Over the shoulders of hugging friends, she caught glimpses of yellow signs. "Free at last!" "God is so good!" A pink sign said "Praise the Lord!"

A friend holding a camcorder called to Steve, who was holding back to let others hug Mary. "Steve, get up here."

Steve stepped closer, the only suit and tie in an army of parkas. He hugged Mary sidewise and wiped tears from his eyes while the cameraman filmed them. "What a happy day!"

Mary could only imagine what the day meant to him. Steve had flexed every legal muscle and poured out his heart and soul to defend her, only to see her convicted and imprisoned for two years. The new trial would be a second chance—no, a third—for both of them.

Kim stood with Steve, supporting the celebration. She was holding Brennan, the baby they had just adopted

Never had Mary felt more supported than in this cocoon of weeping, laughing people who cared. But people on the edges of the cocoon stamped their feet and shivered in the cold. They probably also recognized that this was only the beginning of a very emotional day for Mary, so they began to head for their cars, which lined both sides of the narrow road. Mary also yearned to be with her own family, whom friends and reporters had edged to one side. She crept closer to the family van.

A reporter pushed closer. "Mary, this must be very rough on the Mathes family. What do you have to say to them?"

She was glad she had prepared for the question. "The truth will speak for itself." She turned to the kids. "Let's go, guys."

Seconds later the van sped away, leaving a reporter on the curb who probably would have preferred a more vindictive answer. First stop was Marshalltown, where Mary signed more paperwork. Another crowd met her there with signs and yellow ribbons pinned to their chests. They had tied yellow ribbons to the trees. Mary hugged neighbors and former coworkers and friends from Eldora and Steamboat Rock she hadn't seen for years.

In the courthouse Al Brennecke took off his yellow ribbon with the little angel pin. His wife Jean nudged Mary. "He's been wearing that pin everywhere for two years. He never took it off." She laughed. "He even wore it to bed."

Al handed it to Mary. "I'm not going to need it anymore," he said.

The elder Brennecke lawyer felt the same assurance she did. She would never go back to prison.

In Eldora they pulled up to the white, ranch-style house that was familiar to her family but new to Mary. "Welcome Home" signs and yellow balloons welcomed her once more, along with another crowd of people. She greeted supporters and reporters before walking inside.

Jim had arranged the furniture and likely put the spatula in a totally illogical kitchen drawer, but this was her home. She longed to put her feet up and enjoy a few minutes of quiet. This moment, however, didn't belong entirely to her or even to the family who had waited for her. This moment belonged to all the supporters who had believed in her. They had prayed for her, testified in court, carried clipboards for petition drives, posted signs, washed cars, donated goods, and cooked and baked to raise funds. These people had followed the nightly news as closely as if the case had been their own. In a sense it had.

So many women had written letters to say, "If you were convicted of abusing Melissa, it could just as easily have been me. I'm afraid to baby-sit anymore." Or "I'm afraid to watch my own grandkids." They all flinched at the sting of injustice. This was a victory for them all.

Much of the crowd lingered outside, but many followed her inside. Everywhere she turned people milled about, laughing, crying, sharing their own support group memories. A stranger handed her fifty dollars to take her family out for pizza sometime.

Somehow Mary must have eaten something between the hugs and well-wishes. Reporters edged into the celebration. She gave an interview to each reporter, asking God to help her think clearly through all the interviews. One reporter checked with the cameraman and held a mic close to Mary. "How did it feel to walk out of prison this morning?"

"I was just relieved to get into the family car and drive off. Every time I've left the prison before, I was handcuffed and shackled, and it was just neat not to be handcuffed or shackled and be leaving in a police car, but just to get in the family van and drive off."

"Mary, you maintain your innocence, but you've just spent two years in prison. Are you angry about that?"

"I don't fault the justice system. I try not to be mad, to be angry. It was just a mistake. Mistakes happen. Everyone makes mistakes. I hope it will be corrected."

The reporter continued to dig for an angry reply. "But this 'mistake' has cost you two years of life with your children."

"I don't want to dwell on the things I missed. I just want to concentrate on enjoying each day. Seeing things other than the little room I lived in and the little enclosed yard that we had. I'll enjoy just walking around the neighborhood, to walk down the aisle of a grocery store."

After recording several interviews, Mary was able to watch some of them as various channels showed the breaking news. The reports didn't twist her words or leave out the best parts. She thanked the Lord for helping her to speak and the media to edit.

Among the reports Mary caught a quote about her release from Tessia, who had refused to appear on camera. "We're very disappointed. We believe Judge Goode's ruling on a new trial will be overturned by the state's appeal, and we look forward to that day." Sad comments, but what more could she hope for from the grieving mother? The media had to try to give a balanced view of her case.

By evening the crowd had thinned, then regathered. Celebration wafted in from the kitchen with the scent of casseroles warming in the oven. At five o'clock Jim turned on the TV and began flipping channels until he found Channel 9.

"Hey, everybody," Jim called, "here's the news!" He turned up the volume.

Catherine started bouncing. "There I am!"

Marge Wolfe pulled the girl close and whispered, "And there's your mom and grandpa. Quiet now, sweetheart."

Mary focused on the TV screen, anxious to hear the version of events the media was presenting.

Reporter Mark Thomas flashed on the screen in a heavy trench coat with wind whipping his hair. "Supporters of Mary Weaver are obviously hopeful and optimistic, while the child's family says they can't believe Weaver is out of prison."

Mary's comment about driving away in the family car was back. They balanced that with a report from the other side by Melissa's grandmother, Tessia's mom. "Mary said she was excited today because she got to go home and see her kids. I don't get to see Melissa. Melissa's gone."

The screen flashed back to a smiling picture of Melissa and more trial details. Then back to the grandmother. "We believe it happened Monday in Mary's care. It was a concussion, and she was slowly getting better, and by Friday she was fine. And we believe the job wasn't finished, so she finished it Friday."

Reporter Mark Thomas resumed the report with talk about the different opinions in Marshalltown over her release, but Mary's mind stayed behind on the last report. Her stomach clenched. Soon the grandmother was back on camera. "When you're convicted of murder and you're in prison for life with no parole, that's where you should be and not out walking the streets."

Mary leaned against the wall, put her hand over her thumping heart, and blinked the tears out of her eyes. Accusations of giving Melissa a concussion on Monday, thinking about it for four days, and then finishing the job—it sounded so deliberate, so premeditated, evil beyond belief. But she should have expected this. First-degree murder was always premeditated, deliberate, evil—and she'd been convicted of the charge.

Reporters spoke of how this case had ripped Marshalltown down the middle. In the weeks to come, the media would show both sides of the issue. She would have to brace herself for comments from the opposing side. The parents who had once thanked her for saving their child's life now proclaimed her the killer at every interview.

Today she had gained her freedom. She could walk the streets freely, shop anywhere she wanted, interact with people around Eldora. But her case had divided the Marshalltown area. Many supported her, but some still viewed her as a baby killer.

One observation, however, soothed the pain a bit. The press could evidently find dozens of Mary's supporters eager to speak in her defense. Yet they had to resort to Melissa's family members to find someone to speak out against her.

# CHAPTER 30

Steve sat at his desk fingering Paul Rosenberg's business card. Paul Rosenberg and Associates—as if Paul had any. Paul seemed to enjoy the freedom of working alone. Steve would enjoy second chairing this third trial. He could help bear the heavy workload, but he wondered if Paul would want to share his place at the counsel table.

After Mary was released from prison, Steve had reopened the files from her first two trials and had begun to relive the case. Despair had rusted the legal gears in his brain, but new hope and fresh memories were beginning to free them. He could feel logic and legal strategies engaging again. He knew Mary's case like no one else. This was unfinished business that nagged for a happy ending. But would Paul want an associate, a young attorney who had already represented the client in two trials without clearing her name?

Steve dialed the number on the card.

Paul's secretary answered. "Paul Rosenberg and Associates."

"Steve Brennecke for Paul, please."

"Just a moment. I'll put you through."

Paul's voice broke the silence. "Yeah, Steve?"

Steve assumed the tone of an ardent admirer. "Oh, Mr. Rosenberg, I don't mean to bother you, sir. Please just put me through to one of your associates if you would."

"I fired them all, every last one of them." Both men laughed.

Steve sat forward in his chair and laid Paul's card down on his desk. "Seriously, I'm calling about Mary's trial. I'm wondering how this will work out, how things will mesh."

"You mean how we'll divide up the case? The witnesses?"

"Assuming we are both needed, yeah."

Paul sensed the issue immediately. "Absolutely. We'll do this as a team. Have you talked to Mary about this?"

"Not yet."

"I've read the transcripts, but you've lived through this thing, twice. We definitely want you at counsel table when we try it again."

Steve worked his shoulders and let the tension drain from the tight muscles. "What are you thinking? How should we divide the witnesses?"

"Now that you mention it..." Paul let the line go dead for a few seconds. "You were pretty wild with the doctors."

Steve knew the more experienced lawyer must have critiqued each of Steve's legal tactics as he'd read the transcripts. Steve needed to learn from experience, not guard his feelings. "Wild?"

"Yeah. You quizzed them like a detective about their opinions, findings on the autopsy, details. All that does is highlight their testimony. The doctors don't know what happened. They weren't there." Paul's voice raised a couple of notches. "When you chase after them and stomp on their presumptions and try to pin them to the mat, you just emphasize their testimony. Might as well install a neon sign over them that flashes to the jury, 'Important! Remember at all costs!'"

"So what do you suggest?"

"Questioning an expert witness is like flying a kite. They won't fly if you let go of the string. I'll fiddle with them a bit on cross-examination so the jury will see we're not afraid of them, and then I'll just let them go."

"I can help keep track of their prior testimony and where it differs, if it does."

"And the three ladies. Mrs. Wall, Mrs. Kail, and...the third one."

"Mrs. Braack." Steve jotted their names on a legal pad.

"Right. Mrs. Braack. I handled them at the new trial hearing when they took the prosecutor apart, so I'll do their testimony again. But Mary's testimony is yours. You do a good job handling direct exam, especially Mary's, so why don't you plan on that. And Dr. Ruth Ramsey. She was great, and you know each other now, so you take her as a witness too."

Steve jotted more notes as they finished the call and hung up with a renewed sense of purpose. He slipped Paul's card back into his wallet, searched through the transcripts for Mary's testimony, and began to prepare for the biggest trial of his life.

✿ ✿ ✿

Celebrations of her release helped Mary to focus on her freedom rather than on the years false accusations had stolen. She treasured ordinary moments with her children. Cleaning house and cooking meals brought new delight. Trips to the grocery store invited celebratory hugs and good wishes, some from people she barely knew.

As she entered her church for prayer meeting, Lucille Pierson announced her arrival as if she were a celebrity. "If you don't believe in prayer, just look at that miracle walking through the door."

About fifty of these people had prayed every Wednesday night for the truth to be known and justice to be done in Melissa's case. Other Christians formed prayer groups and prayed as well.

Supporters had kept her case on the front burner before God and men. They raised a large amount of funds. God had blessed the fund-raisers in such a spectacular way that it helped convince many Christians of Mary's innocence.

Jim had also worked continually at paying off the bills, but they still owed $15,000, and the third trial hadn't even begun. With the kids in school most of the day, Mary contemplated getting a job. Under the circumstances she couldn't consider baby-sitting in her home anymore, but she had other good job skills. Unfortunately she also had a prison record. She would need time off to meet with her attorneys and participate in the trial. Though she knew she was innocent and felt God had promised her she wouldn't go back into "captivity," she could offer a prospective employer no guarantees that she would be acquitted.

But Mary didn't have much time to worry about it. Within days of her pretrial release, Donna Blanchard, a former coworker, invited her to lunch. They discussed Mary's recent release and the upcoming trial. In time they began talking about work at Dodger Industries, a manufacturer of athletic clothing. Mary had worked for them for fifteen years before she decided to stay home with her two small children. Donna now worked as credit manager for the company.

Donna set her fork down and shifted in her seat. "Would you consider coming back to work in the credit department? We have an opening."

Mary could only stare at her for a few moments. Her former boss, Dick Ritter, had served as a character witness in both of her trials. He had testified to her ability to handle stressful events at work and respond well under pressure. But she hadn't expected this. This could only be God's provision.

A smile crept over Mary's face. "That's a generous offer. If you really want me, yes, I'd be glad to work there again."

God was good, and at this moment, life was good. Mary pushed away thoughts of the pending trial with its uncertainties and stressful days, and focused on what she had before her. Family, friends, church, job, and freedom to make her own choices. She even enjoyed driving by Iowa cornfields and seeing the long, straight rows waving in the wind.

In April Steve's mom, Jean, hosted a welcome-home reception for Mary at Al and Jean's house. The open house gave Mary three hours on a Sunday afternoon to chat with any of her friends and supporters who came. The celebrations kept coming in spite of the fact that she was only out of prison on bail, waiting for another trial.

As the celebrations settled down, however, Mary began to notice something. Her conviction had stolen two years of her life, and though it was good to be home, things at home had changed. Her family had changed.

In prison Mary had tried to focus on positive things. God had helped her through those years, but they were still the darkest days of her life.

She had spent two years in prison searching for answers from the Bible, growing in the Lord. Meanwhile, Jim had been shouldering all the parenting responsibilities as well as his full-time job. He had worked through the nanny problems, moved to a new house, worried about bills, consulted with attorneys and detectives. Two years of absence hadn't helped their marriage.

And Mary could only imagine the confusion Catherine and John had gone through. When this ordeal started the kids were so young that they were only allowed to watch the blandest of cartoons. Then two men in uniform had come to their house and taken their mommy away. Daddy told them Mommy had to go for a while. They stayed with their grandparents for several weeks. Then they witnessed the upheaval of changes in nannies and finally day care. Months later they could go visit Mommy once a week in a big building, but she could never come home.

Jim and Mary had tried to shield them from the awful truth that Mommy had been convicted of murder and sentenced to life in prison. They were young, but they had to notice people whispering about their mommy in low tones.

Jim and Mary made excuses while Catherine and John passed two birthdays with Mommy in prison. They even marched in a parade, wearing yellow T-shirts that read "I BELIEVE IN MY MOMMY." That was fun, but Mommy still didn't get to come home.

Finally all their friends had thrown a big party, and everyone hugged mommy, which seemed a bit silly. They had always expected Mommy to come home.

Now that she was home, Catherine and John clung to her like little pole bean vines. One day she got held up at work and was fifteen minutes late picking the kids up from school. She found John sitting on the curb. Tears washed clean streaks down his face.

Mary squatted beside him and put her arm around him. "John, what's wrong?"

He grabbed her neck so hard, she nearly toppled over. "I was afraid, Mommy."

Mary forgot her black work skirt and sat on the dirty curb. "Afraid of what?"

John just shook his head.

Mary pushed him away just enough to read his eyes. "What is it, John? If you're afraid of something, you need to tell me."

# CHAPTER 30

John pulled close and nestled his head on her shoulder. "Afraid you wouldn't come back. I don't want to lose you, Mommy."

Mary hugged him close and dabbed at her own tears. She wanted to promise him that she would always come back, that he would never lose her again, but no parent could guarantee that. She, of all people, knew that.

"John, you don't have to be afraid. God is always with us. He will take care of us."

"But I want you, Mommy. Before you came home and we had the big party at our house, you were gone so long. I don't want to lose you again."

Mary stroked his fine red hair. "I know, John. We want to be together, and God has brought us together again. Isn't it great? I try real hard to be on time to pick you and Catherine up, but if I'm ever late again, that doesn't mean...Well, sometimes life makes us late, but that doesn't mean something bad has happened. I love you guys so much, and I just think God's going to keep us together. Okay?"

John sniffed, and Mary knew it was the best answer she could honestly give.

# CHAPTER 31

Steve stared down at the unbelievable letters. How many months had he doubted God, wondered why God kept his hands in his pockets, and shrugged his shoulders while Mary was serving each unjust day of her life sentence? These letters were proof that God had been working all through the silent months of her imprisonment.

Since her conviction in March 1994, Mary's supporters had kept her case alive in editorials and letters. Frank Santiago had raised the profile enormously that August with his two-and-a-half-page article in the *Des Moines Register*. The media attention Steve had expected to move to the back burner still burned on high by October of 1995, when the three ladies stepped forward with their testimony. That evidence was sufficient reason for Judge Goode to grant them a new trial, but God had been working in other ways they couldn't see. The letters proved that.

This high-profile case had captured the attention of Justice Barney Donielson. At the time of Mary's appeal, Judge Donielson was the senior-most member of the court of appeals and one of the original judges appointed in 1976, when the court was created. Although he wasn't on the three-judge panel who heard the oral arguments in Mary's case, he joined in the court's decision to affirm her conviction. But something about the case bothered him. Perhaps it was Judge Sackett's persuasive dissent. Perhaps it was a sense that the decision might have technical merit yet led to the wrong conclusion, a concern the continuing public outcry about Mary's imprisonment boldly reinforced. Whatever the case, he promptly sent a copy of the decision to his breakfast club acquaintance, Dr. Thomas Carlstrom, a prominent Des Moines neurosurgeon.

Dr. Carlstrom reviewed the judicial opinion in which Melissa's autopsy findings were extensively detailed. He shot back a letter to Justice Donielson on October 2, 1995, only ten days after the court of appeals' decision was handed down and a full ten days before Paul would ask the Iowa Supreme Court to grant further review. Steve remembered the dates on the letters to be the very darkest days of Mary's case.

Steve scanned the letter from "Dear Barney" to the incredible conclusion.

Given the information that I have, I would find it very hard to rule that Mary Weaver caused the death of this child. The fact that there was a significant head injury seven to ten days prior, particularly with the subdural hematoma, the intracerebral hemorrhage, and the edema, all indicate to me that this child's brain was extremely vulnerable to a very mild re-injury, perhaps even something like a cough or a sneeze. In particular, the pathological notation of sagittal sinus thrombosis disturbs me. This is an almost 100% fatal complication of head injuries, and when it occurs, death occurs rapidly. The sagittal sinus thrombosis could cause all of the findings noted in the pathology that were described as acute. It would seem to me much more likely that this child died of the sagittal sinus thrombosis, acutely. Based on the information that I read here, and the information from the paper, it would seem to me that Mrs. Weaver is entirely innocent in this particular case.

Steve let the letter drop to his desk. Carlstrom agreed with Rose and DiMaio. He believed that Melissa could have easily died from her older injuries, completely apart from any new injuries that last Friday. Judge Donielson had passed away on January 30, 1996, the day before Mary's new trial was granted, but Carlstrom hadn't let the matter drop.

Steve reread a second letter dated April 29, 1996, that Carlstrom had dictated and sent to Paul Rosenberg. Steve skimmed the first paragraph to focus on the golden words of the last.

"In summary," Carlstrom wrote, "I think the injury that caused this child's death was inflicted a week to ten days prior to the incident for which Mrs. Weaver has been charged. I would be happy to speak with you about this if you wish."

If you wish? Did a drowning man wish to grab a life preserver? This wasn't three housewives exchanging words with a mother in Hardee's. This was a neurosurgeon who practiced medicine on live patients with injuries like Melissa's. Bennett performed autopsies and spent time testifying and building a resume that looked like the Des Moines phone book. Carlstrom was too busy doing brain surgery and saving lives to build an impressive resume, but he understood brain injuries. The jury would see Carlstrom as a doctor they would trust if their own brain was injured. He had reviewed the case and felt so strongly about it that he was willing to initiate contact with Mary's lawyers.

Steve set the letters aside and rubbed his eyes. In the darkest hours of Mary's case, after her conviction and before any new evidence had come to light, God had been preparing an even better defense than she had enjoyed during her first trials. Steve was beginning to see how God caused events to come together in a precise timing that worked for Mary's good. The thought was reassuring and troubling at the same time. If he accepted God's timing as perfect, that God was truly in control, then logic led him to an inevitable conclusion. God must have allowed Mary to go to prison for a good reason. Steve had a hard time getting his head around that.

Even now, the thought that Mary could once again be convicted forced him to tether his high hopes with a solid rope of reality. Though Judge Goode had granted them a new trial, that decision was still on appeal. They couldn't be sure of getting a new trial until the Iowa Supreme Court affirmed it. After the oral arguments in July, the court could reverse Goode's decision and send her back to prison, or they could affirm Goode's decision and let the case proceed to trial.

Nothing was guaranteed yet.

✿ ✿ ✿

On July 18, Mary and Jim sat across the aisle from Brad and Tessia in the Iowa Supreme Court. Again Mary's supporters filled the chairs and left many standing in the gallery. Prosecutors asked the high court to reject Judge Goode's ruling that granted Mary a new trial on the basis of the testimony of the three ladies.

The state, represented at the arguments by the Iowa Attorney General's office, argued that Judge Goode had used the wrong legal standard to grant Mary a new trial. They argued that Goode determined that the women's statements could have possibly affected the outcome of Mary's second trial. Instead, he should have determined whether their statements probably would have affected the outcome. The court should overturn Goode's decision to grant Mary a new trial because of his "erroneous use of judicial standard."

Paul never flinched. Standing before the packed supreme court gallery, facing five justices of the court, Paul argued from the solid legal justifications outlined in Goode's order.

Mary reminded herself of Paul's reassurances prior to the hearing. Judge Goode's ruling was thorough. The supreme court would reverse his decision only if the judge had "abused his discretion" and if his decision was "clearly unreasonable." She knew she had a strong case for a new trial.

When the arguments were over, Mary began another period of waiting for their decision. Two months later, nearly six months after her release from prison, Paul informed Mary that the ruling on her case would be handed down the morning of September 18.

That Wednesday morning Mary gathered with about thirty of her supporters outside Jim's auto parts store in Eldora. Mary's dad, Jerry Bartlett, hung close to her as she hovered by the phone chatting excitedly with supporters.

The phone only had to ring once. Mary grabbed it.

"It's unanimous," Paul said. "You got a new trial!"

"Woo-hoo!" Mary cheered, holding the phone high in the air. "Unanimous decision for a new trial!"

Her dad hugged her so hard her glasses almost fell off.

Cameras clicked from every direction. "Praise the Lord!" echoed over and over again across the crowd. Farmers, business people, and housewives all exchanged hugs and pulled out handkerchiefs.

Mary pulled the receiver close to her ear again to listen to more details from Paul. He read parts of the ruling. "The court ruled that the judge who reviewed the new evidence was in the best position to evaluate its potential impact on the case. Chief Justice McGiverin wrote, 'We give weight to the district court's conclusion that the new evidence would change the decision to convict Weaver of first-degree murder.'" Mary couldn't absorb it all over the phone, but this much she understood very clearly: she would have one more chance to clear her name.

# CHAPTER 31

She pushed her concerns aside to hug supporters. These people had ridden with her as her roller coaster ride to justice plunged to dark depths of uncertainty. Her case would likely include some more drops and rolls, but today they would enjoy the exhilaration of high hopes and celebration. The justices of the Iowa Supreme Court seemed to favor her chances of winning, and they had spoken unanimously.

During some of her most difficult days, God had whispered so softly it was hard to hear his voice, but today even doubters couldn't ignore the sounds of hope. God was speaking to those who would listen, "I've been there all the time."

Soon after Mary returned home the phone rang. Two years after his initial interview with her, Frank Santiago was still following her case in the *Des Moines Register.* Mary felt God had stirred his interest in her case to keep the case alive.

Frank exchanged greetings and talked about the morning's phone call. "Obviously, this is good news, Mary. Tell me how you feel right now."

Mary forced herself to focus. She trusted Frank, but she had to give him good answers. Anything she said could be quoted many times over. "I feel so relieved that this part is over. It renews my confidence in the legal system."

"Melissa died more than three and a half years ago. You've been through two trials and two years in prison. Prosecutors can choose to retry the case or drop the charges. What do you hope will happen at this point?"

Mary was glad she had already considered the question before the ruling came down. "I hope they retry the case, even though that means I would risk being convicted again. Of course, I want my name to be cleared, but we also want the truth to come out. We want to know what caused that first injury."

At the end of their conversation, Santiago asked the question Mary had learned to expect with every interview. "Mary, you've been through some very traumatic years since you were first accused of Melissa's murder. Some doctors think the fatal injury occurred shortly before Melissa died, and some think the injury was inflicted seven to ten days before her death. Her injuries obviously point to a very severe, intentional trauma. Who do you think caused Melissa's death?"

Mary breathed deeply and considered her words carefully. "I have to remind myself that I don't know what happened to Melissa. I was falsely accused, and I'm not going to accuse somebody when I don't know."

After the excitement outside Jim's auto parts store, Mary waited week after week to hear from the court system as they scheduled a time to try her case. Mostly she tried to forget about the upcoming trial and just keep to a normal routine with her family.

Finally the scheduling order was issued, and Paul called to inform Mary: her trial date was set for February 18, 1997. More than four years after Melissa's death, Mary would get one more chance to clear her name. In another four months it could all be over.

☆ ☆ ☆

Steve added another file to the stack of files on his desk. One more case closed. One more job done. These simple cases were composed mostly of criminal defense cases for indigent clients, child-in-need-of-assistance cases, real estate matters, and a smattering of civil litigation for small-town clients. These were the bread-and-butter cases of a small-town Iowa lawyer. They paid the bills. They kept him in touch with people in great need, and that realization filled him with a sense of satisfaction. Each time he closed a file, he felt he had helped mankind a little.

Before her conviction, Mary's complex case had dominated much of his life. His conversations with Kim often centered on the case. When his mind was bogged down in the morass of medical testimony from scores of the state's witnesses, Kim's insight became invaluable. Mary's case hovered on the edge of every thought and conversation. He even kept a legal pad on the nightstand for times when strategies for Mary's defense called more loudly than sleep.

Now that Paul Rosenberg was leading her defense, the pressure had eased. They would divide up the witnesses for this final effort, which would free both of them to focus more intently on countering each bit of testimony that would be aimed at Mary. Sharing the load made the labor more enjoyable, and the friendly banter that formed naturally among Paul, Steve, and Mary eased the friction and stresses they faced together. After all, she was still being tried for murder in the first degree. Her freedom was still in jeopardy.

Steve hadn't really talked to Mary much lately. The only news about her case had been a change of venue. The trial would be held in Fort Dodge so the jurors would be less likely to be tainted by all the newspaper publicity and activities of the support group in Marshalltown. It was time to talk, to catch up on things, and to begin to turn her attention to the trial that was looming ahead.

He leaned back in his chair and dialed the number. Mary chatted about family picnics and the sweet corn harvest. Finally Steve turned the conversation toward the trial.

"I'm sure it's been good to be back with your family. Catherine and John really need you. I feel bad that you had to miss two years of their life."

Mary's voice became serious, intense. "For the record, Steve, my conviction was not your fault. I don't feel like you cost me two years of my life in prison or anything like that. God allowed it. We don't know why, but I know you did your best to represent me."

"I'm glad you're back at home now, enjoying your family, rebuilding your life, but we've got to get ready for your third trial. It's great to have the three ladies now and Dr. Carlstrom, but we're going to face the same medical experts we faced in your first two trials, and by now we can't surprise them with much of anything."

"I know. No guarantees."

"Paul's the best appellate lawyer in the state, but we're going to have to give this trial our best preparation and effort."

"Of course."

Steve hunted for words, wanting to delve deeper, but not sure how to begin. "You always seem so cheerful, but I know your time in prison must have had an impact. You must have some difficult adjustments. How are you really doing, Mary?"

Silence filled the line for several moments. Steve prepared himself for the darker side of reality.

"I love being with my family. Even cleaning house is a treat after prison. I know I have a lot to be thankful for, but I do have one real problem."

"What's that?"

"I feel more distant from God now. I had some dark days in prison, but God seemed so close to me there. I know he hasn't left me or anything. I'm just busy with things. In prison I had all the time I wanted to read the Bible and pray. But since I got out, my life has been so…distracted."

Steve searched for an answer to that, finally muttered something, and ended the call. After he hung up, he spent several quiet moments burning her answer into his memory.

When Mary went to prison, Steve had begun the fiercest struggle with faith he had ever experienced. Meanwhile, this ordinary

# CHAPTER 31

baby-sitter, separated from her family and with little evidence to give her hope for the future, was building a simple but powerful faith in God. Prison hadn't wounded her faith. It had made it stronger.

# Chapter 32

**M**ary stroked the pink snowsuit Melissa had been wearing when she quit breathing. Three and a half years had passed since that awful day, but Mary could still remember it clearly. How many times had she relived those dreadful minutes when she struggled to save the baby's life?

Mary, Paul, and Steve sat around a huge table of evidence. The state's attorneys, Douglas Marek and Virginia Barchman, both assistant attorneys general for the state of Iowa, sifted through the same materials. Any evidence to be used for or against Mary during the third trial had been laid out on this table for both sides to review.

Mary dropped the snowsuit to examine other items. Today they were reviewing the pieces of evidence, not revisiting grief. Thankfully Paul and Steve kept these moments light, even joking between themselves. That made it so much easier.

Mary skimmed over police reports, medical records, and curriculum vitae for the various doctors. She'd leave them for the lawyers. Audiotapes of the 9-1-1 call and police interviews formed another pile. Steve had already pulled transcripts of these tapes from the first two trials. Mary shuffled through some photos: the Cookie Monster chair Tessia said Melissa had fallen out of, the recliner Melissa had evidently hit, the Kool-Aid smile.

## CHAPTER 32

Mary stared at the last picture, a key piece of evidence in the state's case. A happy, normal Melissa held her Kool-Aid cup. A red curve of Kool-Aid accented her grin. Brad and Tessia had testified that this picture with Melissa's grandma was taken on Thursday evening before Melissa's seizure. The prosecution claimed it was the last photo of Melissa taken while she was alive, that the next pictures were taken at her autopsy. The state had used the photo to suggest Melissa had recovered from her earlier illness and would be alive today if Mary hadn't abused and killed her the following morning.

Mary flipped past that picture, a cropped enlargement, to find the original photograph. Wait! Something was wrong here. During the first two trials Ms. Tomlinson had displayed a cropped version of the picture. This original contradicted the prosecution's story. Mary moved on to other photos to hide her interest but came back to the original twice to confirm her first impression. This picture proved someone was lying. In fact, more than one person was lying.

She forced herself to move on. She held CT scans up to the light as if she could read them, but didn't even pretend to examine the grisly autopsy pictures. When enough time had passed, she strolled over to Steve.

She fingered some bound medical reports. "Finding anything?"

Steve rifled through a report file. "Seems like we've seen all this stuff before, but it can't hurt to look again."

Steve and Paul moved close to the photos. Mary moved with them. She glanced at the state's attorneys to make sure their eyes were averted, then tapped the photo of the Kool-Aid smile with a little more force than was necessary. She arched a meaningful eyebrow at her attorneys. "Melissa was a little sweetie."

267

Steve caught the eyebrow signal with the benign words and studied the picture more closely. He and Paul exchanged gestures of confusion.

At the end of their examination, Mary and her two lawyers strolled to the elevator, rode it to the first floor, and found the exit. Outside the building Paul nudged Steve. "What were you guys looking at in there?"

Mary blinked extra moisture from her eyes. "The secret of the Kool-Aid smile. The state has been using a cropped version, but the original tells a part of the story we haven't heard before."

Steve shook his head. "Were you looking at the calendar on the fridge in the background? I was trying to read it, but I couldn't quite make it out."

"I didn't even look at the calendar, but I did notice the sunlight streaming in the window. A little unusual for an Iowa evening in January, wouldn't you say?"

✡ ✡ ✡

Mary sipped coffee and watched the dust particles dance in the light from the window. Nothing unusual on a winter's day in her living room but totally unbelievable on a winter's evening.

She considered the implications of their newfound evidence. During the first two trials, she had felt compassion for the Mathes family. She knew they had to be hiding something, but she didn't know what had injured the baby. She wondered if it could have possibly been an accidental injury the family had covered up. Or possibly they had suspected who may have inflicted the fatal injuries but kept quiet because they weren't sure.

Now she knew the picture couldn't have been taken the evening before Melissa's seizure as Tessia had testified. Brad and Tessia had produced the photo for the prosecutor to use, and

# CHAPTER 32

Tessia had deliberately lied about it. They had to have known Mary wasn't guilty and that the photo helped frame her for murder. Mary tried to think of some other explanation for the discrepancy, but she knew there was none.

Mary had provided loving child care for this family for six months. She had fought to save Melissa's life after the terrifying seizure. And Tessia had repaid her by using a photo from a happier time to intentionally frame Mary for murder. The realization stabbed her stomach like a knife, deeply plunged, and twisted for maximum damage.

Anger churned inside her, stealing her peace with God. Dr. Bennett may have cut corners on the autopsy to get a conviction. Dr. Smith and Dr. Alexander may have spoken with more confidence than they should have. But at least they must have truly believed she was guilty. Brad and Tessia had to have known she wasn't guilty but were willing to frame her for murder anyway.

Mary deserted her coffee, filled a bucket with hot, soapy water, and began scrubbing her kitchen floor on her hands and knees.

She could understand why Brad and Tessia would lie about a detail like this. They had to be shielding someone. But why would God allow this false testimony to go unchallenged? Why would he allow her to go to prison for a crime she didn't commit?

Mary scrubbed the floor with more vigor than usual, working off the destructive emotions.

The revelation about the photo changed nothing. Someone had hurt Melissa. Mary wasn't the one who hurt her. The true killer hadn't been revealed. Someone was hiding evidence to protect the true killer. Same as always, but a new realization of an old truth stung like salt in an old wound.

God wasn't done with her case yet. Very soon the lies behind the photo would be challenged. They had discovered the photo in time for her new trial.

Mary scrubbed the corners of the floor close to the cupboards. They would begin this third trial with new evidence, new witnesses. Perhaps this time they would clear her name. It seemed like an awfully long process, and she didn't understand why God allowed it to take so long or why he allowed her to go to prison. But she had a choice. She could focus on her feelings of betrayal and become a bitter, angry person. Or she could let God work out the situation and concentrate on spending time with her family and enjoying every day of freedom.

She continued to scrub until the dirt was gone and she was afraid of stripping the gloss off the linoleum. Then she dumped the water and collapsed onto the couch. Her arms ached, and her emotions were raw.

She considered her options. Anger would imprison her spirit and destroy her life. Submission to God would free her spirit to enjoy life. Anger was far too heavy a burden for her to carry. She had to let it go. This wasn't a victory she could win in a day. She would fight this battle day after day, but she would fight it. She wouldn't allow bitterness to rob her of any more life.

Mostly Mary tried to forget about the trial and just keep to a normal routine in her family, but even normal life presented challenges. At one point Mary caught a cold with a never-ending cough. John sneaked into her bedroom one afternoon while she was napping and poked her awake.

Mary's eyes popped open. A dull headache persisted in spite of pain relievers. She turned to her son. "Mommy was sleeping, John. What do you want?"

He stared at the carpet like a puppy who had forgotten his paper training. "I just wanted to know…"

# CHAPTER 32

Mary rubbed her forehead, willing the ache to subside. "What, John? What did you want to know?"

"If you were dead."

Mary stroked his cheek. "I'm very much alive. I'm not feeling very good. I'm sick. Everyone gets sick. But in a few days I'll feel better again."

He bunched the blanket into a knot around his fingers. "I hope so. I don't want you to die. Promise me, Mommy. Promise me you won't die."

Mary considered appropriate promises and discarded them all. "No one can promise that, John. No one knows how long he'll live. But God has worked so hard to bring us together again that I really think he plans to keep us together for a long time."

John walked around the bed, lifted the covers, and crawled in beside Mary, dirty tennis shoes and all. He grabbed onto her germ-laden hand and wouldn't let go.

Mary prayed that God would help her know how to deal with the confusion, anger, and fears that had grown in her children. Jim and Mary had worked hard to protect the hearts of their kids from realities that were too harsh for them to understand. They refused to lie, but even their excuses left plenty of room for confusion.

Day by day Mary weathered the challenges, focusing on the fact that the worst was behind her. After two years in prison, life could only get better. She couldn't believe she would return to prison.

But why was it easier to trust God with her own problems than with the problems of her family? Mary prayed that the third trial would end in a clear acquittal that would decisively clear her name. Then her family could jump past the confusion of Melissa's death and return to their role as a normal Iowa family.

Then she could promise her kids that she would never go back to prison. Her name would be cleared. In time her kids would lose their constant fear of losing their mommy.

In the middle of the night, when Mary couldn't sleep, she tried to focus on the new evidence they had for the third trial. Surely that would make the difference. But Mary knew she had no guarantees. The prosecution had the two previous trials to teach them how to hone their strategies. Juries were unpredictable. A case might seem clear to the judge or the people in the gallery, but only the jury could decide the verdict.

So while Mary remained optimistic, during nights when sleep refused to come, she knew she needed to answer these questions: What if she was convicted again and sent back to prison? What would her kids think when their mommy was taken away a second time? Would she still trust God? She didn't think she'd be convicted, but then she hadn't thought she'd be convicted the first time. She couldn't imagine why God would let her go back to prison, but she didn't know why he'd allowed her to go to prison in the first place.

✦ ✦ ✦

As the trial date neared, Mary knew very soon she would face the accusations all over again. A higher level of prosecutors would cross-examine her. Jury members and a courtroom of people would watch her reaction. Cameras would record it. TV viewers across Iowa would want to know if her faith was real or only an act.

She would remain optimistic, but here in the quietness of the night she needed to prepare for any eventuality. Days before the trial, Mary settled the matter in her heart. While Jim snored beside her in bed, she talked to God.

# CHAPTER 32

"Lord, make me real," she prayed. "I really think I'm going to be acquitted this time. But I know that your faithfulness doesn't depend on an acquittal. You were faithful to me in prison, and I know you'll keep on being faithful, whatever the verdict is. I want to see Melissa's true killer found and brought to justice, but I'm going to leave that in your hands too.

"God, you know why everything happens, and that is enough. You're in control of my life and this verdict. I'm glad I'm not. I could never figure out these things.

"Lord, I ask you to clear my name in this next trial. I believe you will. But just for the record, Lord, even if for some reason I'm convicted again, I'll still trust you."

With that she fell asleep.

The next morning Mary went into Catherine's room to change the sheets. As she pulled the fitted sheet off the bed, an envelope fell to the floor. Mary picked it up and examined the address. It was addressed to "Jim, Catherine, and John Weaver." She recognized the return address of a distant friend. The postmark was over a year old.

Mary opened the envelope and pulled out a card with flowers on the front. Written inside the card was one word. "Prayers."

Jim kept a huge box in the closet of all the letters Mary had received in prison. But Mary hadn't given much thought to the cards and letters that friends and supporters had sent to her family. Catherine had evidently pulled this card from their personal stash. Dog-eared corners and sticky finger marks revealed what a treasure it was to the seven-year-old.

Mary clutched the letter to her heart and whispered to God.

"Lord, thank you for putting into the mind of this friend, over a year ago, to write this simple one-word letter. You knew it could reach the heart of a little girl who missed her mommy and didn't understand why her mommy couldn't come home."

She brushed a tear from her cheek. "My heart grieved for my children. I longed to be with them, but that was not part of your plan. Instead you gave them aunties and uncles to care for them, give them presents, take them swimming, and include them in family activities. You surrounded them with the love of others, who became family for them. When I couldn't put my arms around my children, you used the arms of others.

"My prison years have been hard on all of the family. It will take time to heal, and in time I believe it'll make us strong. But Lord God, you have provided for me and my family so well during our darkest days in the past. I know I can also trust you with our future."

# Chapter 33

Tomorrow Steve would get his chance at redemption. His chance to right a wrong, to correct a failure. Mary's third trial would begin and Steve determined to get it right this time. It might be their last chance to keep Mary out of prison and clear her name.

He turned down the heater in his Fort Dodge hotel room and removed his sweater. The heater ticked off. Temperature highs had reached the upper fifties today, a rare warm spell in an Iowa winter. Steve knew the weather had no bearing on the trial, but somehow it raised his hopes even higher.

*Failure.* For months the word had knotted his stomach and caused his shoulders to slump. Had he failed during the first two trials? He had done his best, but already he had learned from Paul some things he could have done better. Paul's skill and insight had been honed and refined through years of trial experience. The older lawyer had read the transcripts from the earlier trials, hearings, and depositions—and patiently shared his insights with Steve.

During the first two trials Steve had aggressively questioned the doctors. Paul advised Steve not to go after doctors like that. Steve wasn't a doctor, and doctors could talk circles around him.

Steve had also tried to show that other people could be guilty, thus absolving Mary of guilt. He had introduced the evidence of Tessia's inquiry into the cost of a grave space before her baby died. Paul didn't even want to raise that issue in the third trial. He said it was too risky. It pushed the jury toward the one conclusion that was harder to accept than convicting the baby-sitter—convicting a family member. Steve wished he had known that two trials earlier.

As Steve was learning new trial strategies, he was also attempting to refine his belief about God. Had he failed during the first two trials, or had God? Or was failure part of the plan? Steve was just beginning to trust again, even when the line between failure and success proved hard to discern.

He felt like a toddler in the school of theology, but even as a child in the faith, he knew these things: God was good. God loved him and Mary and their families. God had stuck his hands in his pockets and watched Mary be sentenced to life in prison for a crime she didn't commit. Steve didn't understand this, but he realized he'd been walking by sight, not by faith. It was time for him to be a faith walker.

The entire community had followed Mary's second trial and the aftermath. The media had given them great coverage, listing reasons to doubt Mary's guilt and showcasing her clear Christian testimony and trust in God. The guilty verdict had divided the town of Marshalltown and much of the state, though the majority seemed to support Mary's claim of innocence. Many wondered: With so much reasonable doubt, how could Judge Peterson have found her guilty? And If Mary was innocent, who was the true killer?

Hard questions, but this one was more difficult: If Mary was innocent, how could God have allowed her to be convicted and the true killer to go free? Mary's reputation wasn't the only one at stake here. God was on trial too.

# CHAPTER 33

They had to win this next trial. The stakes were too high to consider any other possibility. Somebody had to stop those who were overzealous in their pursuit of shaken-baby cases.

"Somebody's got to stop these guys." Steve smiled at the memory of their first meeting with Carlstrom. He and Paul had met him in this office one afternoon. The doctor was short but solid and carried himself like someone you didn't want to mess with.

Paul asked him what he thought after reading the court of appeals' summary of the case.

"Why aren't authorities looking into Melissa's prior injury?" Carlstrom asked. "That's what I want to know. That injury made it much more likely she would suffer a second, life-threatening injury. It may have even been inflicted unintentionally."

Paul leaned back in the comfortable office chair. "Guess you can't blame the police. Bennett, Smith, and Alexander seem to be ignoring the prior injuries too."

Carlstrom perched one hip on the edge of his desk, ready to jump into the battle. "They talk like all the research supports their shaken-baby theories. What about the study in Philadelphia of forty-eight real babies and young children who were diagnosed with SBS? Those researchers concluded that an otherwise normal baby is unlikely to get that kind of injuries by shaking alone. An impact had to occur as well. But you don't hear much about those studies, do you?"

Steve cleared his throat and broke into the conversation. "Bennett, Smith, and Alexander all seemed to place a lot of emphasis on retinal hemorrhages. What do you think?"

Carlstrom waved the thought away. "Yeah, all these shaken-baby believers want to set retinal hemorrhages and brain swelling as markers for shaking babies—like there's no other cause of those injuries. That's just not true. Bunch of stinking pathologists don't know what they're talking about. Believe me, I know. I work on live people, not cadavers like Bennett."

Paul never so much as shifted in his seat, but his eyes probed deeper. "You think Bennett's a little overzealous?"

"Sure. Bennett and his cronies. Prosecutors too. In rare cases babies may be shaken to death, but they make it sound like it happens all the time, and I suspect innocent people are being sent to jail. Of course it makes Bennett look good when he gets a child abuser convicted. Looks like they're winning the war on child abuse. Who wouldn't want that? So what if we're sending innocent people to prison?" He punched his fist into his other hand. "These pathologists need to be more careful about their testimony. But no one wants to challenge them because it makes you look like you support child abuse. What idiot would be stupid enough to do that?"

Paul grinned. "Evidently you are."

"Somebody's got to stop these guys."

Now Steve sat in his hotel room, preparing to do just that. They could only do their best and then leave the verdict in God's hands. He had already given them new hope.

Muffled voices passed by in the hallway.

Steve dragged a heavy box over the carpet to a spot by the easy chair. Filled with the equivalent of about four thick Des Moines phone books, this box contained bound transcripts from Mary's second trial along with medical records, police records, depositions, and hearings. Markers and sticky notes protruded from the open edges. One of Steve's jobs in this trial would be to follow the testimony of witnesses and compare it to earlier trials. Steve had studied the transcripts until his head was so crammed full of information he could hardly sleep at night. Right now Steve used the heavy box as an end table.

# CHAPTER 33

Weary from reading the transcripts but unwilling to waste his last evening before the trial, he opened his briefcase and pulled out James McElhaney's book, *Litigation.* He flipped through the book and reread highlighted passages about new strategies they would try during this third trial.

The author's theory on primacy maintained that what you hear first is what you are more likely to accept as true. The recency principle stated that you could more easily recall the last thing you heard. Since some of the doctors would testify for more than two hours, these theories could help him and Paul determine the order to ask their questions to make the strongest impact on the jury. Steve needed to rearrange his questions for Mary's testimony.

McElhaney said a trial was like a play, broken up into acts and scenes. The jury was the audience. The lawyers and witnesses were the actors. The jury decided which team of lawyers to believe and trust. A lawyer's goal was simple. With each witness he wanted the jury to conclude that he was the "good guy" and his opponent was the "bad guy." When the jury could see that they were trying to reveal the truth, they would wear the white hat. If their objections made them look like they were trying to hide something, they would wear the black hat.

If Steve and Paul could keep wearing white hats when the state wore black ones, they would keep the jury on their side.

This concept was new to Steve, and he had resolved to look for examples of this in the coming trial. He hoped to use this to encourage them during the arduous next few weeks.

Steve set the book on his makeshift end table and scribbled a few reminders on a legal pad.

Today, after the jury was selected, Steve and Paul had discussed their strategies for this third trial.

"We're not going to pit our forensic pathologists toe-to-toe with theirs," Paul said. "That just turns the whole thing into an argument between brainiacs about dead tissue from dead bodies."

"Then what are you thinking?"

"The jury's going to love Dr. Carlstrom. He can testify about Melissa's case as a practitioner who would try to help her cling to life. I think he'll bring a whole new feel to the case. His testimony about the skull fracture and older fatal injuries will do away with this silly notion that Melissa was fine when Mary picked her up. Carlstrom is our strongest witness. He's going to clinch this case for us."

Maybe this time they could show Mary wasn't the killer clearly enough to force the police to search for the true killer. Mary's acquittal was their top priority, but the injustice of a baby killer who walked free still burned within him. Police weren't even looking for the person who had inflicted the baby's fatal blows. Steve wouldn't consider this case closed until that person was justly convicted of the crime.

Then he could move on with his life. This case had eaten up four years of his life with failures, doubts, and second guesses. Some of those days had been the blackest in his life, when he'd felt far from God and didn't know how to get back. Though he had learned to trust God again, he could scarcely imagine the relief he would feel when this case was over. He could spend more time with his family. Smile more, worry less. Help needy people with smaller problems that didn't keep him awake at night.

Steve could hardly wait to file this case away for good and be done with it—forever. Yet another drama hovered just around the corner. One he didn't even want to think about.

Steve reached for another file from his briefcase and flipped it open. He lifted a newspaper article and stared at another baby's face. Like his own newly adopted baby, this one was named Brennan. On Christmas Eve the Hutchinsons had held their six-month-old son in Decorah, Iowa. After hours of showing flu-like symptoms, the baby died in his mother's arms. Bennett performed the autopsy and diagnosed shaken baby syndrome.

Steve reached for another article. On February 8, just days ago in Charles City, three-month-old Levi Sansgard's parents had found him dead in his crib. The family doctor, also the Floyd County medical examiner, diagnosed SIDS. Bennett called it SBS.

A third article showed that some researchers believed that several hundred baby deaths a year, once diagnosed as SIDS, were actually SBS. The writer of the article felt many more deaths should be attributed to SBS. Carlstrom was right when he said this diagnosing innocent deaths as SBS was becoming a very dangerous growing trend.

Only God knew what had truly happened in these hundreds of SIDS cases. Steve's lawyer hunches told him that perhaps some of the cases were murders, but most of them probably weren't. The parents were innocent people like Mary who'd had the misfortune of being alone with a baby who died. Medical experts were taught to spot abuse, but sometimes they couldn't know which cases were caused by abuse and which deaths had other causes. How could they catch abuse without accusing innocent people? How many other innocent people were victims of a presumption of guilt?

Somebody needed to fight for other innocent people who, like Mary, had been accused of murder.

Steve closed the file and stuffed it in his briefcase. This wasn't his problem. He was a young lawyer with two small children at home. He had already given four years to defend Mary. Her case had raised the profile of the problem, helped the cause. But he was battle weary. Now reinforcements needed to march into the fray and challenge medical and legal experts not to cut corners to get a conviction.

Someone other than him needed to slow this freight train of SBS accusations. Greater caution might mean the occasional child abuser would go unpunished, but American law was clear about the need for presumption of innocence. It maintained that it was better to let ninety-nine guilty people go free than to take the liberties of one innocent person. Without presumption of innocence, average Americans were in grave danger.

Mary Weaver could be the poster mom for innocent mothers accused of murder, but they would have to look elsewhere for a poster lawyer.

Steve snapped his briefcase shut at the sound of a low but determined knock on his door.

He heard Paul call his name and yanked the door open.

Paul had lost his smile and worry lines furrowed his brow. "Cindy Carlstrom is dead. Dr. Carlstrom's wife."

Steve stared at Paul in disbelief. "What happened?"

"Just saw it on the news. You know that nice weather we've been having? It melted the snow so fast that it caused rising water levels and ice jams on the Raccoon River. Cindy's car was swept away into a gravel pit. She drowned."

Would Carlstrom testify for them within days of his beloved wife's funeral? Steve felt guilty for even considering the thought at this time of grief for the neurosurgeon, but he knew Paul was thinking the same thing.

In the battle for Mary's acquittal, they may have just lost their most potent weapon.

# Chapter 34

Steve tossed and turned for hours before he finally drifted off to sleep. As soon as his eyes popped open the next morning, he scooted to the door and reached out for the newspaper. "Swept to her death," the headline of the *Des Moines Register* read. A photo of Lucinda Carlstrom, a short-haired blonde, shared the front page with the photo of her bereaved husband.

The article told how Cindy Carlstrom was driving to a bridge lesson at her country club when she got into trouble. Floodwater swept her 1997 Oldsmobile Bravada a thousand feet from the road to a gravel pit filled with water. "As the deceptively powerful floodwater pushed her south," it said, "Carlstrom used her cellular telephone to dial 9-1-1 at 9:18 a.m. The call ended abruptly before she could give her location to Des Moines Police Department dispatchers...The same water that swept Carlstrom away prevented rescue crews from reaching the site before boats could be brought in by the various units comprising the Central Iowa Search and Rescue team."

Steve read in horror as the article described a 9-1-1 call that had started calmly but escalated to panic within seconds. Her final words were, "I need help right away! I'm going under water!"

9-1-1. "I'm going under water!" "I have a baby that's stopped breathing!" The voices of Cindy Carlstrom and Mary mingled in Steve's mind.

Steve finished the article, then returned to the front page to study the photo of the neurosurgeon with the familiar receding hairline. His head was buried in the shoulder of some unknown person. His hands were clasped around the person's shoulders. He hung onto the person as if he had insufficient strength to support his own weight. The photo spelled out devastation of a man who had lost his high school sweetheart and wife of thirty years.

The heartbreaking pictures printed indelible images on his mind. The attractive Cindy Carlstrom with hundreds of friends and a heart for her family. The grieving doctor, who had so suddenly joined the ranks of grieving widowers. Divers and rescue workers in a boat preparing to search for her vehicle.

Steve prayed for God's comfort for this generous man. His concern was for Dr. Carlstrom first of all, but Steve's lawyer mind couldn't help wonder how this death would affect their case. Was there any possibility Carlstrom would still testify?

He gazed upward. "Well, Lord, what now? I still trust you, but I don't know how we're going to win this case without Carlstrom."

Later that morning Steve plunked his briefcase on the counsel table like a prop in a play being reenacted on the stage of real life. Cameramen and journalists were already claiming seats and checking viewfinders. Perhaps the first two trials were mere rehearsals for this third trial when God would rewrite the ending of Mary's case and good would triumph over evil.

Many of the doctors and witnesses on both sides had practiced their testimonies in depositions, hearings, and trials until the surprise element had been replaced by well-rehearsed lines. Until yesterday that fact hadn't bothered him. Carlstrom had given him hope. Steve would pit his neurosurgeon against their pathologists any day.

But now Carlstrom was gone. Probably. Uncertainty had crept back into their case. Would three older ladies, a new judge and jury, and a new lawyer be enough to change the outcome?

Right on cue with his thoughts, Paul Rosenberg strolled up to the counsel table and plunked his briefcase beside Steve's. The curly-haired lawyer slapped him on the back but kept his voice respectfully low. "Hey, Brennecke, I see you got here early so you could get a good parking space. Looks like we're going to have a crowd, even if most of the spectators have to drive a couple hours to see the show."

"Think Carlstrom will testify?"

Paul shrugged. "I'll call his office when we get a break. Don't imagine anybody will know anything for sure for several days."

If Paul was worried, he didn't show it. His natural optimism and skill in the courtroom inspired hope for a good ending to this trial. Steve could hardly wait to get started. He believed this was the time for God to show himself strong and the state of Iowa's justice system to do the right thing.

Mary arrived at the courtroom and greeted her supporters. Soon the courtroom was humming with the low conversation of ordinary Iowans, most of whom realized that if Mary could be convicted for this crime, so could they.

At 9:00 a.m. the Honorable Judge Goode entered the courtroom and pounded his gavel. Then the drama began. The judge had met with the lawyers from both sides the day before after jury selection. He made it clear he would call the shots in this trial. He would give them latitude to try their case but wouldn't allow them to waste his time or that of the jurors.

Judge Goode wasted no time with preliminaries but moved quickly to the opening statements. The 9-1-1 responders came next with the ER doctors and Melissa's pediatrician. All gave familiar testimony similar to the other trials.

The next day the state called Melissa's parents. The state had prepared Tessia for every question that was likely to be asked. Steve felt sure that the state's attorneys had read every word of the transcripts from the first two trials carefully and sifted through Dr. Carlstrom's deposition. They would have given his deposition to Bennett and the state's experts too so they could counter everything Carlstrom might say.

Except now Carlstrom might not be coming.

✿ ✿ ✿

During the first two trials Mary had felt compassion for the grieving mother as she stepped up to the witness stand, but the Kool-Aid smile photo had changed all that. Now she knew the lies must be exposed so the truth would become clear.

Friday morning the pale-faced mother of the murdered baby slipped up to the witness stand for the third time since her baby's death. Tessia's hand trembled as she swore to tell the truth, the whole truth, and nothing but the truth.

If only she would.

Though the state's attorneys were probably hesitant to call this bereaved mother, only Tessia could testify about Melissa's life that last week. Tessia could establish that the baby was acting normally when Mary picked her up.

As Tessia settled into the witness stand, Steve rose from his chair beside Mary and pulled a bound copy of one-third of the transcripts from the second trial. He dropped the heavy volume on the counsel table and opened the book to the beginning of Tessia's previous testimony. Yellow Post-it notes protruded from the edges. Tessia's eyes darted in Steve's direction. She had to know he would be tracking her prior testimony for any inconsistencies.

The attorneys for the state chose the female of the two of them to question the young mother. Barchman eyed Tessia and visibly softened her normal attack style. "Boy, you look nervous."

Tessia glanced at the attorney. "Yes."

Barchman pointed to a glass of water that had been left for Tessia, reminded her to speak loudly, and asked about support people Tessia had in the courtroom. The attorney remained seated at the counsel table and began with routine questions about Tessia's age and how long she'd been married to Brad. Mary knew from her own experience that these questions were designed to make Tessia more comfortable before the tough questions had to be asked.

When the prosecutor asked about Tessia's children, Melissa and a boy who had been born since her death, Tessia broke into tears.

Barchman glanced up from her notes uncomfortably, as if wondering if she should proceed. "Okay. I didn't think I'd lose you so fast. You're okay?"

Tessia blew her nose, took a deep breath. "I'm okay."

"If you need to take a break at any time, you can."

The reassurance rang hollow to Mary. Tessia had to testify, and she could hardly take a break mere minutes into her testimony.

Tessia talked about the way she used to play with Melissa— pretending to chase her, holding her upside down, and making her laugh. The nostalgia caused a fresh river of tears to stream down her face, and Barchman got up from her table and handed her a box of Kleenex. Tessia pulled the last one from the box, and Barchman offered to get more.

The same old stories came out about Melissa's bruises and her falls, a reminder to Mary that this frail mother had falsely accused her of inflicting those bruises. Tessia described the baby's illness during the week of her death. In time Tessia regained strength and seemed to relax a little.

More than an hour into Tessia's testimony, Barchman called for a fifteen-minute break. When the case resumed, Barchman laid out the Kool-Aid photos on her table and addressed Tessia. Her questions picked up where they had left off: the Thursday night before Melissa died. "When Brad's mother was over, what kinds of things did you and Melissa and Brad's mother do?"

Tessia scanned the familiar photos some fifteen feet away. "We played, and Brad's mom gave her a little bit of Kool-Aid."

"You guys took some pictures of her that night, didn't you?"

Tessia nodded before the question was out. "Yeah."

Barchman rose from the table and strode to Tessia's side. She showed Tessia two pictures of Melissa's Kool-Aid smile marked Exhibit 28 and Exhibit 29. Tessia took the pictures and gazed at them.

"What were you trying to show in that picture?"

"Her Kool-Aid smile." The mother lingered over the photos, then returned them to Barchman, who handed them to the nearest juror so they could be passed around the jury box.

"And you got it, didn't you?"

"Yes."

Barchman moved on to other questions, but Mary knew she had made her point. Thursday evening, roughly fifteen hours before Mary picked her up, Melissa had recovered from her illness and was a normal, happy, Kool-Aid-smiling child.

This argument wouldn't help them much, however, when it was exposed as a deliberate lie.

In time Barchman moved to the weekend before Melissa died. Everyone agreed Melissa had acted normally until that weekend. Brad and Tessia had to know more about that weekend than they were saying. If only Tessia would tell the whole truth, Mary believed the true killer would be revealed.

The tragedy of this case wasn't just that the police suspected Mary but that by suspecting her, they had failed to search diligently for the true killer. As much as Mary wanted to have her name cleared, she also longed for justice for Melissa. Police had gathered testimony about the weekend before Melissa died, but the stories just didn't match up. Instead of questioning the stories, they let Bennett shave a couple of days off the original time frame for the older injuries, making it easier to accuse Mary.

Barchman's questions centered on late Saturday evening after Tessia's time at the casino. "When you got Melissa back from your sister, about what time of the day was that?"

"It was at night," Tessia said. "Around ten, I think."

"Brad has told us that you and he and his parents drove out to Conrad to pick Melissa up. What was Melissa doing when you got there?"

"She was sitting on my sister's lap, playing with these toy blocks that connect together."

"Did she seem to be herself?"

"Very much so."

"Did she seem to have any injuries on her anywhere?"

"No."

By now Mary understood what Barchman was doing. The attorney knew all the witnesses the defense would call. After reading transcripts from the earlier trials, depositions, and hearings, Barchman and Marek could predict practically everything the witnesses would say. Since the prosecution got first turn to present their case, they could anticipate coming testimonies and cut the fires from the fuses before they ever got lit.

Just now Barchman was anticipating the testimony of Brad's parents, Cindy's boyfriend, and another witness who had seen

Melissa that Saturday. They would testify that Melissa had been fussy that evening, that she had been whining and crying. That testimony would make the injury likely to have happened on Saturday when Melissa wasn't with Mary.

Barchman had countered their arguments before they stepped foot in the witness stand. If the parents didn't think Melissa had been fussy that night, the jury might believe that all this fussiness was just a matter of opinion and not worthy of consideration.

Next Barchman moved one day forward to the Sunday before Melissa died. She knew from the transcripts that Paul would ask Tessia about this as well as each of the Matheses, so she cut the spark from another fuse.

Brad and Tessia had been having supper with Brad's parents when Tessia's parents stopped by. Tessia said Melissa was sleeping.

"Did you tell them they couldn't see Melissa?"

Tessia hesitated. "Not exactly."

"What did you tell them?"

"I told them that Melissa had only been down maybe ten minutes for a nap. She hadn't slept all day, and I was joking around with them. They didn't really want to go wake her up. And I'm like, 'You wake her up, you get to hold her while I eat.'"

"Okay. And did they decide to wake her up?"

"No, they didn't want to wake her up."

Defuse the explosive situation with humor, Mary thought. Very effective.

The prosecutor nodded slightly, and Tessia's shoulders visibly relaxed. Barchman moved to the topic of dressing Melissa in her snowsuit. Now the attorney would try to defuse the testimony of the three ladies who would testify for the defense.

Barchman asked about the process of putting Melissa in her snowsuit.

# CHAPTER 34

Tessia described the process. Melissa was always on the floor, Tessia said. Melissa never stood up until she had it on.

"As you were putting Melissa's snowsuit on her, did she throw her head back and smack herself on the coffee table?"

"She was already laying on the floor. Our coffee table was in the middle of our living room, and we were off to the side."

"Did Melissa hit her head on anything while you were putting on her snowsuit?"

Tessia stared at her lap, clasping her hands tightly, and shook her head. "No."

"Other than the tumble from the Cookie Monster chair that morning, did Melissa bump her head on anything?"

"No, nothing else besides on the recliner."

"While you were putting on Melissa's snowsuit, did Melissa become unconscious at all?"

"No." She shook her head and continued to do so even as Barchman framed her questions.

"If your child had bumped her head at any time in her life and become unconscious, what would you have done?"

"I would have taken her to the emergency room or called 9-1-1."

"Would you have been calm about it?"

"No." Faster head shaking.

"Would you have sent her to the baby-sitter?"

"No." Her head never stopped.

"Would you have gone to work?"

"No." She spoke with finality, meeting the prosecutor's gaze.

Mary could only guess why Tessia had told five other ladies a different snowsuit story.

Barchman changed her pace and moved to the next topic to defuse some more future testimony.

"Did you and your husband and your families try to figure out how Melissa could have been hurt?"

"Yes."

"At that time, did you ever think Mary Weaver could have hurt her?"

"No."

"Did anybody ever suggest to you that—did you think about something happening at the baby-sitter's?"

"Some people said that. We told them there is no way."

"Could you have told Robin McElroy at church that you didn't think Mary Weaver would have done anything?"

"Yes."

"After Melissa's death, did you and Brad sit down and try to think of every bruise and bump Melissa had ever had?"

"Yes."

"Mrs. Mathes, do you know of anything that happened while you saw Melissa that could have caused a serious head injury to your child?"

"No."

"I have no more questions for you right now."

Mary could imagine Tessia's thoughts because she had been in the same position. Done with the questions from the lawyer on my side. Next come the questions designed to trip me up.

Tessia shifted in her chair and met Paul's eyes.

Paul fingered his notes and searched Tessia's face. As he began his cross-examination, Mary marveled anew at the transformation that came over him in a courtroom. Gone was the ever-present humor that Paul used to defuse tension. In its place was an unreadable mask a poker player would envy.

"Mrs. Mathes, you normally got off work at seven p.m. Is that correct?"

"Correct."

"Now these photographs that were shown to the jury after Melissa had the Kool-Aid—those were taken Thursday evening."

"Yes, they were."

"And Brad was there, too?"

"Yes, he was."

"So Sunday, January seventeenth. That would be the day your parents came over…"

Steve scribbled a note and shoved it toward Mary. "Master at work!"

She had to agree. Paul knew how to work important events into his examination without giving a hint of the impact the statements would have later. But perhaps Steve had sensed the tension of betrayal Mary felt on this issue and was just trying to distract her.

Paul brought Tessia's testimony to the point on that Sunday when her parents had stopped by the house while Brad and Tessia were having supper with his parents.

"So you had four grandparents there at that time. Do you recall telling them that they couldn't see—"

"No. I did not tell them that." She shook her head vigorously. Tessia's voice lacked conviction or defiance, but she knew what was coming and was prepared to counter the impressions of the grandparents. Paul turned to Steve, who handed him the transcripts of Tessia's testimony from several occasions.

"At the time your deposition was taken, did you say that"—Paul held the transcripts high—"'I wouldn't let them wake her because she didn't have a nap all day and she didn't have a nap Saturday and she was tired'?"

"I wasn't going to let them wake her up, but they could have went in the room and looked at her."

Paul handed the transcript to Steve and turned back to Tessia. She was staring at her lap again, wringing her hands. Mary knew Paul was trying to suggest that Melissa's grandparents might have been worried about Melissa from the night before.

They may have come by Brad and Tessia's house on Sunday to check on Melissa, but they weren't allowed to see her.

"You know Robin McElroy, don't you?"

"I know who she is." Tessia agreed that she had run into Mrs. McElroy at a local Baptist church during the weeks following Melissa's death.

"And did you tell her at that time that you were putting the baby's coat on and that she threw herself backwards and hit her head on the table?"

"No." Simple denial, no explanation.

"Do you know a person by the name of Mistry Lovig?"

Tessia said she had worked with her at Hardee's.

"Sometime about three or four weeks after Melissa had died, did you have a conversation with Mistry Lovig in which you would have said that you were putting her snowsuit on, and she threw her head back and hit it on the coffee table? She was crying and continued to cry?"

"No."

Paul asked about the three ladies: Flossie Wall, Elaine Kail, and Evelyn Braack.

Tessia recalled that they often came to Hardee's on Wednesdays. Tessia had been off work two weeks after Melissa died.

Paul asked if Tessia recalled having a conversation with the ladies after she returned to work.

"I'm sure I talked to them."

"Did you tell those three ladies that when you were dressing Melissa the morning that she went to the hospital and got sick and had a respiratory arrest, that she had thrown her head back and hit it on the table, and she was knocked unconscious?"

Tessia's words held more certainty than her tone. "I did not say that."

# CHAPTER 34

Paul ended his questioning, and Ms. Barchman made one last attempt at damage control.

"Mrs. Mathes, did you talk to Mary Weaver about what had happened to Melissa at her house?"

"Yes."

"And did Mary Weaver tell you that she was putting on Melissa's snowsuit, Melissa's eyes rolled back in her head, and she quit breathing?"

"Yes."

"Could you have told Robin McElroy, Mistry Lovig, the three ladies from Hardee's, and anyone else who asked you what happened to your baby—"

"Yeah."

"—that Mary Weaver was putting on her snowsuit, that her eyes rolled back in her head, and she quit breathing?"

"Yes."

Mary forced herself to take a deep breath. Tessia's testimony wouldn't go unchallenged. An acquaintance at a church Tessia had visited, a coworker, and three customers at Hardee's all agreed about their conversations with Tessia. Next week they would all testify that Tessia had told them something happened at the Mathes' home on Friday morning of the day Melissa died. Melissa had hit her head on a coffee table, and Tessia had told several of them that Melissa had become unconscious.

This was the best slant Barchman could put on the story: at three different times Tessia told the same story to different people, who didn't know each other and didn't know her well. In the minds of all five, the story of what actually happened on the carpet at Mary's house had become confused. The five now all believed the incident had happened over the coffee table at Tessia's house.

Surely the jury would find that fact far from convincing.

In a couple hours of testimony, Tessia had pitted her word against that of three people who had visited the home of Tessia's sister, against Mary, and against five ladies who had no motivation to lie. In the closing arguments Paul would also reveal the secret of the Kool-Aid smile.

No wonder the young mother looked so nervous.

So far this trial had a much more positive feel to it than the last one. Still, Mary hadn't been able to read the jury accurately during the first trial. She couldn't decide on a clear definition of God's promises. And Dr. Carlstrom's office wasn't making any promises about his testimony.

# Chapter 35

On Monday morning a voice from the past entered the courtroom and waited to be heard. This voice would be 100 percent accurate. Steve couldn't wait to see what affect a little reality would have on the next witness's ever-changing testimony.

Dr. Wilbur Smith stepped up to the stand. During the first trial Smith had said Melissa died of shaken baby syndrome from two events. The older event had to have occurred seven to ten days before her death.

During his cross-examination Paul pointed to this earlier testimony. He even read from a previous statement in which the doctor had called the five- to ten-day assessment "a mistake." But now Smith maintained that the five- to ten-day time frame was correct.

"So you changed your opinion?" Paul said.

Smith straightened his shoulders, evidently undeterred by the question. "I believe that I have slightly." Still he insisted that the earlier injury played no role in Melissa's death.

Paul moved to the acute injury. He wanted to show that Smith's testimony had changed to match the testimony of other doctors and convict Mary. From his first look at the CT scans until the first trial, Smith had tightened his testimony about the time of the fatal injury from a full day to a mere sixty minutes.

"Moving to the second event, the acute injury which caused Melissa to die, what do you believe to be the time frame of that injury?"

"Melissa suffered the fatal injuries just before she stopped breathing."

"During the last forty-two minutes while she was in Mary Weaver's care?"

"Yes." Smith propped his elbows on the armrest and peered smugly over his low-slung half glasses.

Steve suppressed a smile. The doctor had no idea what was coming.

Paul stepped to a cart behind the counsel table, which held a tape recorder and speakers. He rolled it to a position directly in front of the jury. Jury members shifted in their seats, eying the recorder with curiosity.

Paul adjusted the speakers. "Dr. Smith, do you recall your initial telephone conversation with Lieutenant Buffington?"

The doctor glanced at the tape player, then back at Paul. The glance hinted that until this moment he had no idea that the voice recording of his conversation still existed. Steve had read from a typed transcript during the earlier trials.

Smith conceded that he remembered the conversation.

Paul tapped the "play" button. "Would hearing that conversation refresh your recollection about your exact words at that time?"

Dr. Smith stared at Barchman, who popped out of her chair. "Objection, Your Honor. The foundation for this tape is lacking."

Judge Goode glanced at Paul, who shrugged.

Paul caught the prosecutor's eye. "This tape was provided by the state. It's a phone conversation Lieutenant Buffington of the Marshalltown police recorded between himself and Dr. Smith."

Judge Goode frowned. Establishing a foundation for this tape would mean calling Buffington to come from Marshalltown. The objection was technically correct, but it was an unnecessary delay of the inevitable. With a deep sigh the judge checked the wall clock. "We will reconvene in twenty minutes. Counsel, let's meet in my chambers."

Paul strolled to the counsel table and leaned toward Steve. "I can't see the sense in this. Are they going to fight their own chain of custody of the police department's tapes?"

Steve shrugged, and they followed Barchman and Marek to the judge's office. As the door clicked shut, Goode glared at the prosecutors.

"Is it the state's position that the defense has somehow substituted a different tape?"

Barchman cleared her throat. "No, our objection is simply that the foundation is lacking."

"Do you have reason to believe the original tape is lost?"

"No, Your Honor."

"Is there concern that this tape does not contain the voice of Dr. Smith?"

"Again, our objection is as to the foundation. Someone recorded this, whether it accurately—"

"Then we will take all the time we need." The judge emphasized the words with finger jabs on his desk. His tone softened as he turned to Paul. "If you need to subpoena your foundation witnesses, whether that's Lieutenant Buffington or the entire Marshalltown police force for that matter, go right ahead. Dr. Smith will be glad to wait."

The judge turned back to the prosecutors, "We will lay that foundation if it takes four hours!" With that he unzipped his robe and threw in onto his chair. "You are dismissed."

Back in the courtroom, Barchman, Marek, and Smith conferred in urgent whispers. Paul stood at the counsel table, quietly reviewing the Iowa Rules of Evidence. The break gave Steve more time to locate Dr. Smith's parallel testimony from earlier proceedings concerning Smith's telephone conversation.

Barchman finally called across the room to the defense lawyers. "We will withdraw our objection."

Steve knew they had won a minor victory. Their objection to the tape had only announced to the jury that they were hiding something important. They had effectively donned their black hats.

When the trial reconvened, Paul focused Smith's attention back on his original phone call to the Marshalltown Police Department and pushed the button on the tape player.

The doctor's confident, authoritative voice spoke to a full courtroom. "I am afraid that with the pattern that I have got, I can't put it any better than twenty-four hours or so. So within twenty-four hours of the time of the seizure is when the injury occurred by the X rays. The problem that I have got is that it is not that massive of an injury, so it depends on how reliable this sitter is. You can get fooled by a little baby with cerebral edema. They can be just minimally tired, or they can even drink and all with the cerebral edema pattern and then rapidly deteriorate and get their seizure."

Any hint of uncertainty had disappeared. He couldn't narrow the time frame to any less than twenty-four hours. But the figure who now sat in the witness chair had lost his air of confidence, and his thin, little eyebrows arched in confusion.

On redirect exam, Smith explained that he had changed his time frame for the injury after conferring with the other doctors and learning more about how the baby was acting when Mary picked her up.

# CHAPTER 35

Returning to the final injury, Smith described the force needed to cause the damage inside Melissa's brain as similar to a fall from a second-story window.

When Barchman called Dr. Randell Alexander to the stand, he changed Smith's estimate. He doubted the baby could have sustained the kind of injuries he had seen by banging her head on a coffee table.

"Falling out of a four-story window onto a coffee table isn't going to cause this kind of injury," he said. "Immediately after getting this kind of injury, you'll always look terrible, like you need 9-1-1."

Paul scribbled, "Smith—2 stories, Alexander—4" on a legal pad, then leaned close to Steve. "First, it was a two-story fall. Now it's four. How high do you think we can get this fall: Five stories? Ten stories?"

"Seems they want to outbid each other."

"Wanna bet these guys will lose to Bennett? The state medical examiner gets to bid last."

Barchman asked Alexander what kind of shaking caused shaken baby syndrome.

"We're talking about somebody basically going all out to injure a child." At her invitation he stepped down from the witness stand to demonstrate. He accepted a doll from her and held it under the arms. He spread his feet wide, stabilizing himself, and pumped his arms back and forth furiously until he was completely disheveled. He handed the doll back to Barchman, then straightened his shirt and ran his fingers through his hair.

The prosecution wound up its case on Wednesday with its eighth doctor, Dr. Thomas Bennett. The state medical examiner strutted up to the witness stand like an expert who never found it necessary to question his opinions. He "improved" on the testimonies of Smith and Alexander. "A child hitting a coffee table five hundred times would never have sustained the kind of injuries Melissa sustained," Bennett said. He compared the force needed to cause the injuries to a fall from a four- or five-story building.

Mary shielded her hands from the jury's view and held out five fingers. Steve and Paul caught her look and answered with their own five fingers. The testimony was becoming ludicrous.

Bennett repeated the state's mantra: the older injuries hadn't caused Melissa's death. The skull fracture would have made the baby's head less stable, but it played no role in her death. Melissa died because of the injuries she suffered right before Mary called 9-1-1.

Even though the child's skull may have been imperfect, he said it provided enough protection against normal bumps and scratches, and didn't predispose her to death. The eye injuries were caused by at least two to three seconds of very violent shaking, enough force to cause her brain to shift inside the skull.

Steve still couldn't understand how these doctors could totally ignore Melissa's skull fracture and severe preexisting brain injuries, saying they had nothing to do with the baby's death.

When Paul got his turn to cross-examine Bennett, he asked the glaringly obvious question that Steve had been asking for years. "If, as you say, Melissa's head was slammed onto a hard surface with a force equivalent to a thirty-five-mile-per-hour car crash or a fall from a four- or five-story building, why do you think her head didn't show any outward sign of injury? Wouldn't there be a bruise or bump or swelling that would be obvious to the doctors upon her admission to the Marshalltown hospital?"

Bennett regarded Paul with the condescension of a medical prodigy lecturing a class of failing, first-year students. "I'm not surprised Melissa's head didn't show outward signs of injury because her head would offer compression, and it might not crush."

Steve wondered if Bennett's logic made sense even to himself. He talked about Mary shaking Melissa so violently that her brain shifted inside her skull. He spoke of slamming Melissa's head against a hard surface with the force of a four- or five-story fall. Yet a careful doctor hadn't even been able to find a bump the size of the ones kids often got when they fell off tricycles.

Thankfully, if he couldn't swallow this argument, the jury was likely to choke on it too.

# CHAPTER 36

**W**atching an overly aggressive prosecutor badger three elderly ladies on your behalf didn't make for a relaxing morning. Steve and Paul didn't seem worried, but Mary was glad for a lunch break. She and a group of her supporters bundled up and strolled to a little café on a side street near the courthouse. Seven ladies, mostly older than Mary, pulled extra chairs around a chrome table.

Lunch provided a good break from the strain of the trial. This third trial certainly had a better feel to it than the first two, but it was never easy reliving Melissa's seizure and being indirectly accused of murder by witness after witness. This morning she had listened to Melissa's grandparents testify that the Kool-Aid photo was taken on a January evening despite the sunshine in the photo. Betrayal by former friends always hurt the most. She couldn't forget their words, but she could choose not to dwell on them—which was what she was trying to do right now without much success.

A middle-aged waitress pulled an order pad from her apron pocket. "Hi, girls. Looks like the Mary Weaver fan club again today. What can I get you? The pork roast special's awful nice with applesauce."

The ladies ordered seven pork specials with separate checks. The group began a lively discussion of the morning's events.

Mary never got much distance from the trial these days, but at least she could unwind with people who believed in her. She leaned back in her chair and sipped Diet Coke while the comments floated around her.

"I think Elaine, Flossie, and Evelyn did a fine job testifying. It's not easy talking in front of all those people. I'd be scared to death."

"But wasn't that Mr. Marek mean? If he asks a question, he ought to give them time to answer it, is what I think. What's he got to hide anyway?"

"Plenty. He doesn't want to hear the truth. He just wants to convict Mary."

"Maybe he's just doing his job."

"His job ought to be getting to the truth, that's what. And here these ladies are trying to tell the truth, and he's cutting them off before they get their story out. And Mr. Marek begging the judge to make them just answer his questions and no more. Why not let the whole truth come out? That's just rude, is what I say."

"Me, too. If I were that Mr. Marek's mama, I'd bend him over my knee."

"What do you think, Mary?"

Mary shook herself out of a daze. Her mind had been busy trying to block negative thoughts from her mind. "Huh?"

"Don't you think that Mr. Marek was more aggressive than he needed to be?"

"He was a bit hard on those ladies, but you know me. All I want is the truth to come out. That's all I ever wanted." Truth, the end to this trial, and a clear acquittal would do.

The waitress arrived with the pork specials and set one before each lady. The meat's aroma wafted over the table, awakening their hunger. Several bowed their heads briefly before eating.

When the last head came up, Marge Wolfe turned to Mary. "So is Cindy Butler going to come testify tomorrow or not?"

Mary chewed a bite and swallowed. "No. She's going to her father's funeral. They've rescheduled her testimony for Monday."

"First that nice Dr. Carlstrom's wife dies the day before testimony begins." Diana Bulanek punctuated her sentence with fork stabs in the air. "Then Cindy's dad hits his head and dies, and they schedule the funeral for the day she's scheduled as a character witness. Seems strange."

"And then there's Frank Santiago," Mary said, "the reporter from the *Des Moines Register,* who kept my case active in the public eye. He hasn't covered this trial because his wife is dying from cancer."

Lucille Pierson clucked her tongue and shook her head. "All in a couple of weeks. Makes you wonder why, doesn't it? Mary, I'd think you'd go crazy wondering why all this stuff happens."

Mary took a big gulp of Diet Coke and considered her answer carefully. Be real. Be honest.

"Asking why can drive you crazy." Mary dabbed at her mouth with a napkin. "For two years in prison I studied the Bible, trying to make sense out of my life. Why did God allow Melissa to die and me to be convicted of a murder I didn't commit? I still don't know. I just know I experienced God's faithfulness every day. He carried me through the roughest days, and I came out of prison stronger than I went in. I came away knowing God has a plan for my life."

Wilma Luiken raised her eyebrows. "You think two years in prison is part of that plan?"

Mary shrugged. "Must be."

"But the legal system failed you." It was Mabel Meyer this time. "People lied and sent you to prison."

"And those lies are about to be exposed," Mary said. "The legal system gets it wrong sometimes, but God can put it right."

Wilma set down her fork and focused on Mary. "Why would God do that to a nice person like you?"

Mary stabbed her meat and cut it, stalling for words. "I don't have an answer for that," she finally admitted. "I know we live in a world where a lot of stuff happens that must grieve him. He doesn't stop all the bad stuff, but he's still in control. I don't understand a lot of things, but I know I can trust him. He paints beautiful sunsets and unleashes wild tornados. I don't like tornados, but I know I can trust the God who controls them. I'm just glad he's in control and I'm not. Can you imagine keeping the planets spinning for even one day? And solving all the world's problems while everyone takes credit for the good stuff in their lives and blames you for all the bad stuff? No, I wouldn't want to be God. I have enough work to do just to move forward with my life."

Marge Wolfe squeezed Mary's hand. "That's right. And now we get to watch God correct the mistakes of the legal system. Your name could be completely cleared in another week. God has worked in much too obvious ways to be sending you back to prison. You're going to be okay."

"I'll be okay—even if I go back to prison." Mary grinned. "But if it's all the same to God, I'd rather not."

☼ ☼ ☼

Steve pictured the agitated form of the prosecuting attorney. With each objection Douglas Marek made, his face grew a deeper shade of red.

As Steve looked back on the morning's testimony, he decided it was nice of the prosecution to help them out so much. Paul had begun his defense by calling Elaine Kail, Flossie Wall, and Evelyn Braack, who did a fine job testifying on their own. When Marek cross-examined them he continually interrupted them and tried to limit their answers. When they tried to break free of his restraints and tell the whole story, Marek objected and asked the judge to instruct them to answer only the question asked and not to volunteer any additional information.

Steve knew the ladies were frustrated, but he and Paul never objected. Asking a judge to constrain elderly ladies certainly put a black hat on the prosecution. And each of Marek's objections shouted to the jury, "This testimony is important! The prosecution is trying to hide something!"

After that Brad's parents and two others testified that Melissa acted fussy on the Saturday night before her death. Paul led the parents nonchalantly into the story of the Kool-Aid smile. Both testified that the incident took place the Thursday evening before Melissa died. Paul also called witnesses to verify Mary's version of the events on that Friday after Melissa stopped breathing.

Friday Paul called six character witnesses, who testified again to Mary's patience under pressure.

Then Steve questioned Dr. Ruth Ramsey. She had gained even more confidence and was much more at ease in front of the jury than during the first trials. This time she asked Steve for a light box so she could display the CT scans to the jury. She taught the jury as if she were teaching a class of med students. She clipped the first scan to the light box and switched on the light. Then she showed the jury different examples of various head injuries from CT scans of other patients and compared them to Melissa's. One scan displayed a classic "goose egg," the bloated swelling from a blow to the head. Then she pulled that scan down and displayed Melissa's. No "goose egg" was visible.

# CHAPTER 36

The state's medical experts had rambled on until the jury seemed to be fighting to stay awake. Ramsey kept her testimony professional and concise, and the jury seemed to follow her logic with interest.

Ramsey said her examination of the CT scans taken of Melissa's brain produced no evidence that she had been shaken and slammed violently. Instead the scans were more consistent with a child whose brain hadn't received enough oxygen. This testimony was consistent with what Mary had told the 9-1-1 dispatcher on the tape—that the baby wasn't breathing.

Together Paul and Steve built their case for Mary's defense stone by stone like a stone arch. Each testimony was designed to add strength and credibility, but Carlstrom's testimony was the keystone that locked the other testimonial stones into position and allowed the defense's arch to bear weight. Steve and Paul had passed anxious days, wondering if Carlstrom would be available to testify. Steve began to realize that presenting a doctor who routinely saved lives was a strategic and brilliant move—if he came.

# CHAPTER 37

On Friday, nine days after his wife died, Paul called Dr. Thomas Carlstrom as his next witness. Dr. Carlstrom entered the courtroom from the back doors, accompanied by his son. The doctor shuffled down the aisle and took the oath to tell the truth. He collapsed into the witness chair and stared at Paul with vacant eyes.

Steve wondered, now that Carlstrom was here, how well he would be able to testify after the devastating loss of his wife.

When asked to describe his background, Carlstrom slipped into a daze. He focused on the carpet just in front of the witness stand and answered Paul's questions in a monotone. He'd been a neurosurgeon since 1979. As a neurosurgeon he diagnosed and treated problems with the nervous system, including head and brain trauma.

Steve noticed the doctor wasn't connecting to the jury. He scribbled a note to Paul. "You're losing him."

Paul cleared his throat loudly and asked the doctor to describe for the jury the most common complications he saw in cases of severe head trauma.

Carlstrom glanced up at Paul, then at the jury. The most significant head injury complication, Carlstrom said, was elevated intercranial pressure from the brain swelling or a blood clot that prevented the brain from draining blood.

# CHAPTER 37

Paul grabbed a marker, scurried to the doctor, and asked him to explain those conditions to the jury using a diagram, if necessary.

Carlstrom rallied his energies, accepted the marker, and approached a whiteboard. He drew a chart to illustrate the sharp and fatal rise in intercranial pressure common to cases like Melissa's. The teacher in him kicked into gear as he explained that the brain normally regulates its own pressure. Arteries carry blood into the brain; veins carry it back out.

"If you have too much pressure, the brain will push against the skull walls." Carlstrom added arrows to the diagram. "But it can't push out because the skull wouldn't let it, so it pushes on itself"—more arrows—"and it squeezes itself. The adult brain does this a lot better than a child's brain. When a child has an injury, it's relatively common for them to lose this autoregulation, causing the pressure in the brain to build up. The younger the child is, the more chance he has of losing his autoregulation.

"For a period of time after a child has a head injury, there's impaired autoregulation in the child's head, and another blow is potentially a serious blow, even though it wasn't any worse than the last one; and it might not have even been as bad as the first one, but their autoregulation is impaired, and they can't handle another injury as well as the first.

Carlstrom set the marker down. "The important part of that is that as the pressure goes up, you can get to the point where, all of a sudden, a very small increment in volume is going to cause an extremely large elevation in pressure, which can be very— well, it can be fatal."

Paul allowed Carlstrom time to answer but kept his voice intense, hoping to hold on to the fervor that had been building in the neurosurgeon's voice. "And during what period after a severe head injury would a patient be vulnerable to a seizure?"

"Seizures are very common in head injuries. They're fairly common in the first week after a head injury and taper off after that. A first seizure can occur months and months after a head injury."

Paul paused long enough for the jury to realize this statement contradicted testimony of medical experts, who had maintained that Melissa's injury had to have been inflicted just prior to her seizure. "Could a seizure cause a respiratory arrest?"

"Most of them eventually will cause a respiratory arrest, but it will be a brief one."

Carlstrom returned to the witness chair. Paul handed the doctor Melissa's autopsy report, known in this courtroom as Exhibit 5. He asked Carlstrom to list Melissa's injuries that were dated as seven to ten days old.

The doctor read a list and began to explain the various injuries.

After Carlstrom covered the most serious older injuries, Paul moved to those that had been described as acute, the ones some medical experts said must have been inflicted Friday morning.

The subarachnoid bleeding could have come from the old injury. Melissa's brain had been so fragile that any type of relatively minor trauma could have caused this condition as a complication of the sagittal sinus thrombosis, the clot between the hemispheres of Melissa's brain.

Retinal hemorrhages were key to Melissa's case. Bennett and Alexander had set them as a marker for shaken baby syndrome. The state's medical experts had pointed to this bleeding in the eye as one of their strongest indications that Melissa had been shaken at least once and certainly shaken just prior to her respiratory arrest that last Friday morning.

Carlstrom believed the bulk of the retinal hemorrhages were from the old injury and from the events following, being resuscitated and on a respirator.

# CHAPTER 37

Carlstrom had begun to slump in his chair again during the recital of the various injuries.

Paul stepped forward to remove the autopsy report from the doctor's hand. "Several doctors have testified that retinal hemorrhages are almost exclusively caused by abusive head trauma or shaking. Do you agree with that?"

Carlstrom pushed himself up in his chair, resting his elbows on the armrests. "Absolutely not."

"How often do you see retinal hemorrhages in your practice?"

"I see them often enough. A child or even an adult with a severe head injury, on a respirator, getting all the various things that we do, almost uniformly has retinal hemorrhages."

"Would chronic intercranial pressure or a rush of intercranial pressure cause retinal hemorrhages?"

"Either one could."

Paul sorted through his notes just long enough for the jury to realize that retinal hemorrhages didn't guarantee Melissa had been shaken.

He put his finger under a note he'd made from the testimony of the state's medical experts. "Dr. Carlstrom, doctors have described the trauma Melissa suffered as equivalent to a fall from a four- or five-story building, an auto accident, thirty-five miles an hour, various analogies like that. Do you see in Melissa, to a reasonable degree of medical certainty, the type of symptoms you would normally expect if this were the case?"

"No. I think it's hard to quantify a head injury, and I think sometimes we try to make it sound worse than it really is. I've seen children fall from a third-floor window with absolutely no injuries whatsoever. I've also seen them die from that kind of a fall. If an infant fell five stories on her head, it would normally be much, much more severe than Melissa's injuries. But the seven- to ten-day prior injury was significant. It made her extremely susceptible to mild trauma, and by mild trauma I might even mean a cough or something like that. She did not show any evidence of any kind of a direct blow to the head that was newer than the seven to ten days that was noted in the autopsy report."

Steve admired the neurosurgeon for admitting that medicine was an inexact science. He didn't dance on the edge of truth with claims he couldn't substantiate. No five-story buildings, eight-hundred-pound gorillas, or five hundred blows on a coffee table.

With Melissa's prior skull fracture, Carlstrom said, any new trauma would have caused fresh bleeding. Bennett and Robinson had described the seven- to fourteen-day-old subdural hematoma as "clotted and adhering both to the dura and the brain when the skull was opened." Carlstrom said if Melissa had been shaken violently that Friday morning, there would have been disruption of the blood clot that was becoming scar tissue. Their findings were inconsistent with shaking.

"Dr. Carlstrom, testimony has been presented here that Melissa's mother told several individuals that Melissa had thrown her head back and hit it on a coffee table prior to when Mary Weaver took charge of the child," Paul said. "Do you have any opinion on what you would expect to see from such a blow with Melissa's prior injuries?"

"I think the story of hitting the head, losing consciousness, is a very believable one given the fact that there is a week-old injury."

"After hitting the coffee table, would you expect the symptoms to be immediate or delayed?"

"They could be immediate, like half a second, or they could be delayed. Our ability to predict exactly what's going to happen after a head injury is fair and not much more than that. A second head trauma is even less predictable than the first."

# CHAPTER 37

"Doctor, to a reasonable degree of medical certainty, do you have an opinion on whether Melissa Mathes suffered a severe shaking equivalent in force to a thirty-five-mile-per-hour car accident or a slam to the back of her head equivalent to a four- or five-story fall on January twenty-second, 1993?"

"Yes. I do not think that happened."

As Paul finished his questions, the tall, blonde prosecutor straightened in her seat. The jury wouldn't want her to openly attack this doctor, who had so recently lost his wife, but she couldn't afford to take it easy on this doctor who was the keystone of their defense.

Barchman moved quickly to retinal hemorrhages, which, according to her medical experts, was a mark of a shaken baby. "How many cases a year do you believe you have with retinal hemorrhages not associated with violent shaking or a car accident in children under three?"

"As an enthusiastic young doctor," Carlstrom said, "I always looked at the retina of all of my head-injured patients, and I found hemorrhages many, many, many times. Retinal hemorrhages and severe head injury go hand in hand, and I honestly don't look in retinas any more. We have so many monitors of other types that we use that there is, in my opinion, little value in looking for retinal hemorrhages, so I just don't."

Each time Barchman thrust a question at him, Carlstrom parried the blow. With each new attack he seemed to draw new strength.

"Do you have an opinion as to what caused Melissa's respiratory arrest on the morning of January twenty-second while she was in Mary Weaver's care?"

"If you're asking me to sort of solve the problem, no." Carlstrom must have sensed the importance of the question because he turned to face the jury. "But there are a number of possibilities. A simple loss of consciousness with food in her mouth. There was food in her lungs. It got there, I guess, because she vomited. She could very well have had a short loss of consciousness caused by a loss of autoregulation or seizure or the sagittal sinus thrombosis."

"You've told us that there didn't necessarily have to be a fresh traumatic injury?" Barchman crossed her arms. Convince me.

Carlstrom leaned forward. "It depends on what you mean by 'trauma.' Sitting down hard or striking the head on a coffee table can be head trauma. It can be enough to trigger a fragile brain into a series of events that can cause a problem."

"If Melissa, in a standing position, had jerked back and struck the back of her head on a coffee table, you would expect to see some evidence of that, wouldn't you?"

Steel shone in the doctor's eyes. "In her case, events that you would not normally consider to be head trauma can be head trauma. She would not have had to hit the head very hard to set off a series of events that would cause her to lose consciousness."

"If Melissa, while still at home with her mother at about nine o'clock in the morning, had thrown herself backwards onto the coffee table with sufficient force to become unconscious and set off this chain of events, what symptoms would you expect to follow?"

"She could remain unconscious, and she could go on then and die, or"—Carlstrom shrugged—"she might just wake up and be fine or anything in between."

Barchman raised a skeptical eyebrow. "She could wake up and be laughing and giggling and talkative, eating, and then three hours later deteriorate and simply stop breathing?"

"I think that's possible, sure." He crossed his arms, matching hers. "Three hours later the brain is no better than it was three hours before because of the relatively trivial nature of whatever it was that occurred at nine o'clock. It's not going to be necessarily a whole lot worse. But I don't have the answer to what happened here. I'm just saying that there are plenty of possibilities that are extremely likely given the fact that this brain was fragile because it had been injured a week earlier."

Steve scrawled "reasonable doubt" on his pad and shoved it close to Mary.

Barchman was losing ground here. Carlstrom had used every question she asked to advance Mary's defense.

Barchman tried to get him to disagree with Ramsey—that if you expected to see the subdural clot on the CT scan, it should be there.

Carlstrom remained polite but firm. "I think she and I are just saying the same thing. It was there. We know it was there, but we just don't see it. If I'm pressed, I can tell you that I see it; but I don't think I would have read it had I seen the scan."

The prosecutor asked him if he agreed with Alexander's statement that 999 out of 1,000 children with retinal hemorrhages, for reasons not explained by a car crash or enormous fall, would be the result of abusive head trauma.

But Carlstrom refused to be backed into a corner. "No. Nine hundred ninety-nine out of a thousand—that's almost like saying for sure. I don't say anything for sure about medical things. Any blow to the head strong enough to give a skull fracture can give retinal hemorrhage."

Barchman ended with questions about testimony from Dr. Folberg, the eye pathologist. The prosecutor claimed he had said that some particular retinal hemorrhages in Melissa's eyes were caused by violent shaking.

Carlstrom assured her that he had read Folberg's notation in the autopsy and didn't believe Folberg was dogmatic about that. "I don't think he said that the retinal hemorrhages that he saw were pathic and emblematic of shaken baby syndrome. I didn't read it that way."

Barchman sat tall, straightening her stack of notes. "Well, I guess the jury will decide what he told them. In any event, it's not your major field of study to study the causes and the locations and all the little minutia regarding the eyes?"

Carlstrom held her gaze. "That's correct."

Barchman had no further questions. Steve unclenched his fists and relaxed his shoulder muscles. Carlstrom had refused to be shaken by Barchman's cross-examination. At a time of intense grief, this doctor had been willing to stand for his beliefs against a majority of doctors without even compensation for his time and travel.

When the trial broke for lunch, Carlstrom came to talk to Mary, even hugged her briefly. Steve and Paul thanked him for his testimony.

The keystone of their defense was now in place. A straight path to a "not guilty" verdict stretched before the jury. If they stuck to the presumption of innocence and remembered that a conviction assumed guilt beyond reasonable doubt, Mary was home free.

But would they follow the clear path, or would side issues distract them?

# CHAPTER 38

Steve was going to ignore the advice he'd learned at law school.

The professors were all clear on this point: "Always prepare a witness for trial." When your client was going to waive her Fifth Amendment right to remain silent in her trial for first-degree murder, this advice became even more urgent.

But Friday afternoon, after seven days of testimony, Steve decided he wasn't going to use the weekend to prepare Mary for her testimony.

Mary had already testified in two previous trials. She had spent two years in prison thinking about the day Melissa died, reliving those events. Her story about Melissa acting normally when she picked her up made her look guilty. But she never wavered from the truth, even when the prosecution used it to push her into a prison cell.

Steve explained his decision to Mary at the end of the court day on Friday. "I still think if I coach you it will sound rehearsed. If the jury senses you are reciting a script, they will reject your testimony and side with the grieving parents."

Mary could have reminded him that he had said the same thing at her first two trials. She nodded instead. "I understand." But worry lines wrinkled her brow.

"It's not worth the risk. We have always done your testimony as if we are having a conversation. Sometimes it may seem clumsy rather than polished and smooth. But those moments make your testimony real."

"Okay."

Steve marveled at the simple faith Mary put in him and God. He just hoped he could live up to his side of that equation.

"Just remember, make eye contact with the jury so they can assess your honesty." He pointed two fingers at his eyes then away.

"Eye contact. Got it." Mary smiled. "We've been through this twice before. Maybe this time we'll get it right!"

Humor was always a good sign. Steve put his hand on her shoulder. "You're an easy client. You've always told the truth, and that has made this job of defending you very simple. Tell the truth, and…" He paused.

"The truth will make you free." They chanted the words together, grinned, and parted for the weekend.

Mary grabbed her purse and pulled out her car keys.

Steve headed for his car. Though Mary had testified at two previous trials, this time his approach was going to be completely different. He hoped she would be ready for anything.

On Monday, as Mary settled into the witness stand, Steve raised his voice and interrogated her like a police officer. "Mary, did you harm Melissa?"

"No."

"Did you shake her forcefully or slam her head on the counter?"

"No"

"Did you ever hurt her in any way?"

"No, I did not."

Mary had that deer-in-the-headlights look for the first few minutes. She relaxed a bit when Steve returned to the more typical direct examination style he had used during the first two trials. He asked her about her life, her family, and how she came to be Melissa's baby-sitter.

He led her through the last seven days of Melissa's life, focusing on how Melissa had behaved during those days. He had Mary walk the jury through that last Friday when Melissa quit breathing. Mary relived her forty-two minutes. Feeding Melissa. Noticing the time had come to leave. Laying Melissa down. Feeding her legs into the snowsuit. Lifting the back of her shoulders and head so she'd be in a sitting position. With fresh grief she told how the baby's eyes rolled back, her body slumped, and she quit breathing. Mary retold the rescue efforts as if it were yesterday.

When Steve had finished asking her about Melissa's last days, he finished with a flurry of questions, just like the questions he'd started with.

"Did you harm Melissa?"

"Did you shake her with force or slam her against anything?"

"Have you ever done anything to hurt her in any way?"

Each time Mary's voice was clear, emphatic. She had done no wrong to the baby.

As Steve leaned back in his chair, Paul scribbled on his pad, "Nice. Primacy and recency, eh, professor?"

But it was too soon to celebrate. Marek was pushing up his wire-framed glasses and clearing his throat for cross-examination.

Steve picked up a pencil and prepared to take notes, listening carefully to Marek's initial questions. Mary had only been cross-examined by Diann Wilder-Tomlinson, a locally elected county attorney. How would she fare when a staff member of the Iowa Attorney General's office cross-examined her?

Early in his questioning Marek stood, grabbed the snowsuit Melissa had worn that last Friday, and marched to the witness stand. He held the tiny pink snowsuit by the shoulders, displaying it for Mary and the jury as a store clerk would to a customer. Mittens swung from each sleeve by strings. He asked Mary to identify the snowsuit, confirming it was Melissa's.

Suddenly he shifted into attack mode. "How much do you weigh?"

Mary's mouth fell open. She blinked a few times. Heat flushed her face.

Steve stared at Paul. Should he object? This question was absolutely irrelevant, not to mention humiliating. Paul motioned for Steve to let it go.

Several women jurors studied their laps, red-faced like Mary. The clock ticked loudly.

Marek glared at Mary. Courtroom lights reflected across the bald top of his head.

Mary glanced at Steve, waiting for him to react, do something. Steve avoided her eyes, let the embarrassing question hang in the shocked courtroom, undignified by an argument.

For the first time in all her criminal proceedings, Steve sensed that Mary didn't know what to say. Finally, she glanced back at Marek. She mumbled her weight, agreed that she was overweight.

But Marek wasn't done yet. "Would you agree that you were many times the size of little Melissa Mathes?"

As if overweight adults were more likely to abuse children than skinny ones.

Now Steve's mouth hung open. Supporters in the gallery gasped. Jurors, several of them overweight themselves, shifted uneasily in their seats.

Mary cleared her throat. "Yes. Of course. I'm many times the size of Melissa."

"If he insists on hanging himself," Paul whispered, "I guess we should let him."

Steve scrawled a black hat on a legal pad. Marek couldn't have found a better way to lose the jury's sympathy.

Soon after that Mary finished her testimony and stepped down from the stand.

Tuesday morning the prosecution presented a couple of rebuttal witnesses and then the evidence was all in. All done but the closing arguments.

Steve glanced at Mary. Her shoulders were relaxed. Her face showed no signs of strain. During this four-year fight to clear her name, he had thought her naïve. Now he realized simple, uncluttered faith had brought her through the dark days of this long process. She seemed to accept the harshest aspects of an unjust sentence simply because God was in control. Now she continued to trust him to work things out.

As Virginia Barchman stepped forward to address the jury for her closing arguments, she wore her law degree like a pair of worn work boots, determined to stomp out injustice. The soft slipper approach she had used with Tessia's testimony had disappeared with the spent box of Kleenex.

Barchman described the forty-two minutes Mary had spent with Melissa on that last day. "Mary Weaver had many priorities that morning as she strapped an active, playful baby into car seat. Melissa was not one of those priorities. Mary did errands, picked the baby up at Tessia's home, dropped books off at the library, parked the car seat on her kitchen counter. Then she proceeded to unload the car and put groceries away. I submit to you that Melissa was a distraction from more important things in Mary Weaver's life that morning. Mary jammed baby food into the baby's mouth between unloading groceries and filling her cupboards."

Several supporters in the gallery gasped.

"Mary Weaver was short on time that morning. She needed to pick up her own children at preschool, and she had to feed the baby first. She became frustrated and committed a hideous act of violence. Mary Weaver violently shook the baby or slammed the baby until the baby stopped breathing. Then, to cover her act of violence, she performed resuscitation efforts, which were meager at best."

Doug Marek brought Melissa's pink snowsuit with him to offer his closing arguments. He spread the snowsuit on the floor so the jury could picture those last moments of the baby with her sitter. He said Mary lost control and shook the baby. This act was the only reasonable explanation for the events on that fatal Friday. He discounted the statement of the three ladies who ate at Hardee's, saying they had used their collective memory to reconstruct what they heard many months before. He believed their witness was unreliable.

Paul returned verbal fire with the skill of a marksman. "Consider the character of Mary Weaver," he said. "Never in her life has she committed a crime. The prosecution searched diligently for one person to say they had ever seen Mary use any violence or display impatience under stress and found no one. Mary was suspected of killing Melissa simply for being alone with her when the baby quit breathing. The 9-1-1 tapes give evidence of Mary's sincere efforts to save Melissa's life, not kill her.

"The prosecution wants you to believe that Mary shook this baby violently and slammed Melissa on the back of her head with a force equivalent to a fall from a five-story building. I ask you, if this is truly what happened, where is the physical evidence of this injury? Why were there no signs of bruises, grip marks, scratches, cuts, scrapes, a goose egg, even redness? Instead we find a skull fracture and severe injuries, which medical experts agree date back seven to ten days before death, when Mary was not with the baby.

"Investigators want us to ignore those older injuries and blame acute injuries for her death. I ask you, if the acute injuries were responsible for her death, if she was violently shaken, why didn't the medical experts find the prior blood clot disturbed and fresh blood near the skull fracture as they would expect?"

"I submit to you that police investigators and some medical experts assumed Mary Weaver was guilty on day one and searched for evidence to prove her guilt. Meanwhile they ignored older injuries and other suspects."

Paul approached the tape recorder again and played the tape of Smith's voice confidently stating that he couldn't narrow the time frame to less than twenty-four hours or so. Paul pointed out that the doctor had changed his testimony over time to come into line with other doctors, who believed Mary was guilty.

"Mary Weaver's story of what happened during the day of Melissa's death never changes. It is unimpeachable.

"Compare that with the word of Brad and Tessia Mathes. Within the Mathes family we have widely differing stories of the baby's demeanor on the Saturday night preceding her death when her parents picked her up at around 10:30.

Paul glanced at his notes. "Tessia maintains that her pediatrician said that Mary was to blame for bruises months earlier in her life, whereas Dr. Grauerholz testifies that she told Tessia she believed those scratches and bruises were self-inflicted.

"Brad, Tessia, and Brad's parents have each testified that this picture of Melissa with the Kool-Aid smile was taken Thursday night, the evening before Melissa quit breathing." Paul held the cropped photo for the jury to see. "As we look at this picture, you and I are asked to notice that Melissa is apparently a happy, normal child the night before Mary picked her up and inflicted fatal injuries on her. That's not hard to believe when you look at the cropped picture that the prosecution has been showing us."

Paul pulled an enlarged photo from an envelope and held it up to the jury. "In this original photo, however, I would ask you to notice the sunlight streaming into the window in the background. Does sunlight stream in your window in Iowa in January after seven p.m.?"

Paul walked close to the jury so they could all study the picture. Steve watched the light of understanding dawn on the jurors' faces one by one as they realized the truth that Mary had found that day on the evidence table.

Paul laid the picture on the railing of the jury box and met the gaze of each juror. "Ladies and gentlemen of the jury, I want you to remember that Mary Weaver is not required to prove her innocence. Every suspect who enters this courtroom is supposed to be presumed innocent until proven guilty. The state carries the burden of proof. When you form your verdict, you must declare my client, Mary Weaver, innocent unless you believe that state has proven that she is guilty beyond all reasonable doubt."

✧ ✧ ✧

At 12:40 the judge gave instructions to the jury, who began deliberations with a well-earned lunch. Mary dashed to the diner with some of her supporters, stuffed the lunch special down, and dashed back to the courthouse. The group paced, speculated, and wondered in a side room. The jury probably wouldn't make a decision that first day, but Mary and the others were there in case they did. The time spent waiting gave them a chance to discuss the third trial and what they thought the outcome might be.

They prayed for the jurors, that they would be able to discern the truth. When the jury asked for equipment to listen to the tapes of the 9-1-1 call and Buffington's call to Smith, they took that as a good sign. Both tapes supported her case. Mary's group reviewed all the positive aspects of the case and ignored the negative ones.

Paul stayed at the courthouse that first day. He and Steve had decided to alternate the days they spent waiting so they would each be able to slip home and get some needed rest. At one point Mary spotted Paul lying on his back on a wooden bench in an empty room with his arm crooked over his eyes. He was fast asleep.

After eight hours of waiting, Mary and her supporters returned home.

Wednesday the same group drove more than an hour to wait at the Webster County Courthouse. The jury in the first trial had taken eight days to deliberate. This time the group wanted the jury to take plenty of time for careful consideration—but hurry up about it.

After four more hours of waiting and wondering, the court attendant informed Steve that the verdict was in, and they could return to the courtroom. The verdict would be announced at 3:30—in fifteen minutes.

Mary raced to call Jim, who was at home in Eldora with the kids. Her supporters scrambled to find seats in the public gallery. Mary sat at the counsel table, folding her arms to keep them from shaking.

She whispered a prayer. "Please, Lord. Show yourself strong. Reveal the truth."

She checked the clock at the back of the courtroom. 3:23. She glanced at Steve and exchanged fleeting smiles.

"Please, Lord. May your truth set me free." 3:27. Another glance. Another wobbly smile.

"I trust you, Lord. No matter what you do, I'll still trust you. But I believe this is the time for truth to prevail." 3:29.

The doorknob twisted. Judge Goode entered the courtroom with his usual noncommittal face.

# Chapter 39

Judge Goode sat at the bench. "The court will come to order." The perfunctory monotone words belied the electricity that kept Mary and everyone else in the room on the edge of their seats. An unnatural hush reigned as the judge turned toward the jury box, where twelve jurors had suddenly become the focal point of the entire proceeding. Though they had sat silently throughout the proceedings, they were about to speak, and their declaration would be heard far and wide.

Judge Goode addressed the foreperson. "Has the jury reached a verdict?"

"We have, Your Honor." The foreperson of the jury rose and handed the black binder to the bailiff who passed it to the judge.

Mary held her breath. She stared at the binder as it moved. The judge laid the binder on the bench and opened it, flipped pages to the back, and silently read the verdict. His face offered no clue to the verdict that would change her life forever.

Finally, after many extremely long seconds, he spoke. "On the charge of first-degree murder, I find the defendant—not guilty."

Mary's mouth fell open. One charge down. One to go.

"On the charge of child endangerment, I find the defendant—not guilty."

Beside her Steve pumped one fist. Mary squeezed his other hand. Four years of uncertainty disappeared.

"Ladies and gentlemen, pursuant to the jury's verdict, the charges against the defendant are dismissed. This case is over."

Mary stood on shaking legs and hugged Steve. This was his victory too. "Isn't God good?"

Steve rubbed tears from his cheeks. "He sure is."

No charges against her. She didn't have to wait to see if she would be charged. She wasn't just out on bail. The charges were gone. She no longer wore the label of "convicted felon." The case was over. No more hearings, appeals, rulings, testimonies, legal arguments. Done.

Mary stepped close to the gallery and hugged a few of her closest supporters. "Praise the Lord! I'm free!"

These friends, relatives, even strangers had attended all three trials, some every day. They had worn yellow ribbons, posted signs, supported her family, written letters, and raised funds. This was their victory too.

Mary pulled away from a tight hug. "Gotta call Jim and the kids!"

A knot of weeping, hugging, celebrating supporters followed her out of the courtroom to a first-floor office. She dialed her home number with shaking hands.

Jim answered on the first ring.

"Great news, Jim! I've been acquitted on both charges, and I'm coming home!"

Mary could hear muffled noises in the background and then the voice of six-year-old John. "Mommy's free! Mommy's free!"

Free.

Soon after she hung up, cameras and microphones pushed close.

"Mrs. Weaver, how do you feel right now?"

Relieved. Joyful. Thankful. Amazed. A thousand emotions pumped into her. "I just can't begin to describe how I feel. I feel like I'm free for the first time in four years."

"Do you have any plans?"

"None."

Beyond today her calendar was blank. She would circle today's date, March 6, 1997, and celebrate it for the rest of her life. She was free. Now she could plan. She had three weeks of housework to catch up on, a job to go back to, a family to love. She could play with her kids and their friends without court-ordered supervision. She didn't have to have the court's permission to travel to Dubuque and visit her parents in their home. She could go anywhere she wanted without asking anybody. Free! It was beginning to sink in.

Mary grinned. "Maybe I'll take a trip to Alaska."

She laughed, but the microphones picked up the travel joke, like so many travel agents arranging a booking.

"You have always claimed to be innocent of Melissa's murder. Who do you think caused it?"

"I don't know, and it wouldn't be fair to speculate."

"In light of the circumstances, do you have any ill feelings for the Mathes family?"

Mary had felt the sting of betrayal, and in this moment she had the chance to grasp one handful of revenge. But Mary knew the sweetness of revenge would quickly turn to bitter regret. God knew the full facts of the case, and he would exact justice in his time. Her part in Melissa's story was done. She wouldn't let the chains of the past shackle her future.

"This has been a long ordeal. I'm just relieved it is over and ready to move on."

Workers left their courthouse offices to congratulate her. Judge Goode found her, shook her hand, and offered his best wishes. The whole courthouse seemed to shift into party mode.

Mary knew this victory belonged to so many people who had done their part to make it happen.

Mary also knew the party spirit would fade. The media spotlight would burn brightly for weeks, and then it would be pushed to the back burner. Her friends would return to their lives, and now she could return to normal life too. She was free.

Free to plan. Free to heal. Free to get on with life. This mommy was never going back to prison again!

✿ ✿ ✿

Steve stepped to the gallery and found Kim, who was beaming and dabbing at tears. They hugged, and he whispered into her ear. "It's over—finally."

"What a happy ending," she whispered back.

He released his wife, moved to the edge of the gallery, hugged a few supporters, and shook a few hands. He pulled out a handkerchief and wiped at his eyes, blew his nose.

Jean Brennecke leaned over the rail with a proud mother's hug. "Steve, it's over."

"Yes. Such a relief. All of Iowa can rejoice today because the jury did the right thing. The people corrected the judicial system's mistake. Sort of renews my hope in the legal process."

"You'll sleep well tonight."

"Sure will. When my adrenaline runs out, I'm going to be one tired attorney. But this is such a happy day. We won't forget this one—ever."

Steve glanced past the happy section of the gallery to where Tessia sobbed against Brad's chest. Reporters snapped photos of the couple but kept a respectful distance.

All the celebrating couldn't block a sadder image from Steve's mind. In a Marshalltown cemetery, these words were etched in

CHAPTER 39

black granite: "Mathes. Melissa Marie. Born February 22, 1992. Died January 23, 1993."

Mary's case was over, but Melissa's killer hadn't been found. For one moment this regret called more loudly than the hugging celebration and thankful cries.

"Praise the Lord."

"Hallelujah."

"It's finally over."

Was it?

The media circus followed Mary out of the courtroom with her mass of supporters. A reporter stuck a microphone close to Steve's face. "Mr. Brennecke, how do you feel now that your client, Mary Weaver, has finally been freed?"

Steve sighed. Euphoria, relief, and exhaustion all fought to be recognized. Euphoria stepped up to the microphone. "I couldn't feel any better. The jury heard all the evidence and came to the right conclusion. Mary Weaver is innocent."

"Mary's first trial ended in a hung jury, her second in a conviction. What do you think made the difference in this trial?"

Steve spoke of new evidence they had presented in this trial.

He had barely begun to answer when the reporter's attention shifted to Lieutenant Buffington, who had grabbed his briefcase and was heading for the door. The microphone moved. "Lieutenant, what do you believe made a difference in this third trial? Was it the new evidence that came forward?"

Buffington scowled. "I didn't hear any new evidence. Some feel that Dr. Carlstrom's testimony made the difference, but we had information from medical experts the day we interviewed the parents. We know it. And where these women came from is beyond me." The detective waved away those thoughts with a quick gesture. "But again the jury had its say. And that's really about all I have to say about it."

"Do you think there's another killer out there who you should be looking for?"

"No. I sure don't."

As Buffington exited the courtroom, Steve's euphoria gave way to a mental tap on the shoulder that his job wasn't complete yet. If Lieutenant Buffington still thought Mary had killed Melissa, then the police case was closed. Her true killer might never be found.

Steve wanted to chase after the detective and yell, "What about the baby's week-old skull fracture? Have you forgotten about that? Your job's not done here!"

Anger at the injustice swelled within Steve, threatening to rob him of inner peace. Just as quickly he shifted the case back to God's jurisdiction. Somehow, some way, sometime, God would exact justice. Steve's job had been to help free Mary, and her case was over. He was done. This was the end.

Yet Steve still felt the stirrings of unfinished business. What about the parents of Brennan Hutchinson and Levi Sansgard? They claimed to be innocent. Could they also be victims of Dr. Bennett's eagerness to diagnose shaken baby syndrome? Across America he felt sure other innocent caregivers were being accused of murder, and some were being convicted. Simply being alone with a baby who died could put anyone at grave risk. As a lawyer, he needed to continue to fight for the principle of presumed innocence.

As he observed the reporters and camera crews working the crowd, hope began to flame within him that Mary's case wouldn't stand alone. This case and cases like it could challenge medical experts and police investigators to guard their presumptions and not rush to judgment. Mary's case was over, but Steve hoped its effects were only beginning.

He found Kim again and hugged her properly. They drew strength from each other and shared relief. He swapped comments of celebration with many who knew him. Soon he worked to the edge of the jubilant crowd and found a phone on the first floor of the courthouse. He dialed Paul's number.

Paul answered on the first ring. "Hey, Brennecke, I heard the great news! Here I was, dead on the couch, watching TV, when they broke into the program with a live verdict. I've been jumping around and yelling and calling people ever since."

"With a few minor exceptions, the courthouse is one big party. I guess Mary can get back to living in freedom again." Steve sighed. "This has been one wild ride, but we've finally got a fair and just outcome. Amazing."

"It's one for the record books. That's for sure."

"I can hardly believe it's over. Guess I'm just numb. You did a great job, Paul."

"Sure. I'm a legal magician." Paul laughed. "You know, other lawyers are going to line up, asking for our secret for winning this case. What are we supposed to tell them? One innocent client, two bumbling attorneys, three trials. It takes more than that to add up to today's verdict. You and I know the secret."

Paul's laughter died, and reverence tinged his words.

"Divine intervention."

# Epilogue

Teresa Engberg-Lehmer sat in her cell at the Mitchellville prison, reading and rereading a letter to the editor of the *Des Moines Register*. S. Brennecke's letter pointed out that Dr. Thomas Bennett, the state medical examiner, had been paid by the hour for his testimony in criminal cases—a clear conflict of interest by which he stood to gain financially if he found a child had died of suspicious causes.

Dr. Bennett had been in the news a lot lately. After he and Dr. Carlstrom had testified in Mary Weaver's third trial, the two had fought a very public debate about shaken baby syndrome. Both doctors called for better scrutiny of expert witnesses for SBS. Dr. Carlstrom felt that deaths by SBS were rare if they existed at all. He suspected that innocent people were accused of shaking a baby to death and were being sent to prison. Bennett, on the other hand, felt prosecutors were missing cases of SBS. He felt that disbelief in shaken baby syndrome was like doubting the existence of headaches.

Teresa's interest in Dr. Bennett was personal. Four months earlier she had put her three-month-old Jonathan in his crib early in the evening. When she went in to give him a bottle around midnight, he wasn't breathing. She called 9-1-1. By the time the baby reached the ER, he had no pulse. Doctors pronounced her sweet baby dead. Though he had no sign of injury, they ordered an autopsy, done by Dr. Bennett.

Dr. Bennett found no obvious wounds, fractures, injuries, or bleeding in the eyes. On the basis of four small blotches of blood, which he found after he popped the skull cap off, he diagnosed shaken baby syndrome and called the death a homicide.

Teresa and her husband, Joel, were terrified. They knew they weren't guilty, but if they agreed to a trial, a jury could find them guilty of first-degree murder. Even second-degree murder would send them to prison for forty-two years. Their court-appointed lawyers encouraged them to plead to involuntary manslaughter and child endangerment, which would give them each fifteen-year sentences. After all, the lawyers said, Dr. Bennett was nationally known as an excellent courtroom witness.

Teresa and her husband refused to plead guilty, but, facing life sentences, they each accepted an Alford plea as an alternative. They claimed innocence but admitted that the county attorney could prove his case. What else could they do? If they went to trial and tried to prove their innocence, they could be sentenced to life in prison.

For the last four months in prison, however, Teresa felt like she had been free-falling into a bottomless pit. While she was grieving over the loss of her only son, Bennett's shocking accusation of murder compounded the tragedy. The legal system had followed his lead. Now she was a convicted felon serving the first days of a sentence that felt like it would never end. Even when she was released from prison, would the world always see her as the one who murdered her own baby?

Teresa began to regret her decision to accept the Alford plea, though at the time they had been given little choice. Now this editorial gave her fresh hope. Less than a month before Jonathan died, Mary Weaver had won a similar case. This S. Brennecke from Grinnell had written about it in the editorial. Was it too late for her and Joel? They might not be able to reverse their sentence, but it couldn't hurt to try.

Teresa pulled out a pen and a tablet of paper. "To Mr. S. Brennecke," she wrote. "My name is Teresa Lehmer...We, my husband and myself, both feel that we are a victim of circumstances, probably due to Dr. Bennett..."

☆ ☆ ☆

Dr. Thomas Bennett was determined to stamp out child abuse—a worthy cause. One of the biggest hindrances in the battle against abuse, however, is uncertainty. Doctors often look at injuries and think abuse may be indicated, but they're unsure. What can they do? If they don't report cases, don't testify to the abuse, the abusers can go on to continue their abuse. But if they are wrong about the cause of injury, innocent people may be punished.

Barry Siegel noted in the *LA Times*: "It's that child in the ER—or morgue—who finally makes the shaken baby controversy most complicated. Say what you will, it's hard to challenge someone who's campaigning against baby killers. To do so isn't politically palatable, or, for many, personally appealing. Dismay over child abuse trumps concern for civil liberties."

Trauma teams applauded Dr. Bennett because he would testify to a diagnosis of shaken baby syndrome when other doctors were slow to do so. From 1989 to 1997 Bennett diagnosed SBS in seventeen of his autopsies. He served as an expert witness on other SBS cases. Other doctors, however, wondered about some of Bennett's cases. Siegel said: "Here and there, it looked as if Bennett had diagnosed shaken baby syndrome based on microscopic evidence—tiny tears and leaks in the brain—rather than the customary gross bleeds visible to the naked eye."

On Christmas Eve 1996, six-month-old Brennan Hutchinson died in Decorah, Iowa, after hours of flu-like symptoms. Bennett found minute drops of blood in the brain and diagnosed SBS.

On February 8, 1997, three-month-old Levi Sansgard was found dead in his crib in Charles City. The medical examiner who did the autopsy called it SIDS. Bennett reviewed the autopsy and called it homicide on the basis of some small spots of blood in the brain.

Then Jonathan Lehmer died on April 4, 1997, one month after the end of Mary's trial. Bennett labeled the death a homicide by SBS. Teresa and her husband chose the Alford plea and began fifteen-year sentences.

But Mary's third trial had raised issues about SBS. Carlstrom entered the battle this time. "It's hard to underestimate Carlstrom's impact," Siegel said, "not just on the Weaver case but on all that followed. The brain specialist proved as potent a courtroom weapon as Bennett. He helped the defense shape its opening argument and questions. Then he took the witness stand, to great effect. On March 6, the jury acquitted Mary Weaver."

After Mary was acquitted, Bennett and Carlstrom began their public debate about SBS in the papers. Other forensic pathologists who questioned Bennett's methods now spoke out. Dr. Peter Stephens, a former deputy state medical examiner, offered to review Bennett's cases for free and serve as a free witness if the cases merited it. Five pathologists, including Dr. Earl Rose, reviewed Brennan Hutchinson's case. All five believed Brennan had not died by SBS.

On October 2, 1997, Teresa Lehmer and her husband entered the Alford plea. Two weeks later Dr. Bennett resigned as

Iowa State Medical Examiner while facing a state investigation of his administration.

At this point Steve reentered the fray with a letter to the editor about a flaw in the system that basically gave financial advantages to the state medical examiner for diagnosing suspicious causes of death.

Teresa Lehmer heard that Dr. Peter Stephens had offered to review Bennett's cases for free. She wrote her letter to Steve.

When Steve contacted Stephens, the doctor asked Steve to get him the full Lehmer file. Steve inquired about the files at the state medical examiner's office but received no response. After several weeks the attorney general's office returned Steve's phone calls. Siegel said, "Inadvertently, the office explained, all slides and tissue samples from the Lehmer case had been destroyed back in January. Not just the Lehmer case: In the wake of Bennett's resignation, someone at the state crime lab had improperly destroyed samples from 356 autopsies conducted by Bennett from 1995 to 1997. Five involved infant deaths. Four of those five were shaken baby homicides. The four shaken baby cases, as it happened, received special treatment: In those, the crime lab destroyed not just tissue samples but all biological materials."

In the wake of the destruction of all tissue samples in the case, Dr. Stephens couldn't look at all the evidence in the Lehmer case. He could only look at the handful of photographs that were part of the state medical examiner's file and compare those to the written autopsy findings. Those photographs clearly showed this wasn't a case of intentional trauma.

Steve drove to Council Bluffs to copy the Lehmer file. The prosecutor, Rick Crowl, had won two convictions in the Lehmer case, but he had never felt good about it. The couple had always maintained their innocence. Crowl had gone along with

Bennett's autopsy, but he felt the medical evidence was pretty thin.

Crowl chatted with Steve in his office as Steve copied the prosecutor's entire file, complete with the hospital records, court pleadings, and police reports. As they talked, Crowl began to doubt the Lehmer's guilt. After Steve left, Crowl reconsidered the verdict. Naturally the defendant's expert was going to say the defendant was innocent, but Crowl had never been comfortable with this verdict. He couldn't turn to Bennett, who had left office.

Later Crowl called Steve from his office in Council Bluffs. He told Steve to call Dr. Jerry Jones, the medical examiner who worked across the river in Omaha, Nebraska. If Steve could convince Jones that Jonathan had died of innocent causes, then Crowl might reconsider the convictions and agree to new trials for the Lehmers. Steve agreed and sent the typed autopsy report and photographs to Dr. Jones.

Jones reviewed the autopsy and the photographs, and called Crowl. Jones insisted that the Lehmers were innocent. He explained that there were three cardinal points necessary to diagnose SBS: retinal hemorrhages, a subdural hemorrhage, and no other injuries. The Lehmer case had no retinal hemorrhages and no subdural hemorrhage. "This is a bad conviction," he told the prosecutor.

On September 28, 1998, Teresa Lehmer walked out of the Mitchellville prison as a free woman. Steve presented her with a large bouquet of flowers. Now she could grieve the loss of her child.

On the same day, several hundred miles away, Joel Lehmer was also released from prison.

Their lives, like Mary's, would start over again.

Five medical experts also reviewed Brennan Hutchinson's case. All five agreed he had died of natural causes. Charges were dropped.

Levi Sansgard's mother had been charged with first-degree murder. Six medical experts reviewed the case and agreed that the baby hadn't been shaken. Charges were dismissed on the third day of her jury selection.

Today SBS is usually known as abusive head trauma. While we mourn the loss of any baby who is truly killed by shaking, we maintain that the presumption of innocence is crucial to the safety of caregivers everywhere.

# To the Reader

Names and descriptions of all inmates and prison workers have been changed to protect their privacy.

Much of the information for the epilogue was taken from this excellent article: Barry Siegel, "Judging Parents as Murderers on 4 Specks of Blood," *LA Times,* July 11, 1999, http://articles. latimes.com/1999/jul/11/news/mn-54984

Here is a link to a summary of the study mentioned by Dr. Carlstrom in chapter 33:

http://medicalmisdiagnosisresearch.wordpress. com/2010/05/18/a-joint-clinical-study-of-shaken-baby-syndrome/

If you enjoyed reading this book, please consider requesting it at your public library so others may enjoy it too.

# How Accurate Is This Story?

This is the true story of Mary Weaver from the viewpoint of Mary and Steve Brennecke. The basic facts are all true. Though fifteen years passed from the time Mary was acquitted to the time of writing, and memories have faded, we had a wealth of written records about her case to help make this story accurate. We had a large portion of the transcripts from the three trials as well as police and medical reports, depositions, and hearings. We also had many newspaper articles, support group newsletters, and videotapes of news clips and two national talk shows where Mary appeared. Most of the trial testimony came directly from written transcripts.

We worked especially hard to keep the words of the Mathes family, the medical experts, and police investigators as accurate as possible. Minor actions were added that show Mary and Steve's interpretations of their demeanor in any given scene.

We did, however, create a few scenes to help the story flow. These are true to the spirit of the story but are not true to actual detail. John was afraid Mary would die but didn't exactly express his fear as we have portrayed it in the book. Catherine did keep the note that said "Prayers," but Mary didn't necessarily find it by her pillow. We also created several scenes in which Mary and Steve think about certain aspects of their lives. While these scenes are true to what they were thinking at the time, these scenes didn't necessarily happen exactly as the book portrays them.

Throughout the book we created conversations that reflect the general truth of real conversations. Mary and Steve obviously can't remember these conversations word for word, but we tried to represent general content.

So we added details to personalize this story, but we tried not to misrepresent the story or overplay negative characteristics of anyone. We endeavored to be as accurate and as fair as possible and still tell this personal story. We apologize for very minor inaccuracies where they may occur.

# Acknowledgments

Many people played a part in helping to bring about a happy ending to this true story. Mary and Steve want to thank Dr. Thomas Carlstrom, Dr. Ruth Ramsey, Dr. Vincent DiMaio, Dr. Earl Rose (posthumously), and other doctors whose testimony helped Mary's defense. A big thanks goes to Frank Santiago for keeping Mary's case in the public eye with his thorough newspaper articles. Thanks to all the witnesses who bravely spoke out in Mary's defense..

Mary wishes to thank her support group who gave of their time, money, and encouragement to support her and her family during her time in prison. Special thanks to Nancy Pins, Lisa Murphy, Jim and Marge Wolfe, and Al Brennecke for leading this group. You'll never know how much your support meant to Mary's family during that difficult time. She wants to especially thank Paul Rosenberg who contributed so much to her defense.

Steve wants to thank his wife, Kim, for her invaluable contributions to Mary's defense through all three trials. Kim was more than a sounding board, and her keen memory of strands of testimony from prior proceedings helped to bolster Mary's defense. Paul Rosenberg brought to Mary's defense a caliber of legal work seldom seen, along with a great sense of humor and humility. Paul's skill in the courtroom and in his appellate work were unmatched.

Deb wants to thank Marge Wolfe for saving newspaper articles, agendas for support group meetings, support group newsletters, photos, and videos of newscasts and talk shows Mary appeared on. This material made it possible to write this book with a high degree of accuracy. Thanks to Dr. Annette Fischer for reading the manuscript for medical accuracy and helping to make corrections. Deb also wants to thank her husband, Art who lived this book with her for more than two years and gave great assistance in many of the practical aspects of bringing this book to publication.

And Mary, thank you for living by faith. During your difficult years, you clung to a simple promise from the pages of Scripture: "The truth will set you free." Steve and Deb thank God that you lived to see your prison doors open once more.

# More about Mary, Steve, and Deb

**D**eb first heard the Mary Weaver story while riding down the road in New Zealand in December 2010. As Steve told Deb and her husband, Art, the story, Deb couldn't escape the compelling nature of it. She believed the story needed to be told and that she could be involved in bringing the story to print.

Deb interviewed both Mary and Steve while in the States. After a great deal of research, she started close communication with Mary and Steve to craft a personal and in-depth retelling of their story. Mary trusted Deb with the personal details of her story and reviewed writing at various stages. Steve wrote most of the scenes from his viewpoint, gave advice on legal aspects of the book, and worked through the entire book with Deb, who directed the writing process.

Mary now lives in a small, scenic village along the Iowa River. After her place of employment closed two years ago, Mary returned to college, graduated, and is the executive assistant in finance at a local college. Catherine and John are grown, have both graduated from college, and own homes nearby. Mary says, "God has blessed us with a nice young man who will be a great addition to our family when he and Catherine marry later this year (2013)."

Steve is an Iowa native. He graduated from Southern Methodist University in 1983 and from the University of Iowa College of Law in 1986. After Mary's case was closed and the Lehmers were free from prison, Steve and Kim devoted themselves to ministry, serving overseas in a missionary endeavor with Baptist Mid-Missions (BMM). Today Steve serves as the field administrator for BMM. Steve, Kim, and their children live in Ohio.

Deb grew up in Colorado. She graduated from Faith Baptist Bible College in 1977. She has been writing for publication for over thirty years. She has authored a wide variety of materials including four novels through Bob Jones University Press. Along with writing, she and her husband have been involved in church planting ministries in Taiwan and New Zealand since 1980. Deb is mother to two married daughters and grandma to two grandsons. You can find out more about Deb and her writing and ministry at http://www.DebBrammer.com.

Maybe you are wondering:
Why did God allow this to happen to Mary?

Which leads to more personal questions:
- If God is in control, why is my world a disaster?
- Why doesn't life make more sense?
- If God is good, why does he allow senseless suffering?

# Companion
# Bible Study
# to
## *EDGES OF*
## *TRUTH*

This ten-week Bible study about unfairness will help you think through these questions. Each lesson uses illustrations from *Edges of Truth*. You'll look at five Bible characters who were treated unfairly and see how they survived their spiritual disasters.

You can use this study for your personal devotions or discuss the issues in a group Bible study.

For more information see: www.MaryWeaverStory.com.

CPSIA information can be obtained at www.ICGtesting.com
Printed in the USA
LVOW08s2331200115

423685LV00011B/299/P